THE PO...

Applied
Social Psychology
Annual

VOLUME

1

Editorial Advisory Board

Publication of the APPLIED SOCIAL PSYCHOLOGY ANNUALS is sponsored by the SOCIETY FOR THE PSYCHOLOGICAL STUDY OF SOCIAL ISSUES (SPSSI), Division 9 of the American Psychological Association. SPSSI is—in many ways—a "unique organization," as Harold M. Proshansky noted in his 1972 Presidential Message: "From its very beginning in 1936 it established as the nexus of its concern the application of behavior science research to the major social dilemmas of modern man . . . ." Drawing upon the intellectual traditions of Kurt Lewin—his colleagues and his successors—SPSSI has consistently sought to focus attention on research that is socially useful as well as theoretically meaningful. It is with these aims that SPSSI has undertaken the editorial responsibility for developing and guiding this new annual series—focusing on the broad area where social psychological research interfaces with social problems.

Applied Social Psychology Annual

VOLUME

1

LEONARD BICKMAN
Editor

Sponsored by the Society for the
Psychological Study of Social Issues (SPSSI)

SAGE PUBLICATIONS
BEVERLY HILLS   LONDON

For information address:

SAGE Publications
275 South Beverly Drive
Beverly Hills, California 90212

SAGE Publications Ltd.
28 Banner Street
London ECIY 8QE, England

Printed in the United States of America

International Standard Book Number 0-8039-1401-6 (pbk.)
International Standard Book Number 0-8039-1400-8
International Standard Serial Number 0196-4151

FIRST PRINTING

CONTENTS

LEONARD BICKMAN

INTRODUCTION

APPLIED SOCIAL PSYCHOLOGY, SPSSI, AND KURT LEWIN

This annual presents a perspective that has been virtually lost to social psychology for over three decades. It provides examples and models on how social psychology can be utilized to deal with real-world problems. It focuses on social psychology in the natural setting, a setting which has been largely ignored since Kurt Lewin's work. This perspective grew out of a concern for producing a social psychology which, while maintaining its scientific heritage, provides information which is useful in solving problems. It is this concern that led the Society for the Psychological Study of Social Issues (SPSSI) to sponsor this annual series.

Kurt Lewin, a founder and previous SPSSI president (1942-1943) was probably the foremost proponent of combining applied and theoretical social psychology. Lewin strongly believed that theory development and research on applied problems should occur together. One of Lewin's most well-known statements concerning the practicality of theory includes his perspective on applications:

[Close cooperation between theoretical and applied psychology] can be accomplished ... if the theorist does not look toward applied problems, with highbrow aversion or with a fear of social problems, and if the applied psychologist realizes that there is nothing as practical as a good theory [Lewin, 1951: 169].

Moreover, Lewin stressed that research must accomplish some social good: "Research that produces nothing but books will not suffice" (Lewin, 1948: 203).

Lewin integrated his theoretical thinking and his research so as to support his belief that only scientific research provides reliable guidelines to effective social action. Lewin conducted research on such diverse topics as intergroup conflict, war morale, worker productivity, and leadership. He described these efforts as *action research.* He saw these projects as combinations of experiments and applications. This research, Lewin felt, could bring beneficial changes to society, as well as advance scientific knowledge.

Under Lewin's leadership, the Commission on Community Interrelations (C.C.I.) was formed in 1945 (Marrow, 1969). The purpose of this organization was to use scientific research to combat prejudice. C.C.I. utilized a variety of approaches, including:

(1) *diagnostic action research* —to define the problem and recommend countermeasures

(2) *participant action research* —to involve community members in the research

(3) *empirical action research* —to collect data in a case study type of clinical procedure

(4) *experimental action research* —to conduct a controlled study of the effectiveness of various measures.

This last form of social action research had the greatest potential, but was the most difficult to implement and was clearly a forerunner of modern evaluation research. Some of the projects C.C.I. worked on were: gang behavior, legislation and social change, group loyalty, integrated housing, and sensitivity training—considered to be the origin of the T-group.

Lewin's work did not proceed smoothly. C.C.I. was supported by the American Jewish Congress, but financing such long-range scientific research was difficult. The era of large-scale government-supported research had not yet arrived. Moreover, pressures for quick responses, more militant action, and less research all weighed on C.C.I.'s efforts. But Lewin persisted, and over 50 projects were conducted during C.C.I.'s life.

Lewin's influence on the Society for the Psychological Study of Social Issues is not easily calculated. Clearly, the aims and goals of SPSSI, namely, "to bring theory and practice into focus on human problems of the group, the community, and the nation, as well as the increasingly important ones that have no national boundaries" (SPSSI Statement of Purpose), and Lewin's writings, research, and other activities, continue to be intertwined. In 1947, a memorial meeting was held for Lewin, at the American Psychological Association meeting. The speakers described Lewin's contributions in the fields of theory, social action, and in charting a course for social psychology. At that meeting, SPSSI established the Kurt Lewin Award. This annual award and lecture has continued and is considered to be the nation's highest award in social psychology. This annual represents another effort by SPSSI to advance the Lewinian tradition of action research.

TAKING ANOTHER COURSE

Between the time Lewin's group was active and the late 1960s, the field of social psychology was content with its growth as a social science. The 1950s and early 1960s was a time of complacency for most of society. Social psychologists, too, were content to work within their laboratories and develop their theories.

During this era, social psychology was almost totally concerned with the testing of abstract theoretical notions in the well-controlled environment of the university laboratory. Gone were the concerns Lewin espoused. Social psychology had become academic social psychology with a vengeance.

In retrospect, there appears to be a variety of reasons for ignoring social issues during this period. The belief that well-controlled laboratory research would bring social psychology a legitimacy and acceptability among the "harder" sciences was widely held. In laboratory research, one could conduct true experiments and draw strong causal conclusions. This is a very positive attraction. Moreover, the academic reward system demanded (and still does) many scientific publications for employment and advancement. Thus, research on social problems—with its attendant methodological difficulties, long timespan, and multidisciplinary perspective—was not perceived as a productive area for aspiring academics. Finally, the sensitivity or T-group movement was clearly an alternative path that social-issue-oriented social psychologists could take. Unfortunately, the split between the hard-nosed laboratory-research-oriented psychologists and the more human-relations-oriented psychologists aggravated the isolation of laboratory psychologists. During the ensuing 15 years, laboratory research on theoretical concepts flourished. But the tranquillity and growth was deceptive.

During the late 1960s and early 1970s, social psychology, like the rest of American society, went through a period of anguish. At national, and almost all regional, conferences, self-doubt and concern about the future of social psychology was discussed by eminent figures in the field. There was much concern expressed about its usefulness and the validity and generalizability of its findings. Debates raged concerning whether social psychology was merely a form of history or a real science. While these issues were being discussed, a small number of young social psychologists started to look outside the laboratory for both the setting and the impetus of their research.

A PERSONAL PERSPECTIVE

I was one of those young social psychologists who was dissatisfied with the then-current state of social psychology. During my graduate training at the City University of New York, I was exposed to a mixture of traditional and applied social psychology (environmental psychology) under Hal Proshansky (also a previous SPSSI president). During my last two years there, I became interested in field research as a remedy to the sterility I saw in laboratory research. I felt (and still do) that the control exercised in laboratory research, conducted primarily with college students, results in a biased perspective on human behavior. Studying behavior in a more natural field setting, using the experimental paradigm, seemed to be more relevant to understanding social problems. In 1968, a fellow graduate student and I conducted a field experiment on race and helping behavior, supported by a SPSSI grant-in-aid. At that time, I felt the study contributed to understanding a social problem and was a scientifically worthwhile project. The research was subsequently published in the *Journal of Personality and Social Psychology.* This experience, and others, crystallized my perspective on social psychology and led to the book I coedited with Tom Henchy in 1969 and which was published in 1972.

The new direction in social psychology of the 1970s was characterized by many of the articles published in the Bickman and Henchy text, *Beyond the Laboratory: Field Research in Social Psychology.* During this period, concern was placed on conducting research outside the laboratory. That is, the research setting was the important concern and the utility of the research was taken for granted. However, in retrospect, I see many of these small-scale field studies as no more helpful in dealing with social problems than laboratory research was. This early era was characterized by field research which was rarely applied research. But leaving the laboratory was an important step in breaking with what had become traditional social psychology. However, I now see it as more a movement away from something, rather than toward something. Social psychologists had not yet been taught and were not sensitive to policy implications of their own research. It is the latter that especially characterizes the new trend in applied social psychological research.

In subsequent years, I conducted a fairly large number of small-scale, hypothesis-testing, field studies. However, since moving to Loyola University of Chicago five years ago, my perspectives have changed. I have been involved in numbers of larger, policy-oriented research and evaluation studies, which I believe is one important dimension of applied social psychology.

At Loyola, I extended my research interests in helping behavior by conducting a national evaluation of projects designed to encourage bystanders to report crimes. This study utilized social psychological constructs in attempting to understand the bases of these projects. In addition to interests in crime prevention, I also directed a series of studies for the National Bureau of Standards on human behavior in fire situations. I found social psychological research methods and theories useful in developing recommendations for training standards for nursing homes.

Approximately three years ago, I became associated with the Westinghouse Electric Corporation. Working with Westinghouse has given me the opportunity to direct research, policy, and evaluation projects in a number of diverse areas, under government contracts. Some of the projects have been:

(1) evaluation of captioned television for the deaf
(2) evaluation of shoplifting and employee theft programs
(3) research on the impact of school size
(4) evaluation of a nutrition program for the elderly
(5) evaluation of a curriculum program in school health education.

The purpose of enumerating these projects is simply to indicate that many opportunities exist to conduct applied research. It should be stressed that these projects were not funded by the traditional sources of funds for social psychological research, i.e., National Science Foundation and the National Institute of Mental Health. The sources of these projects included the National Institute of Law Enforcement and Criminal Justice, the National Institute of Education, the Bureau of Education for the Handicapped, and the National Heart, Lung and Blood Institute. These studies are very different from the field studies I conducted earlier in my career in the sense of being more directly applicable to social policy.

WHAT IS APPLIED SOCIAL PSYCHOLOGY?

This annual is an attempt to close the gap that now exists between applied research and basic/theoretical research. The distinction between the two kinds of research can be seen as a matter of degree, rather than of kind. At one end of the continuum, basic research is aimed toward accumulating knowledge about fundamental principles of behavior, while at the other end applied research is intended to provide input into problem solving. This input has an immediacy associated with it that is not usually found in basic research. Basic research may make a contribution to solving practical problems, but the application of such findings usually takes a great deal of time and its contribution is not usually direct. Applied research is generally conducted in a natural setting. But, as noted earlier, research conducted in a field setting is not necessarily applied research.

Thus, applied social psychology is seen as a problem-oriented social psychology. Often, its source of inspiration is not the individual researcher, but a social problem as defined by the government. This is an important distinction and one which will have great impact on the nature of the research conducted. As noted above, all of the projects I have recently worked on are federally funded. Many of them were initiated by an agency issuing a request for proposals and competitively won by submitting an extensive proposal. In most cases, the agency clearly spelled out what work it wanted accomplished. In contrast, the basic researcher working in a laboratory or just with pencil and paper can explore whatever problems he or she desires, within the limits of fiscal and ethical restraints. The purpose here is the development of knowledge, not application. Utility in this narrow definition of basic research is irrelevant.

There is a wide range between these extremes. To a large extent, some of the articles presented in the present volume reflect this individualistic, inner-directed basic science approach. That is, the applied research in this first volume was conducted by academics with a theoretical perspective. Since this dimension of basic-applied is an important construct, some of the research in the present volume can be used to illustrate the differences in the types of research generated along this dimension.

Robert B. Cialdini, in his article "Full-Cycle Social Psychology," provides excellent examples of this type of meld between the basic science approach and concern for applications. Cialdini suggests a movement between the laboratory and the field, in a search for greater generalizability and vigorousness of theory. Cialdini uses the field both as a source of ideas, as well as for a test-bed. However, his concern is not with the solving of specific problems, but instead with the development of a more valid theoretical perspective on social influence. Somewhat more applied along this dimension is the research of Aronson and Osherow. Their research on interpersonal interaction in a desegregated classroom provides an example of research based on social psychological theories, which had as its objective the resolution of this problem. Finally, the chapter by Raven and Haley best represents research which has a more external impetus. The research began as a response to the government's request for proposals dealing with a specific problem. Raven and others proposed a line of inquiry to deal with the government's perception of the problem. Interestingly, Raven and Haley describe how their interaction, one from academia and one from government, produced modifications in both the government's perception of the problem and new research strategies on the part of the academicians. More important, this chapter describes just one part of a very extensive research and evaluation effort.

These government-funded efforts are expected to provide an ever-increasing source of research opportunity for social psychologists.

It is clearly difficult to provide a simple, singular definition for what applied social psychology is. The field is very young and more elaborate definitions will be forthcoming. For the present, however, the reader will have to be content with the natural ambiguity of a newly emerging research area. What applied social psychology is will certainly be dependent upon the research activities over the next decade.

STYLE OF CONTRIBUTIONS

The style used by the authors and the editor in this annual is quite different from most academic publications. This style was encouraged and sometimes pushed upon the authors by the editor. The approach taken by this annual is that research, like any human endeavor, is very personal. Sometimes it appears to the editor that the purpose of textbooks and journals is to remove the individual from the research effort and create a cold and sterile version of science. Often, the process of conducting research may be more rewarding than its particular outcome. For this purpose, the writing style employed in the chapters published in this annual is far more personal and experiential in nature than is usually found in traditional scholarly enterprises. For example, the use of "I" or "we" in writing was encouraged. I felt that it was important to describe how the research was conducted, as well as the research findings. Particular problems encountered in conducting research, which normally do not appear in journal articles, were seen as suitable for publication in this annual. The peculiarities of conducting applied research must be disseminated if we are not to repeat mistakes made by others.

The research presented in this volume demonstrates how one goes about conducting applied research. While its substantive findings are important to discuss, these findings do not overshadow the description of the real research process. Thus, authors recount problems faced and how they were dealt with. Some of these problems may appear idiosyncratic, but in most cases they are not. For example, problems of gaining access to particular environments are common to all applied research. I am grateful to the authors for sharing their failures as well as their successes. It is hoped that the reader will gain a deeper understanding of the applied research process by analyzing the problems encountered and their solutions. The personal nature of the presentations hopefully encourages this analysis.

The self-criticism presented in this annual should indicate that neither the authors nor the editor consider these chapters as perfect examples of applied social psychology. In many cases, the research represents the first attempts of traditionally trained social psychologists to deal with social problems. Many of these attempts can be characterized as small first steps in a path leading to more robust applications. I expect later efforts will be more methodologically and analytically sophisticated, more politically informed, more longitudinal, and will occur in the context of a multidisciplinary team. With additional experience we should be more able to reach the Lewinian ideal of both solving problems and advancing theory.

CONTENT OF THE ANNUAL

The present volume contains 10 original essays representing the state of the art of applied social psychology. Future volumes will contain essays on a variety of topic areas. All methodologies—including experimental, quasi-experimental, correlational designs, case studies, and archival analysis, as well as new statistical techniques—will be considered appropriate for publication in this annual. The present volume is divided into three sections.

ISSUES IN APPLIED SOCIAL PSYCHOLOGY

This section contains chapters that discuss the various issues and problems in applying social psychology. The purpose of this section is to raise general issues important in applying social psychology. This section provides a broader context within which to view specific applications.

As previously noted, Cialdini's perspective on "Full-Cycle Social Psychology" is an example of a more general approach that can be taken in applied social psychology. In this chapter, Cialdini suggests how to combine the laboratory and the outside world in achieving a better understanding of a social phenomenon and a theoretical perspective which is ecologically valid. The next chapter, by Charles A. Kiesler, provides us with some of the wisdom he has developed as Executive Officer for the American Psychological Association. From this perspective, Kiesler has seen the relationship between social psychological research and social policy. This chapter should help the reader focus on the policy implications of social psychological research.

METHODOLOGICAL/ANALYTICAL

Chapters in this section present problems and solutions to those problems which may be seen as unique to applied social psychology. These essays are oriented toward specific techniques and applications and the authors provide some of the tools by which social psychologists who are concerned with applied research can better conduct such research. It should become clear to the reader, from the two chapters in this section, that the traditional research methods taught in social psychological laboratories can no longer totally serve the applied social psychologist. Saxe and Fine provide a methodological perspective on the differences between traditional laboratory social psychology and more field-oriented applied social psychology. They point out the difficulties associated with the older methods and suggest new ways of looking at research.

The chapter by Cook, Dintzer, and Mark provides an additional perspective on analytic methods. Because of the real-world constraints on applied research, the conduct of true experiments in well-controlled settings is often not feasible. The researcher will usually not have the ability or power to manipulate independent variables and examine their effect on specified dependent variables. The researcher must deal with the world as it is already constructed. Data may have been collected which provide some insight concerning the nature of a social problem. Often, data will have been collected over a number of years, by individuals who are not concerned with research but merely with recordkeeping. The chapter by Cook and his associates provides an introduction to a methodology that can be used to analyze such data. The reader should be aware that (unlike many of the other chapters in this annual) this essay is very technical and should provide a challenge to read. This chapter on time series should also serve to highlight the technical problems encountered in conducting research in an applied setting. Because simple true experiments are often not possible, complex analytic methods are often needed to develop confidence in examining causal relationships.

AREAS OF APPLICATION

This last section deals with social psychological research in a variety of substantive areas, each being an area in which new knowledge is produced that contributes to solving particular problems. In the present volume, topics were taken from a number of problem areas, namely, environment, criminal justice, education, and health. Within these problem areas, specific and narrowly defined research projects are presented.

The chapter by Carroll and Coates provides an interesting perspective of the journey of a traditional laboratory-oriented social psychologist to one who is involved with the social policy in the criminal justice area. Carroll and

Coates recount their experience in conducting research on parole decision making. The particular problems in conducting research with parole boards is noted, as well as some of the more general observations about research in applied settings. Importantly, Carroll and Coates present research findings which are relevant not only to social psychologists but also to parole decision makers.

Aronson and Osherow present research in a different institutional setting, the educational system. We can expect that research in educational settings will be an important area of research for social psychologists. In some respects, research in educational settings is similar to the more traditional laboratory research. To a large extent, the subjects (i.e., students) are a captive audience, within a fairly well-controlled environment. However, that is where the similarities end, for the researcher does not control the educational setting as he or she controls the laboratory setting. This chapter provides an account of how the authors became involved in this particular problem and the manner in which social psychological theory was useful in devising an experimental program to deal with a very significant social issue. The results of multiple experiments provide the opportunity to observe how variations on an applied research theme can be conducted. Each variation provided further insight into the nature of the solution proposed.

In contrast to the institutional settings of the previous two chapters, the chapter by Wortman and her associates describes the general approach taken in studying persons who may generally be regarded as victims of uncontrollable negative outcomes. In particular, the victims studied suffered from traumatic accidents which affected their health. Wortman and her associates explain how they developed an interest and a concern for these individuals and how this concern was translated to attempts to provide insight which would be of benefit to these individuals, as well as providing theoretical growth in this area. This chapter exemplifies the concern many social psychologists have with helping others. The notion here is that others can be helped through research, as well as through direct delivery of clinically oriented services. In fact, it can be argued that the promising approach taken by Wortman and others can serve as the basis for assisting untold numbers of individuals in need. Applied research offers an attractive alternative to the clinical, direct therapeutic service form of helping others.

The next two chapters also deal with health-related problems. Raven and Haley describe a research project which is focused on the spread of diseases within hospital settings. The authors point out how social scientists and, in particular, social psychologists can provide a useful perspective on interpersonal relations within this institutional setting. Raven's extensive research on social power, teamed with Haley's knowledge of hospital settings, lead to a multidisciplinary perspective on the problem of infection control. In the future, we can expect such combinations of experts in social psychology and experts in the substantive areas to work together in dealing with problems in a particular area.

Evans's chapter provides an overview of how social psychologists are making contributions in the newly developing area of behavioral medicine. Evans's research, dealing primarily with the causes of smoking among teenagers, demonstrates how social psychological principles and methods can be applied to understanding this social problem. Evans notes other areas of concern, such as cardiovascular disease and stress, which can be explored from a social psychological perspective.

The final three chapters thus provide a perspective on how social psychology can be utilized to deal with problems in the health field. As evidenced by a new division of the American Psychological Association on health psychology, it is clear that this will be a growing area. As social psychologists, we can expect the prevention orientation to be an especially important one in the near future. As treatment becomes prohibitively expensive, new ways will be sought to change behavior and educate individuals about how they can prevent the onset of avoidable diseases.

The chapter by Pallak and his associates represents an attempt to deal with yet a different social problem, that of energy conservation. It will become increasingly clear that energy conservation is an important but often overlooked way to deal with the energy crisis. Pallak applies some principles developed from commitment theory in exploring how the behavior of individuals can be influenced so as to reduce their energy consumption. Clearly, Pallak's effort is just scratching the surface of the energy problem and how social psychologists can deal with it. While Pallak's research is of an applied nature, he notes that no effort was made to disseminate his findings to any government agency or utility company.

If social psychologists are going to have the impact that their findings often deserve, then they must reach out beyond their own scientific community to make their findings available. We can expect that as the field of applied social psychology matures, we will move from conducting socially relevant, but descriptive, research to the development and implementation of social programs that are designed to impact directly on social problems. Moreover, teamed with evaluation research, this approach should bring a new vitality to social psychology.

In the forthcoming volumes of this annual, a variety of substantive areas will be presented. The chapters of this first volume were chosen to present the reader with a broad overview of topic areas and applied research settings. In the future, the last section of the annual will focus on a specific problem area. Next year's volume will feature a special section on social psychology and the criminal justice system, and the following year, applications to health problems will be emphasized.

As SPSSI's President 38 years after Lewin's term of office, I am pleased to be the first editor for this series in applied social psychology. I am honored that SPSSI has judged this venture to be worthy of their sponsorship. During my term as editor, I hope to bring to the field a fresh perspective on social psychology—a perspective that contributes to a renaissance of Kurt Lewin's efforts and the advancement of SPSSI's goals.

REFERENCES

LEWIN, K. (1951) Field Theory in Social Science. Chicago: University of Chicago Press.
———(1948) Resolving Social Conflicts. New York: Harper & Row.
MARROW, A.J. (1969) The Practical Theorist: The Life and Work of Kurt Lewin. New York: Basic Books.

PART

I

**Issues in
Applied Social
Psychology**

ROBERT B. CIALDINI

2

FULL-CYCLE SOCIAL PSYCHOLOGY

An important event in my professional life occurred one day in Columbus, Ohio. It is quite fitting that it took place not on a traditional workday in the excellent Ohio State University library, in my office, or in the labs of the Social Psychology Doctoral Program where I had a visiting appointment that year. Instead, it happened on a Saturday afternoon in the stands of Ohio Stadium where 83,000 people had gathered to delight as a powerful and unbeaten Ohio State team chewed its way through a much weaker opponent. Actually, my day at the stadium had begun considerably earlier. At the time I was there, the social psychology program at Ohio State was located in the football stadium. The stadium is truly immense; and the university was housing some academic units within its bowels. Thus, when I went to my office to do some work that morning, it was to the stadium with the intention of attending the football game later on in the day.

THE TRAPPER AND HIS TRAP

My principal purpose in going to the office was to puzzle over some data I had gotten from a laboratory attitude change study. The data were promising enough in that the means were in the predicted direction, but the effect I was looking for was not statistically significant. I was getting about one-half unit of separation between the two crucial experimental groups on a 7-point scale when, with the amount of error variance present in the situation, I needed a full unit of difference to attain conventional levels of significance.

It appeared as though I had probably uncovered an influence upon the attitude change process that had not been documented before. The problem was to demonstrate that the influence was a real one. I had been in similar positions before, so I was familiar with the task that faced me. If the effect were there, my job was to catch it, to snare it. I knew already that it was a phenomenon that tracked lightly. It would be necessary, then, to build an especially sensitive trap. I had a number of options in this regard that I and

AUTHOR'S NOTE: I am indebted to a number of people for critical comments on this article, especially Chris Paul, Jill Littrell, and Gus Levine.

most of my fellow experimental social psychologists had long since learned to use. I could increase the strength of the experimental manipulations, even though they might thereby become less representative of real-world events. I could switch to an attitude issue that my subjects had virtually no opinions about and would therefore be easier to influence. I could increase the number of scales in my dependent measure to make it a more reliable index of attitude toward the topic at hand. I could cut error variance by reducing from two to one the number of experimenters conducting the study. Or I could simply increase my sample size and, provided everything else stayed the same, increase commensurately the power of my statistical test. Each of the options, and there are others as well, was designed to make my experiment an increasingly effective structure for capturing the phenomenon. By using them singly or in combination, I could build a trap from which the phenomenon, if real, would not likely escape.

As I considered how to best proceed, I noticed that it was nearly game-time. My office was located so that it was possible to walk through a few empty corridors, pass through a pair of little-used doors, and be out of the deserted academic section and into the richly peopled stands of the stadium. Although I made the physical journey easily, my thoughts remained back below the stands with my data, my nonsignificant statistical test, and my experimental trap. So engaged, I moved toward my seat, mostly oblivious to the behavior around me. Not for long, though, because the Ohio State team had left the dressing room and had begun to run onto the field, *merely* to run onto the field. The crowd was suddenly up and shouting. People were bounding about, waving banners, spilling beer on one another, and yelling encouragement to their favorites below. Arcs of tissue paper crossed overhead. The university fight song was being sung. A large group of fans repeatedly roared "We're number one!" while thrusting index fingers upward. I recall quite clearly looking up from thoughts of that additional half unit of movement on a 7-point scale and realizing the power of the tumult around me. "Cialdini," I said to myself, "I think you're studying the *wrong* thing."

A short-term result of the above set of events was the initiation of a program of investigation into the psychology of the sports fan.[1] There was, however, a more important consequence for me. I began to think about and understand my basic orientation to research and the basic orientation of experimental social psychology, as I knew it. It was definitely a trapper's approach. We would usually begin with a theory or formulation that would serve as a kind of map. We would use the map to tell us where to look for effects. Reading the map correctly was pretty much an exercise in logical inference. Certain predictions could be derived from the theory and, if followed as directions, would lead us to find certain social phenomena. Once the theory told us the expected location of these phenomena, we could set our traps for them to see if they actually were there and, consequently, if the map were correct. Trap construction was a crucial step in the enterprise. It was important to build a sensitive and selective mechanism for snaring the predicted effect. Without a sensitive mechanism, the effect we were seeking could slip through our trap and mislead us as to the accuracy of our theory; and without a selective mechanism, some other effect could spring the trap (i.e., produce the predicted results) and again provide misinformation about the correctness of the theory. It was desirable, then, to develop experimental conditions that would (1) register even whisper-light effects and (2) allow no phenomenon but the one under direct study to produce the predicted data pattern.[2]

There is a lot to be said for the trapper's approach. It fosters research with methodological rigor, low error variance, and precise measurement. It gives us good information about the validity of our theories. It often directs us to the investigation of intriguing details of behavior that we would not otherwise have thought to study. And, not unimportantly, it is a fascinating pursuit. When done right, it represents a stimulating, absorbing, and personally gratifying use of time. Were it not for the intellectually challenging character of the work, I am certain that many of its practitioners, myself included, would be doing other things.

But there is a problem with the trapper orientation—the find. Our finely tuned traps allow us to capture phenomena without regard for their importance in the course of naturally occurring human behavior. A number of commentators (e.g., Bickman, 1976; Helmreich, 1975; Smith, 1972) have made the point that social psychology as a discipline has spent far too much time in the study of events that are trivial in size and impact. There seems to be considerable anecdotal support for their position. For instance, I have more than once described some recently obtained finding about which I was both excited and proud to a neighbor or friend, only to be disappointed in the unappreciative reaction I received. In the past, I typically attributed the difficulty to a lack of understanding. I still think that was so, but now I am inclined to believe that the lack was mine. I had failed to realize that in a conversational presentation of my finding, I was providing only the end-product. And the end-product, stripped of the experimental precision and clever design that allowed me to lay claim to a clean and reliable effect was not especially meaningful by itself. So much of the enjoyment and satisfaction I had derived from my investigation had come from technique. Since I could not communicate the subtleties of sophisticated technique to my listeners (e.g., how my design eliminated this or that potential confound), I should not have been surprised that they failed to understand what I was so pleased about. They were telling me something important in their lack of appreciation. But not until 83,000 of such people jumped up and shouted it in unison did I get their message: "Cialdini, you're studying the wrong thing!"

If we accept that the task of a social psychologist is to study normal human behavior, it is odd that so little of current mainstream social psychology *begins* with observation of such everyday behavior. Much more likely, a research project will have its genesis in some theory or in the prior experimental literature. While both of these starting points allow us to infer the presence of social phenomena that can be investigated, neither tells us whether the phenomena are important in the description of human behavior as it normally occurs. A theory, for example, speaks only to the existence of the effects it predicts; it does not speak to the ecological importance of those effects. Questions about the prevalence or prominence of predicted phenomena in the stream of natural human action are not formally addressed by theories.

For instance, attribution theory, in any of its forms, makes a variety of testable predictions about the way the causal inference process works. It says nothing, however, about the relative pervasiveness of that process in the course of mundane social behavior. Do causal inferences have sufficient frequency and impact to warrant the amount of study given them within the discipline? Some evidence (e.g., Langer, 1978) suggests not. Whatever the answer, the theory itself is simply noninformative on this point. Let us take another example, balance theory—a personal favorite of mine. According to the theory, there is a tendency for people to arrange their cognitions in certain harmonious ways. But how strong is the tendency? Is it strong enough to be a genuine influence in a significant portion of our actions? Once again, the theory does not say. It only states that the pressure for cognitive balance is there and, all other things equal, it will show itself. To determine if the theory is correct, we would arrange for experimental procedures that, at best, eliminated or at least held constant all other relevant sources of influence in the situation. But it might well be that these extraneous sources of variance that would interact, interfere, or covary with the action of balance tendencies in our experiment are precisely the ones that are dominant in the natural contexts of the behavior under study. It might well be that by eliminating the action of certain effects in the interest of lower error variance or by controlling the action of other effects in the interest of conceptual precision, we will have uncovered an influence upon human action so inconsequential that it virtually never manifests itself when other factors are allowed to vary.

SCOUTING

So the question remains, if we are interested in more than theory development, how are we to decide what is worth study? One possibility would be to preface our trapping behavior with a period of scouting activity. Just like the trap-setter who scouts an area first to determine what, where, and how plentiful are its big game, we might well begin with systematic observation of the strong and regularly occurring natural effects around us. Perhaps we can reduce the problem of the dubious ecological importance of our derived effects by starting with effects that have already shown themselves to be powerful in the natural social environment. Although this is certainly not a point of initiation that has been previously unknown or unadvocated (e.g., Crano and Brewer, 1973; McGuire, 1973) within social psychology, it does appear quite underused. In determining what to research, we seem to have developed a decided tendency to pay less attention to what the people we are supposed to be studying are doing than to what other social psychologists are doing. There are well-known exceptions, of course. The tradition of research in bystander intervention is an excellent example. Its impetus came from a powerful social event (i.e., the Kitty Genovese case) that did not seem to be one of a kind and that people, generally, cared about. Similarly, Milgram's work on obedience began with the observation of the chilling strength of authority pressures in producing compliance of the sort seen in the concentration camps of Nazi Germany. I think it is instructive that more people outside of social psychology know about these two programs of social psychological investigation than perhaps any other. When I lecture about them to my large undergraduate classes, I am careful to emphasize the incident from which the work sprang. The effect upon the students is quite dramatic. I gain their attention almost as totally as if I had mentioned sex. And the academic issues of interest to college students should not be dismissed airily. Students offer a good approximation of what constitutes the "intelligent laypeople," the administrators, attorneys, politicians, and business people who run the society. If for no other reason than the public regard for what we do, social psychologists would do well to watch carefully what such people find interesting in our work.

In addition to the fact that they have inherent meaning for individuals who are not social psychologists, there is another reason to select effects for study because they appear to represent important behavioral phenomena. Once the decision of *what* to study has been made on this basis, we can more eagerly set out on the intellectual adventure of determining *why* it works the way it does. With enhanced confidence that we are not dealing with a trivial phenomenon, we can feel justified in expending the time and energy to uncover its mediator. With the "what" question out of the way, the sophisticated experimental procedures that are so well-suited to answering the "why" question become appropriate. Recall that the problem with these procedures was, paradoxically enough, their precision; their precision prevented us from knowing whether the things we were studying had any natural impact. But when the task is to explain why an effect already determined to be important exists, we want all the precision we can get. We want to be able to distill the effect to its essence and to differentiate among the possible theoretical explanations for its occurrence. Here, when capturing is once again the order of the day, we should want our experiments to be elegant, sensitive, and selective.

This, then, is the time for clever designs and operations that will allow us to provide evidence for and against one or another of the contending theoretical interpretations for the effect we have observed. Now the fascinating work of testing the applicability of relevant formulations can go on less fettered with worry about its purely academic character. That work is much more than just intellectually engaging, though. It represents the crucial scientific process of theory confirmation/disconfirmation; I will trust that the great significance of such a process for the understanding of human behavior need not be argued here. Granted there are certain advantages to approaching this process in a more deductive fashion than has been suggested in this chapter; the primary benefit appears to lie in the ability to do concentrated theory testing, especially through the prediction of effects that would not otherwise have been expected. Certainly, there are times when this sort of approach is appropriate. There are advantages as well, however, to the more inductive orientation that begins with naturally powerful effects and then seeks to determine their theoretical or conceptual underpinnings. In particular, if such a sequence were regularly employed, one result should be a steadily developing sense of which of our formulations account not just for aspects of human behavior but also for aspects of the behavior that *matter* around us. Earlier in this chapter, I suggested that theories could be viewed as somewhat like maps. To carry the metaphor a bit further, we can see that maps, like theories, may be more accurate in describing certain areas within their boundaries than others. Were I to set off on a trip, let us say through the land of human behavior, I would want to be assured that the map I used represented correctly the important locations of the journey; it would be cold comfort to know that it accurately depicted the inconsequential ones instead.

SOME EXAMPLES

In suggesting instances of the research orientation being advocated in this chapter, I have mentioned the work on bystander intervention in emergencies and on obedience to authority, stemming from the Kitty Genovese incident and Nazi concentration camp experience, respectively. Although these by and large excellent research programs indicate that such an orientation may be profitably applied to the consideration of quite prominent social events, it may just as readily be applied to more commonplace instances of naturally appearing effects. Since part of my charge when invited to contribute the present chapter was to present some of my research on the use of influence strategies in everyday, natural settings, it would be appropriate to do so in a fashion that served to illustrate how the research orientation advocated here was implemented in the investigation of those commonplace effects.

WHEN EVEN A PENNY HELPS

As suggested by the anecdote at the outset of this article, one place to scout for behavioral events worthy of study is in the actions of those around us. An equally suitable place lies in our own actions. Not only are we made aware of the existence of regularly occurring effects in this way but we also may introspect about the processes involved and, thereby, obtain hints as to their conceptual mediators. Powerful personal experiences are often suggestive of powerful and general psychological influences. One such personal experience led me to the investigation of a highly effective fund-raising tactic and its implications for the way compliance decisions are sometimes made.

I answered the door early one evening to find a young woman who was canvassing my neighborhood for the United Way. She identified herself and asked if I would give a monetary donation. It so happened that my home university has an active United Way organization and I had given in-house a few days earlier. It was also the end of the month and my finances were low. Besides, if I gave to all the solicitors for charity who came to my door, I would quickly require such service for myself. As she spoke, I had already decided against a donation and was preparing my reply to incorporate the above reasons. Then it happened. After asking for a contribution, she added five magic words. I know they were *the* magic words because my negative reply to the donation request itself literally caught in my throat when I heard them. "Even a penny will help," she said. And with that, she demolished my anticipated response. All the excuses I had prepared for failing to comply were based on financial considerations. They stated that I could not afford to give to her now or to her, too. But she said, "Even a penny will help" and rendered each of them impotent. How could I claim an inability to help when she claimed that "even a penny" was a legitimate form of aid? I had been neatly finessed into compliance. And there was another interesting feature of our exchange as well. When I stopped coughing (I really had choked on my attempted rejection), I gave her *not* the penny she had mentioned but the amount I usually allot to charity solicitors. At that, she thanked me, smiled innocently, and moved on.

To try to understand the psychology of what had taken place, I enlisted the efforts of a then-graduate student of mine, Dave Schroeder. In analyzing the situation, we realized that the request addendum "Even a penny will help" had not functioned as the invitation to contribute; that had come earlier. Rather, it served as a way of making legitimate even the most minimal sort of help. As such, it engaged, we thought, the action of a pair of powerful sources of influence in the social environment—powerful enough, at least, to change me from adamantly noncompliant in expectation to meekly compliant in reality. First, it removed my excuses for not offering aid of *some* kind. It is very difficult to argue that one does not have the wherewithal to provide as paltry a form of aid as a penny. I needed excuses for my noncompliance. Apparently, it was important that I have reasons to justify my behavior. Without those reasons as anchors, I was easily influenced. Second, by making legitimate a trivial amount of aid, the request had placed some image-maintenance pressures on me. What is the image of someone who will not give even a penny's worth of help to a good cause? It is the image of a decidedly unhelpful person; not the sort of image, public or private, I would like to have associated with me. To avoid such a characterization, compliance seemed required.

It appeared to us, then, that the real function of the phrase "Even a penny will help" was to legitimize the most paltry of contributions, and thereby allow for the action of the two processes described above. But all of this was speculation. We had not yet determined whether the effect was specific to me or substantially more general. The first order of business, then, was to establish that those five magic words did reliably and powerfully increase donations in a naturalistic fund-raising context. So, with the aid of the Phoenix branch of the American Cancer Society, we equipped ourselves with the appropriate identification badges and went soliciting for charity in a nearby middle-income neighborhood.

Our research assistants would go door to door asking for contributions in two ways. The first employed the standard request for funds used by the American Cancer Society's volunteers during its annual area drive: "I'm collecting money for the American Cancer Society. Would you be willing to help by giving a donation?" The other form of request was identical to the first, except that it included the addendum "Even a penny will help." After contacting 42 subjects with each type of request, we counted the money. It became immediately clear that I was not the only patsy in Phoenix. The even-a-penny technique that had worked so well on me a few weeks earlier produced nearly twice as much compliance as the standard technique (50% vs. 28.6%). Moreover, just as had occurred in my case, the even-a-penny subjects did not give only a penny. They gave the amount they normally furnished to such a charity organization. Thus, the median and modal contribution for both kinds of requests was $1. The mean contribution, among those who gave, was also highly alike for the standard and even-a-penny request conditions ($1.54 and $1.44, respectively). It is not surprising, then, that the even-a-penny request provided a significantly higher total yield ($30.34) than the standard request ($18.55).

At this point, we felt comfortable in our belief that we were dealing with an effect worth studying. The first steps of locating the effect and determining its natural impact had been taken. Now it was time to begin the fun of investigating why it worked the way it did. We already had a hypothesis, based on personal introspection, that "Even a penny will help" was effective because it served to legitimize a miniscule form of aid. When the most minimal of monetary contributions is deemed acceptable, excuses for failing to help become inapplicable; and the refusal to bestow such aid might jeopardize one's image as a benevolent person. But there was also a competing conceptual explanation. Perhaps the norm of social responsibility (e.g., Berkowitz and Daniels, 1963) that states that people should help those in need accounts for the effect. That is, it is possible that the words "Even a penny will help" cause people to perceive a greater need for aid than they would had the sentence not been added to the request. For this reason, they might be more likely to donate funds.

Good, we had plausible alternative interpretations, just what experimental social psychologists love to test and just what our trapper techniques are so suited to doing. The rest was the stimulating process of formulation testing. We would have to design an experiment that assessed the ability of the two alternative explanations to account for the effect. We knew, for example, that the social responsibility explanation proposed an increased perception of need by subjects exposed to the even-a-penny request. If we included a measure of perceived need in our next study and found no such enhanced perception, that would be evidence against the social responsibility formulation's applicability to our effect. Thus, when we conducted the study, we incorporated a scale measure of how needful the charity organization (again the American Cancer Society) was of funds, ranging from not at all in need (0) to extremely in need (6).

We also knew that the legitimization-of-small-favors interpretation implied that any statement that had the effect of making a penny seem like a legitimate contribution should result in a greater frequency of compliance. Consequently, we included a condition in our second study that was designed to serve this function without simultaneously implying that the charity agency was badly in need of funds. The solicitor in this condition (social legitimization) legitimized paltry donations by saying "We've already received some contributions ranging from a penny on up." Here, a penny contribution was legitimized via the social comparison-based information that others had given that amount. It was predicted that this condition would produce a compliance level above that of the standard request condition (control)[3] and comparable to the even-a-penny condition.

A final condition was included in our second study to test the derivation from the legitimization hypothesis that it is the legitimization of *minimal* favors that accounts for the effectiveness of the even-a-penny tactic. Subjects in this condition heard the standard request followed by the sentence "Even a dollar will help." Since a person is not as likely to be without excuses for failing to give a dollar and is not as likely to experience image damage in refusing to give a dollar as compared to a penny, the legitimization-of-small-favors explanation would predict that subjects in this condition would not show the high degree of compliance of those in the even-a-penny group; instead, their compliance rate might be expected to be intermediate between the control group and the even-a-penny group.

The results of the second experiment are presented in Table 1. The findings offered no support for the social responsibility explanation based on perceived need. As can be seen in Table 1, there was no significant difference between the even-a-penny and the control conditions in the perceived need scores subjects assigned to those requests, yet there was a substantial difference between them in obtained compliance (58.1% vs. 32.2%), $\chi^2(1) = 4.16$, $p < .05$. It seems unlikely, then, that the even-a-penney effect is mediated by the norm of social responsibility. On the other hand, there was considerable support for the legitimization hypothesis. First, the social legitimization condition that legitimized a penny contribution through social comparison information produced the highest percentage (64.5%) of compliance, a percentage that was comparable with that of the even-a-penny condition. Second, the even-a-dollar request that was designed to weaken the action of the legitimization-of-small-favors process resulted in a percentage of compliance (46.7%) that was intermediate to that of the even-a-penny and control requests. The even-a-dollar condition did not produce significantly

TABLE 1   Percentage of Subjects Donating, Total Amount
Contributed and Need Scores in Experiment 2 of Cialdini and
Schroeder (1976)

| | | TYPE OF REQUEST | | |
	Control	Even-A-Dollar	Even-A-Penny	Social Legitimization
% Donating	32.2	46.7	58.1	64.5
Total Amount Donated (in $)	20.74	19.35	31.30	28.61
Need Scores	3.30	2.67	3.42	2.83

Note. For the donation measures, each condition had 31 subjects per cell, except the even-a-dollar condition which had 30.

enhanced compliance as compared with the control, $\chi^2(1) = 1.34$, ns.[4]

Although the results of our second study support the legitimization interpretation of the even-a-penny effect, a number of additional questions remain unanswered. For example, we have suggested that making a paltry favor appear to be an acceptable one increased compliance for reasons having to do with (1) the elimination of available reasons for noncompliant behavior and (2) image-maintenance pressures. However, the action of these two processes has not been directly shown. Are they really the mediators of the effect? If so, what are their relative contributions to it? Is one the chief influence while the other has little impact? Are there certain conditions under which the first process is the dominant one and others in which the second is paramount? What would such conditions be? But I am beginnning to sound like a trapper again. Exactly. These strike me as interesting, conceptual questions requiring sophisticated experimental techniques to answer. The engaging activity of trapping may now be undertaken with increased assurance that the questions being asked refer back to something that is not just real in a statistical sense but real in a *real* sense.

In the previous example, a research project (Cialdini and Schroeder, 1976) was begun after an accidental encounter with the effect of interest. The same was true of the series of studies (Cialdini et al., 1976; Cialdini and Richardson, in press) that flowed from the earlier-described observation made in the stands of the Ohio State football stadium. There appears to be no good reason, however, for researchers to be so passive about the search for worthwhile effects to study. Certainly it is possible to live our daily lives ready and waiting to be struck by an interesting effect in the behaviors within or around us. But if we have a special topic of interest, it might be advantageous to take a more active, less reactive role. For instance, I am quite interested in the variables that influence compliance decisions. Just what are the factors that affect the likelihood that one person will say yes to another's request? To begin to find out, I have spent the past few summers as an observer, often a participant-observer, in a large number of real-world compliance situations. I wanted to learn which tactics and procedures the practitioners (e.g., merchandisers, fund raisers, con artists, negotiators, advertisers, and so on) thought were effective compliance inducers. Once a sufficiently large sample of such tactics was registered, I could categorize them according to the psychological principles that might explain their efficacy. With the initial scouting done, I could put on my trapper's shoes again and submit the most intriguing or powerful compliance strategies to experimental analysis in order to test the ability of the likely conceptual principles involved to account for the effects.

Without a doubt, these active scouting opportunities have proved to be among the most edifying experiences I have had. Not only have I become less of a sucker for the techniques that underlie the strategies I have observed but I have also learned a lot of social psychology. That is so because the people I have studied know a lot of social psychology, although they do not know that they do. As far as I can tell, there are seven or eight social psychological principles that mediate about 90% of the tactics they regularly and expertly employ. High-pressure sales organizations, legitimate charity agencies, waiters and waitresses, Hare Krishna devotees, Tupperware ladies, they all use procedures that *work*. If the procedures did not work, they or their practitioners would soon disappear; a process not unlike natural selection assures it. Imagine the little-kid-in-the-candy-store feeling for me. There I was, a compliance researcher surrounded by compliance tactics of demonstrated impact but indeterminate cause. It was a trapper's dream. I had my effects, I had my speculations about why they occurred; all that was left was the hunt.

THROWING THE LOW-BALL

During one of the times I was using the technique of participant observation to learn about naturally existing compliance strategies, I came across one that seemed especially intriguing. I had answered an ad for automobile sales trainees and was in the midst of a local auto dealer's program for selecting and training his car salesman. Toward the end of the program, after we had been exposed to a variety of techniques used to get the customer to buy, we were allowed to watch some of the regular salespeople operate. One tactic that enjoyed popularity among the staff is called by a number of names but, for our purposes, can be referred to as "low-balling" or "throwing a low-ball." Although the technique appeared in certain variations, the crucial feature was invariant: The customer was given a price figure substantially below the amount at which the salesperson ever intended to sell the car, in order to induce the customer to agree initially to the purchase.

Once the customer had made the decision for a specific car (and had even begun completing the appropriate forms), the price advantage was deftly removed. This could happen in several ways. Sometimes the customer was told that the initially cited price contained a calculation error or did not include an expensive option that the customer had assumed was part of the offer. More frequently, the initial price offer was rescinded when the salesperson checked with the sales manager who voided the arrangement because "We'd be losing money." The most clever variation required the salesperson to propose an inflated trade-in price for the customer's car that was then cut by the used-car assessor upon close examination; in most cases, the customer knew the true worth of the trade-in and thus considered the second evaluation the fair one. No matter which form of the procedure was used, the result was the same: The reason that the customer made a favorable purchase decision was removed and the performance of the desired behavior was made more costly. Further, the increased cost was such that the final price was equivalent to, and often somewhat above, that of the dealer's competitors. Yet, consistent with car dealership lore, it appeared that more customers remained with their decision to purchase the automobile, even at the adjusted figure, than would have bought it had the final price been disclosed before a purchase decision had been obtained.

I was amazed at the technique's effectiveness. Why should it work so well? After all, the reason these people had originally decided to buy the car rather than some other one was the clear price advantage, and that advantage had been surely removed by the end of the negotiations. But they still bought! What was going on here? I asked the opinions of the old hands at the place. They all said it had to do with getting the customer to make an initial decision to "buy *your* car." After that, their explanations became vague and circular. I should have known. These guys knew what worked; that was their job, and their livelihoods depended on it. But they did not understand why it worked, not in any conceptual sense, at least. That was my job. So, with the invaluable help of three graduate students—John Cacioppo, Rod Bassett, and John Miller—investigation of the low-ball technique began.

From what had been already observed, we surmised that the critical feature of the low-ball technique was the customer's initial decision to buy. More generally, the essence of the procedure is for a requester to induce another individual to resolve to perform a specified target behavior. Once that determination has been made, it is assumed that the decision will tend to persist, even after circumstances have changed to make performance of the target action more costly than before. Of course, at this point, all we had was my nonsystematic set of observations that this technique was effective. It was even possible, though it struck us as unlikely, that automobile dealers had been deluding themselves as to the power of low-balling. The logical first step, as in the prior example, was to establish the effectiveness of the tactic in a natural setting. Since we were not interested in car sales per se, we saw no necessary reason to examine low-balling in the automobile show-room. Indeed, if we could export the technique to some novel context and validate its effectiveness there, we would have valuable evidence for the generality of the effect. It was important, though, to insure that the context we chose demonstrated that the technique had genuine impact in affecting meaningfully sized compliance decisions. Thus, we wanted to show that the technique could significantly influence people to do something that they did not like to do.

One thing we knew that our undergraduate research subjects did not like to do was to get up early to participate in psychology experiments. At the time, any experimenter who put a sign-up sheet that designated openings before 8:00 a.m. probably also believed in the Easter Bunny. We wondered, though, could we get subjects to participate in an early-morning experiment via the low-ball procedure?

Cialdini: "Maybe we should see if we could get subjects to get out of bed and come down here for an early psychology experiment? But how early would be early enough?"

Research Assistant 1: "Eight o'clock, seven-thirty, how about seven?"

Cialdini: "Seven in the *morning,* are you crazy?"

Research Assistant 2: "Yea, let's try seven. Let's see just what we've got here."

Cialdini: "Ok, seven it is. But don't blame me if this flops."

The study itself implemented the low-ball strategy by obtaining a deci-sion from subjects to execute a target behavior (participation in a specific study) and then raising the cost of performing that behavior. The low-ball procedure was contrasted with a control procedure in which subjects were informed of the full cost of the target behavior before being requested to perform it. A confederate blind to the experimental hypothesis phoned Introductory Psychology students and asked them to come to an experiment on thinking processes, for which they would receive an hour of experimental credit. Before they were asked to participate, subjects in the control condi-tion were informed of the 7:00 a.m. starting time. They were also allowed to select one of two days for their participation. A subject making such an appointment was considered verbally compliant. Subjects in the low-ball condition, however, were asked if they would participate in the thinking processes study before being told of the 7:00 a.m. feature. Anyone who declined at this point was included in the data analysis as noncompliant. A subject who agreed to participate was *then* informed that the study would begin at 7:00 a.m. and asked to choose one of the two possible experiment dates. Again, any subject who made such an appointment was considered verbally compliant. In addition to the measure of verbal compliance, we included a measure of behavioral compliance. We counted the number of subjects in each condition who actually appeared for their early-morning appointments, where we saw to it that they did perform in a thinking processes study.

The results were striking. Of the 29 people called in the control condition, 9 agreed to participate and 7 of these actually appeared. Thus, only 24% of our control condition calls produced behaviorally compliant subjects. The low-ball procedure engendered sizably higher success rates, however, as 19 of the 34 subjects called complied verbally and 18 of the 34 (53%) complied behaviorally with the request. These data offered good evidence that the low-ball sequence of obtaining an active decision from a target person to perform an action and only then providing information about the full costs of the action is an effective and powerful way of gaining assent to a request to perform the fully described action.

On the basis of these findings, we felt justified in pursuing the answers to some conceptual questions concerning the phenomenon. One such question that suggested itself to us was whether the low-ball technique in which a requester secures an active decision to perform a target behavior and then raises the cost of performing the behavior is any different from the foot-in-the-door procedure (Freedman and Fraser, 1966). A requester uses the foot-in-the-door technique by inducing an individual to perform an initial favor and subsequently asking that individual to comply with a larger, second request. While both techniques seek to gain performance of a costly action by first obtaining assent to an apparently less costly request, there is at least one important difference. With the low-ball tactic, the behavior requested initially (e.g., buying a certain car) is in fact the target behavior; only the cost of carrying it out changes.

With the foot-in-the-door procedure, the behavior requested initially is not the target behavior itself, although the two may be related. Whether this difference is just a semantic one or is a genuine one that would manifest itself in the differential ability of the two tactics to produce compliance in given situations is, of course, an empirical question. It was our feeling that the procedural difference between the two techniques would empower the low-ball technique as the more effective compliance inducer. That is, an individual who has already decided to perform the target behavior may experience a greater sense of cognitive commitment to the performance of *that* behavior than would someone who has already decided to perform a different, though related, action. As a test, we conducted a field study in which three sets of procedures—low-ball, foot-in-the-door, and control—were used to induce subjects to perform a charitable action. The decision to employ a charity context was made in order to inquire further into the generality of the low-ball tactic. We wanted to know whether the technique could be influential in a charity setting and on benevolent behavior.

Our second low-ball study was performed on male graduate students who answered an experimenter's knock at the door of their dormitory rooms. The experimenter uniformly introduced himself as a representative of the United Way who was asking dorm residents to display United Way posters. The target behavior asked of each subject was the display of two such posters, one designated for the door and one for a window. Control condition subjects learned from the outset that agreeing to display the posters would require that they procure a "poster packet" containing the necessary materials at the downstairs dorm desk within an hour of experimental contact. A subject who agreed to do so and to display both posters was considered verbally compliant.

In the low-ball condition, the script was similar except that subjects did not learn of the required trip to the downstairs desk until they had agreed to post the materials. Then they were asked if they would perform the fully described target behavior. Subjects in the foot-in-the-door condition were initially asked to display a window poster (all agreed and were given the poster); they were then asked to perform the more costly behavior requiring the trip downstairs in order to obtain a door poster for display.

The data were disappointing to us at first. A high and approximately equal percentage of verbal compliance occurred across all conditions. With 10 subjects per group, 80% of the subjects in the low-ball condition and 70% of those in the other two conditions agreed to display the posters after being fully informed of the cost of doing so. It appeared that the very high level of verbal compliance in the control group produced a ceiling effect that prevented any demonstration of the effectiveness of our experimental groups. But, the next day when we measured behavior compliance with our request by counting the subjects who had actually displayed the posters, we found large differences. As hypothesized, the low-ball condition induced significantly greater performance of the target behavior (60%) than the control (20%) and foot-in-the-door (10%) conditions. Further, the superiority of the low-ball treatment maintained itself when only those subjects who verbally complied were considered; that is, 75% (6 of 8) of verbally compliant low-ball subjects complied behaviorally, whereas significantly fewer, 28.6% (2 of 7) and 14.3% (1 of 7) did so in the control and foot-in-the-door conditions, respectively.

We learned two things from our second study. First, the low-ball procedure appears robust across target behaviors and naturalistic situations. Charitable action, a form of behavior quite unlike the target behaviors to which the tactic is typically applied, was strongly affected by the technique in a setting that was different from both the car sales context and the subject recruitment context of our first experiment. Second, the low-ball does not seem to be a simple variant of the foot-in-the-door technique. In this regard, it is instructive to examine the relationship between verbal and behavioral compliance among the three conditions of the design. The behavioral superiority of the low-ball tactic was primarily due to the greater tendency of verbally compliant subjects in that condition to execute the target behavior they agreed to perform.

One plausible explanation for the form of these data supports our prior hypothesizing and underscores the need for compliance researchers to obtain behavioral measures of compliance. It was our feeling that a high percentage of the verbally compliant subjects in the foot-in-the-door and control conditions never intended to perform the target behavior; since the full cost of the target action was known to these subjects before they agreed to do it, many may have privately decided not to perform the costly action but rather to provide only the impression that they would, in order to avoid immediate social disapproval. The comparable subjects of the low-ball procedure, however, were induced to decide to execute the target behavior when it seemed to involve minimal cost; the resultant cognitive commitment to the performance of the target action should have existed privately from the outset for them and, thus, may have mediated the behavioral superiority of the technique. Whether or not the above account is the correct one, the form of the results does indicate that the low-ball procedure is not identical in effect to the foot-in-the-door, in that the two techniques produced distinct data patterns.

All right, at this point we were satisfied that we had located a powerful and cross-situationally robust influence upon the compliance process that was not a simple variant of an already-demonstrated technique. Now the real fun could begin. How could we account for the effect? In this case, there was a bonanza of possibilities. First, the effect might be explained with Heider's (1958) notion that a behavior often "engulfs the total field" and swamps the influence of other pertinent variables (e.g., volition; Jones and Harris, 1967) in the situation. Once an individual has behaved by making an active decision, the perception that the decisional behavior had occurred could overpower the influence of other relevant considerations such as subsequent changes in the cost of implementing the decision, thereby increasing the probability that the decision would be carried out.

Second, self-perception theory (Bem, 1967) might explain the phenomenon. It suggests that a person who perceives him- or herself freely behaving in a certain manner toward some object will self-attribute an attitude toward the object on the basis of that behavior. Such a process could explain the effectiveness of the low-ball procedures in our prior two studies. The perception of the initial, free agreement to take specified action may have caused our subjects to self-attribute favorability toward the action that would enhance the likelihood of its occurrence, even after it had later become more costly.

Third, a cognitive dissonance theory interpretation could explain the effect. Postdecisional dissonance resulting from the initial choice to perform an action could be expected to dispose the actor to become more favorable toward the chosen action; that enhanced favorability would then work to increase the chance that the action would be performed, even if it were rendered more costly by subsequent events.

Finally, a possible account of the low-ball effect lies in the commitment formulation presented by Kiesler (1971). It suggests that a major function of commitment is to impart resistance to change. To the extent that one is committed to a decision, for instance, the decision becomes less changeable. According to Kiesler's analysis, one who makes a decision behaviorally and with choice will be cognitively committed to the decision and disinclined to change it. The applicability of the commitment formulation to the low-ball phenomenon seems straightforward: An active initial decision to behave positively toward some object will tend to persist because the active decision will create commitment, that is, a resistance to change that will tend to be impervious to the influence of subsequent data concerning the wisdom of the decision.

We were wealthy with possible mediators for the effect and, thus, provided with the opportunity for some fancy trapping. If we were to assess the applicability of the various accounts in a third study, we knew we would first have to establish the ways in which the formulations were different in their predictions concerning the phenomenon. Then we would have to incorporate these differences into our experimental design so that the respective predictions could be confirmed or disconfirmed. There seemed to us to be three such areas of difference that could be experimentally mined.

Volition in the initial decision. Only one of our contenders—the notion that behavior engulfs the field—would predict that the low-ball phenomenon should occur when an individual makes an initial, active decision, whether or not the decision was made with a high degree of choice. The perception that a behavior had been performed should, by this account, trivialize the effect of other relevant variables such as volition (e.g., Jones and Harris, 1967). Each of the other three formulations, however, does stress the importance of the factor of volition and would expect the low-ball procedure to work only when freedom of choice existed for the preliminary behavior decision. Consequently, a manipulation of volition of decision was included in the third study.

Attitude toward the target action. Another experimental feature that would allow a discrimination among the alternative explanations would be the inclusion of an attitude measure. Two of the formulations—self-perception and dissonance—argue that an individual who has made a favorable behavioral decision toward an object will tend to persevere in the decision, even in the face of newly negative circumstances, because the individual has come to view the object more positively than before as a result of the decision itself. Thus, these two theories would expect a low-ball effect to be accompanied by a mediating attitude change effect. Although the idea that behavior engulfs the field is nonpredictive concerning this point, the commitment formulation is clear in its expectation that a shift in attitude would not accompany a simple increase in commitment. Kiesler (1971) has argued that commitment itself does not produce attitude change and has presented data to support his position (e.g., Kiesler and Sakumura, 1966).

Justification for the initial decision. A final experimental component that would allow us to assess the predictive power of the alternative explanations for the effect would involve a somewhat different operationalization of the low-ball sequence than was employed in our first two experiments. In those studies, a subject was initially induced to agree to perform an action and the cost of the action was then increased when the requester *added* some rather noxious further conditions. Although legitimate, such a way of enacting the low-ball tactic does not differentiate among the possible mediators of the phenomenon.

Another, equally legitimate operationalization—in which the requester initially obtains an agreement by describing specific positive properties of the target action that make it more attractive than alternative actions and then increases the cost of the target action by *removing* those positive properties—would provide such differentiation, however. This latter implementation can be seen to be comparable to that of the car sales context in which the customer is induced to decide to purchase a particular car on the basis of a clear price advantage which is then removed after the active decision has been made. Such a procedural sequence would allow a test among the various explanatory formulations because the clear advantage initially offered by the requester provides a wholly external justification for the decision to perform the target action.

Self-perception and dissonance theories would not expect the low-ball effect to occur under such conditions. That is, since the target behavior was initially presented in a way that made it easily the most attractive alternative, deciding to perform it would result neither in postdecisional dissonance (Brehm, 1956) nor in a revised self-perception of attitude (Bem, 1967); consequently, without the mediating effect of initial attitude change, the decision to perform the target behavior should not be expected to persist after circumstances have changed to make the behavior a more costly one. Neither of the other two possible mediators of the phenomenon would make a similar prediction; A behavioral decision would be expected to engulf the field and a behavioral decision would be expected to produce commitment whether or not the decision was perfectly justified.

In order to provide evidence concerning the conceptual mediator of the low-ball phenomenon, a laboratory study was conducted that included the above-described form of low-balling, an attitude change measurement, and a manipulation of choice. A laboratory study now seemed warranted, given the prior demonstration of the effect's impact in naturalistic settings. The study contained three conditions, each of which required subjects to make an initial decision to take one of two alternative personality tests. In the two experimental conditions, subjects were informed before the initial selection that one of the tests (the target test) would produce twice as much experimental credit as the other. In one of these experimental conditions (low-ball/high volition), the subjects were given free choice in making the initial selection between the tests. In the other experimental condition (low-ball/low volition), the subjects were initially required to select the test that provided the greater amount of credit.

After the initial selection, subjects in both experimental conditions recorded their attitudes toward the alternatives. Then they learned that the earlier credit information had been in error and that they would receive the small amount of credit for taking either personality test. At that point subjects were allowed to decide again, freely in all cases, which test they wished to have administered to them. A control condition, in which subjects made an initial free selection between the alternatives at the lower amount of credit production, provided the baseline information necessary to assess the effectiveness of the two low-ball conditions.

The four possible explanations of the low-ball effect would make different predictions in the experimental situation. From the simple notion that behavior engulfs the field, we should expect that subjects who initially selected the personality test providing the larger amount of credit would remain with that selection after the credit superiority of the test had been eliminated; further, this would be the case whether or not the initial selection was made with a high degree of volition. The self-perception and dissonance formulations would predict that, since the initial decision for the test offering more credit was wholly justified by the credit difference, the experimental subjects should not experience more favorable attitudes toward the chosen alternative; consequently, these subjects should not be expected to maintain their initial decisions to any enhanced degrees after the credit level of the selected test was reduced to that of the nonselected test. The commitment formulation, on the other hand, would expect that subjects who initially selected the test offering the higher amount of credit would not experience positive attitude shifts toward the selected test but would, nevertheless, retain that decision after the test's credit advantages had been removed; additionally, the commitment interpretation would predict that this perseverance of the first decision would result only when subjects had been allowed free choice in making the decision. These varying predictions are represented in Figure 1.

Formulation	Volition in initial decision	Attitude change toward target action	Justification for initial decision	Prediction
Behavior engulfs the field	Unnecessary for effect to occur	?	Does not preclude effect	Effect should occur in both experimental conditions
Self-perception	Necessary for effect to occur	Necessary for effect to occur	Precludes effect	Effect should not occur in either experimental condition
Dissonance	Necessary for effect to occur	Necessary for effect to occur	Precludes effect	Effect should not occur in either experimental condition
Commitment	Necessary for effect to occur	Unnecessary for effect to occur	Does not preclude effect	Effect should occur only in low-ball/high volition condition

FIGURE 1   Areas of Differentiation

Before examining the tendencies of our subjects to choose between the available personality tests, we looked at their rated attitudes toward the tests. Attractiveness ratings had been taken both before and after the initial test selection had been made. Quite simply, there were no significant changes in attractiveness of the tests as a result of the initial selection in any condition. Turning to the behavioral data, we find an entirely different story.

Table 2 shows the percentages of subjects choosing to take the target test, both at the initial decision point (when low-ball subjects thought the test produced twice the standard allotment of experimental credit) as well as at the final decision point (when the credit advantage had already been removed). As the table indicates, the low-ball/high volition procedures were much more successful in inducing subjects to make an initial selection of the target test than control procedures (81% vs. 31%). Of course, 100% of the low-ball/low volition subjects initially selected the target test, since it was assigned to them. The crucial test of superiority of the technique, however, must be seen in the data of the final decision, when all subjects selected freely between the tests that had by then been rendered comparable in credit production. Here, the low-ball/high volition condition produced significantly greater selection of the target test (61%) than either its low volition counterpart (42%) or the control condition (31%).

TABLE 2 Percentages of Initial and Final Selections of the Target Test of Experiment 3 in Cialdini et al. (1978)

	Initial Selection	Final Selection
Low-ball/high volition	81	61
Low-ball/low volition	assigned	42
Control	31	31

Note. Each condition contained 48 subjects.

Although each of the possible explanations we have considered for the low-ball effect could account for aspects of the data of Experiment 3, the findings are wholly consistent only with the commitment interpretation. That is, only Kiesler's (1971) commitment formulation would have entirely predicted the obtained pattern of results that (1) the low-ball technique would produce greater final selection of the target activity than a control treatment, (2) the technique would be effective despite a lack of attitude change effects associated with the initial decision, and (3) the technique would only be more effective than a control treatment when the initial decision was made with free choice. Of course, it should be recalled that Experiment 3 was designed specifically to eliminate the explanatory relevance of dissonance and self-perception theories. In other settings such as those of Experiments 1 and 2 as well as a variety of naturally occurring situations, dissonance or self-perception factors may well play a role in enhancing the efficacy of the low-ball tactic. Thus, while it appears that commitment to perform an action is the determining condition for the occurrence of a low-ball effect, such a commitment might well produce augmented effects if it also engaged the action of dissonance or self-perception principles.

Together the results of the three studies indicate that the low-ball phenomenon is reliable, robust, and mediated by a commitment to an initial, uncoerced decision to perform a behavior. It is interesting to speculate as to why the factor of volition plays a crucial role in the technique's effectiveness if, as Experiment 3 showed, it does not necessarily result in attitude shifts. Kiesler (1971) has suggested that the perception of choice carries with it the perception of responsibility. Thus, one who freely chooses to perform an action should feel responsible for the action. In fact, Kiesler goes on to suggest that the entire basis of commitment may lie within the concept of self-responsibility: One is commited to something when one feels responsible for it. The reason we are less likely to change once committed is that reversing what we feel responsible for results in a variety of negative self-perceptions (e.g., hastiness; a lack of intelligence, judgment, or appropriate caution; and so on); consequently, we will resist such change.

Another possibility is that situations requiring free choice between alternatives involve a certain amount of strain; that is, abnormally high degrees of information vigilance and awareness are necessary so that the proper decision can be made. Once a resolution has been attained, especially in the instance of a large-scale decision such as an automobile purchase, we may find ourselves loath to destroy the resultant sense of completion and begin again the stressful task of processing choice-relevant information. A test of the validity of these speculations was, of course, beyond the intended scope of the present research; nonetheless, these speculations do offer plausible underlying conceptual frameworks within which to place our results and, consequently, the opportunity for still further challenging work.

FULL-CYCLE SOCIAL PSYCHOLOGY

From the outset of this piece, I have advocated that social psychological investigators begin work, with much more frequency than at present, from naturally occurring instances of social phenomena. Progressive steps should then be taken to establish the power, generality, and theoretical/conceptual underpinnings of the phenomenon of interest. However, natural observation should not be restricted to the beginnings of the research venture; it should be used as well to complete the final arc in the circle. That is, naturally occurring instances should be employed not only to identify effects suitable for experimental study but also to check on the validity of the findings from that experimentation. For example, in the above-described low-ball project, we determined that the action of the variable of commitment was limited to a situation involving the perception of free choice. If we look back to the car sales context that originally brought the low-ball technique to light for us, we can see that a customer's perception of decisional freedom is represented in that setting. Had it not been the case, we should have doubted the ecological validity of our laboratory findings.

It is noteworthy that, in referring to the natural environment to check on this aspect of our results, we can see that not all tactics designed by practitioners to enhance compliance seem to require that free choice be represented. Those that employ the factor of reciprocation, for example, do not. The followers of Krishna, who approach airport visitors to pin flowers on them first and then ask for donations, try to engage the cultural rule for reciprocation of favors (Gouldner, 1960) without asking their targets' choice in the matter of the instigating first favor. The same is true of the disabled veterans organizations which mail us unsolicited address labels, greeting cards, or ballpoint pens along with their request for a contribution. Unlike the low-ball practitioners, these requesters seemingly feel that their tactics (which are among the most cost-effective I have observed) will produce a profitable exchange without the target person's free agreement to the initial stage of the interaction. This sort of comparison between observed compliance procedures cannot help but lead to testable speculation concerning the conditions under which the perception of choice is necessary for the occurrence of compliance. The cycle thus, begins again.

The proposal, then, is for a "full-cycle" approach, wherein initial natural observation gives direction to subsequent controlled experimentation, the outcomes of which can then be given external validation through further natural observation that may stimulate still further experimentation. Systematic recourse to the evidence of the real world both before and after performance of the experimental work may thereby reduce the extent to which current social psychological research can be criticized as artificial and epiphenomenal.

APPLICATION

It does not require a careful reading of this chapter to see that, for a piece in a volume on applied social psychology, there is little suggestion of how to apply the discipline of social psychology to the real world for the sake of society. Instead it has been suggested that we apply the real world to social psychology for the sake of the discipline. Nonetheless, the two approaches are not independent. If one accepts that it is the discipline's social responsibility to identify principles that can be applied to areas of societal concern (Cialdini et al., 1979) then it is important to have prior confidence in the strength of those principles to affect behavior in natural settings. For example, there is an enormous problem of noncompliance in the area of health behavior. It has been estimated that well over half of physicians' regimens for the remission or prevention of disorders are not complied with by patients. Anyone attempting to design a program to reduce such noncompliance would be wise to look to the techniques that have been determined to be powerful in other natural compliance settings. And if the mediating principles that underlie these techniques have also been determined by previous experimentation, the probability of a successful transplant to the health context should be greatly enhanced. Without that vital mediational information, the functional essence of a selected technique is liable to get lost in the translation. Perhaps the most attractive feature of full-cycle social psychology, then, is its ability to foster the performance of solid social science that lends itself easily to social service.

Note, however, that the distinction between science and service remains. Application is *not* the final step in the full-cycle model; it is not even a necessary step. Rather, it is a potential bonus. The model's primary purpose is scientific. It is intended to lead to more realistic information about the factors that influence the preponderance of human behavior. One extremely valuable by-product of such information, however, is a science that is more directly applicable to real problem settings. Clear applicability is such a desirable commodity and yet is in such short supply within much of social psychology that a shift toward a full-cycle approach might be worth a try on that basis alone. After all, even a smidgen more applicability would help.

NOTES

1. Although the approach taken in that research is relevant to this article, the content area is not. Accordingly, the interested reader may look elsewhere for reports of the work (Cialdini et al., 1976; Cialdini and Richardson, in press).

2. It might be a good idea to distinguish at this point between the term *trapping* as I have used it and the term *stage managing* as employed by McGuire (1973). Trapping refers to the honest attempt to test whether a theoretically derived phenomenon can be said to occur under the conditions required by the theory. Stage managing, on the other hand, refers to the arrangement of experimental procedures so that an effect already presumed to occur will surely be demonstrated to occur.

3. In order to keep the standard request as comparable as possible to the social legitimization condition, the standard request was modified slightly from that of our first study. In the present study, the standard request was, "We've already received some contributions, and I wonder if you would be willing to help by giving a donation."

4. If we assume that, for many of our subjects, a one-dollar request by the American Cancer Society was perceived as a small one, the intermediate level of compliance in the even-a-dollar condition fits nicely with the legitimization-of-small-favors hypothesis. In support of that

assumption, among the donors in the control conditions of our studies, nearly a third spontaneously gave more than a dollar contribution, with the smallest such donation being twice as large as the dollar request and the average being more than three and one-half times as great. Thus, while it is likely that all of the subjects in the even-a-penny condition saw the penny request as a small one, it appears that a substantial portion of subjects in the even-a-dollar condition saw the dollar request as a small one as well.

REFERENCES

BEM, D. (1967) "Self-perception: an alternative interpretation of cognitive dissonance phenomena." *Psychological Review* 74: 183-200.

BERKOWITZ, L. and L. DANIELS (1963) "Responsibility and dependency." Journal of Abnormal and Social Psychology 65: 429-436.

BICKMAN, L. (1976) "The gap between basic research findings and applications: can it be closed?" Presented at the meeting of the Midwestern Psychological Association, Chicago, May.

BREHM, J. (1956) "Postdecision changes in the desirability of alternatives." Journal of Abnormal and Social Psychology 52: 384-389.

CIALDINI, R.B., L. BICKMAN, and J.T. CACIOPPO (1979) "An example of consumeristic social psychology: bargaining tough in the new car showroom." Journal of Applied Social Psychology 9: 115-126.

————— R.J. BORDEN, A. THORNE, M.R. WALKER, S. FREEMAN, and L.R. SLOAN (1976) "Basking in reflected glory: three (football) field studies." Journal of Personality and Social Psychology 34:366-375.

————— J.T. CACIOPPO, R. BASSETT, and J.A. MILLER (1978) "Low-ball procedure for producing compliance: commitment then cost." Journal of Personality and Social Psychology 36:463-476.

————— and K.D. RICHARDSON (in press) "Two indirect tactics of image management: basking and blasting." Journal of Personality and Social Psychology.

————— and D.A. SCHROEDER (1976) "Increasing contributions by legitimizing paltry contributions: when even a penny helps." Journal of Personality and Social Psychology 34:599-604.

CRANO, W.D. and M.B. BREWER (1973) Principles of Research in Social Psychology. New York: McGraw-Hill.

FREEDMAN, J.L. and S. FRASER (1966) "Compliance without pressure: the foot-in-the-door technique." Journal of Personality and Social Psychology 4: 195-202.

GOULDNER, A.W. (1960) "The norm of reciprocity: a preliminary statement." American Sociological Review 25: 161-178.

HEIDER, F. (1958) The Psychology of Interpersonal Relations. New York: John Wiley.

HELMREICH, R. (1975) "Applied social psychology: the unfulfilled promise." Personality and Social Psychology Bulletin 1: 548-560.

JONES, E.E. and V.E. HARRIS (1967) "The attribution of attitude." Journal of Experimental Social Psychology 3: 1-24.

KIESLER, C.A. (1971) The Psychology of Commitment. New York: Academic Press.

————— and J. Sakumura (1966) "A test of a model for commitment." Journal of Personality and Social Psychology 3: 349-353.

LANGER, E.J. (1978) "Rethinking the role of thought in social interaction," in J.H. Harvey et al. (eds.), New Directions in Attribution Research (Vol. 2) Potomac, MD: Erlbaum.

McGUIRE, W.J. (1973) "The yin and yang of progress in social psychology: seven koan." Journal of Personality and Social Psychology 26: 446-456.

SMITH, MB. (1972) "Is experimental social psychology advancing." Journal of Experimental Social Psychology 8: 86-96.

CHARLES A. KIESLER   **3**

PSYCHOLOGY AND PUBLIC POLICY

The relationship of psychology to public policy is a broad topic. This article describes needs for scientifically based information on human behavior for public policy; problems that psychology faces in relating to the analysis, formation, and change of public policy; changes in psychology and the behavioral sciences which must occur in the next decade if these efforts are to crystallize; and the problems that such changes would produce for graduate training in psychology.

Some of the country's largest and most persistent problems directly relate to human behavior: our mutual insensitivity to each other, our beliefs which inadvertently affect the freedom and happiness of others, our collective threats to future generations. As citizens, we are aware of social problems receiving considerable legislative attention. In the last 45 years, the American voter has rather consistently supported an increasing array of social programs and social legislation. The federal government now spends approximately $200 billion (or about one-half the total federal budget) in the areas of health, education, welfare, employment, housing, environment, and criminal justice. Perhaps even more public funds are spent at the state, county, and city governmental levels. For example, in the 750 community mental health centers around the country, nonfederal public sources (state, county, and city funds) contribute three times as much as the federal government.

Considerable amounts of money are also spent studying these programs, their development and implementation, and feasibility of various alternative programs, and, to a much lesser extent, their effectiveness. According to a recent analysis by Abt (1976), the federal government annually spends about $1 billion on applied social research. Abt's analysis is noteworthy because he attempts a broad cost/benefit analysis of applied social research. There are some difficult problems and debatable assumptions inherent in his analysis,

AUTHOR'S NOTE: Adapted from "The Policy Implications of Psychology," Invited Address, SPSSI, presented at the meeting of the American Psychological Association, Toronto, Canada, 1978.

since it is often difficult to tell what *is* research. Most of the federal statistics are accumulated on the basis of research *and development* (R&D) expenditures. The definition of "development" is left unclear and, in summary statistics, the relationship of development to research is often tenuous.

Sometimes, in the guise of development, applied research is even actively avoided. Once when I was a young assistant professor at Yale, I was approached by a woman who said she had access to $2 million in research and development funds to study and assist in the hiring of the handicapped. She was very public spirited and asked if I would be part-time director of a center set up for that purpose. My major professional interest was attitude and behavior change, and my interest was caught by some of the intriguing possibilities. I immediately outlined a potential program of research and implementation. I suggested that we study the problem from both directions: the acceptability of the handicapped by potential employers, including the variables contributing to their effectiveness and satisfaction as employees, and the variables which affect the willingness of the handicapped to apply for jobs in industry. In this way, we could study how to entice employers and potential employees to become attracted to each other and emphasize the variables leading to long-term satisfaction on both sides. It seemed to me to be the perfect opportunity to turn my basic research interest into some interesting applied area with socially beneficial results.

My proposal was greeted with the amused tolerance that often falls on the exuberant and idealistic child. She patiently explained to me that my proposal was basic research and the funding sources were not interested in basic research; they were interested in development. They had in mind renting a building which would become a clearinghouse for movies and perhaps other literature dealing with the employment of the handicapped. They wanted to ask employers and the handicapped to come see the movies. They thought perhaps I could give some questionnaires after the movies to tell how much effect that they had had. Undaunted, I pointed out that the literature indicated that movies with self-selected audiences were unlikely to have any dramatic effect on hiring practices. The answer was that both she and the funding sources were convinced that movies were one of the dominant influences in our culture, and they were certain that a center housing a number of such films was just what the country needed. An extended discussion followed, with both sides budging not a bit, and I finally not so politely withdrew from any contact with the proposed center. I never found out what happened, but I sincerely hope that no one spent $2 million on a project with such dubious value.

It is important to note that this sort of money might well be classified as research and development expenditures by the federal government. The

R&D figures the federal government uses are likely to be distorted with ill-conceived development costs being lumped together with thoughtful applied social research. The difficult problems inherent in any cost/benefit analysis of applied social research are magnified by such ambiguities in the federal statistics. According to Abt, between 1965 and 1968 alone some 500 new social programs were legislated and implemented in the United States and a thousand new programs were implemented between 1965 and 1975. Between 1965 and 1975, Abt identified $1 trillion ($1,000 billion) spent in social programs in the United States, and $7.4 billion in applied social research. Thus, $7 were spent for research for every $1,000 directly spent on social programs.

Abt then tries to look at the consequences of applied social research for specific programs. He tries to make a best guess about outcomes of specific recommendations contained in applied social research. These varied from the Department of Health, Education and Welfare maternal and child health study, which Abt feels led to reduced infant mortality, and to the Manhattan bail bond experiment and evaluation, which led to the 1966 bail reform act and saved $50 million a year in detention costs. The examples illustrate the difficulty in obtaining consensual agreement on specific effects. There are obviously important ambiguities in assessing the outcome of applied social research. At this stage of understanding, one must make assumptions regarding the recommendations of research, their specific outcomes, and whether the outcomes would have occurred in the absence of any research. But best guesses are still useful in a preliminary analysis such as this.

Abt's preliminary analysis shows $100 worth of increased impact for every dollar spent on applied social research. This figure is particularly interesting given the fact that most applied social research goes into smaller social programs. Roughly 75% of applied social research is spent on about 25% of social policies and programs. For example, welfare and social security account for about half of the $1 trillion spent over the decade on social programs, but these programs spent, on the average, only .2% of their total funds on applied social research, the lowest of the 10 categories of programs. Abt's analysis is a very complicated and surely controversial one, but very promising as a first-cut study of the relationship between applied social research and social outcome.

The important point for psychology is that all of these programs—all one thousand billion dollars worth—were designed to benefit human beings. All were based on certain fundamental, although often unarticulated, assumptions about human behavior. And in every instance, it was assumed that a particular program would provide more benefit than alternative ones. Abt's analysis shows that those programs with more applied social research had more effect. More research dollars led to more demonstrated benefit in the cost/benefit analysis. Although many aspects of applied social research are controversial and not all social scientists even think it worthwhile, most would agree that we need more and better research regarding alternative policy decisions.

An intimate involvement of psychology and the behavioral sciences with social policy is badly needed. Discussions of federal policy need to be better informed regarding the underlying issues of human behavior. The uneasy relationship between technology and society could be enhanced by a better public understanding of human behavior and our scientific knowledge of it.

There are a number of problems which prohibit better use of psychology in social policy, not the least of which is the fact that social "policy" more often reflects a series of pragmatic political or bureaucratic decisions than it does a thoughtful consideration and analysis of the social problem itself. For example, a variety of federal funds for health are now distributed by major categories, with specific decisions on the allocations of funds to be made regionally or by states. It is conceivable, indeed a serious danger, that various research funds associated with health (including mental health) could also ultimately be processed in such a decentralized fashion. That decision might be made politically as a result of the pressures on the Congress, without any serious or detailed consideration of the ability of the states or regions to review and decide upon requests for funding in basic science in the fields of health and mental health. Too, public decision makers often find secrecy advantageous. "Policymakers wish to keep their considerations of the options confidential, lest they stir up a public debate that threatens the acceptance of the preferred alternative by confounding the issues or raising the saliency of undesired alternatives" (Abt, 1976: 16). Further, the pressures of special interest groups on the Congress and on federal agencies regarding social programs can be so intense as to leave the scientific questions submerged in a political discussion. It is not unusual in congressional hearings to have a series of special interest groups testifying on a particular proposed bill, but not a single scientist or scientific group.

Questions of behavioral science should not dominate discussions of legislative programs involving or affecting humans. However, it is certainly desirable that fundamental knowledge about human beings become an integral part of the discussion of alternative social programs. Improvement on this dimension could be helped along in several ways.

There is not now any clear conception of national experiments in the area of social programs. Campbell's (1969) concept of the experimenting society is an appropriate model for national experiments on public programs, but it is certainly a long way from popular acceptance. For example, discussions of national health insurance have been frequent in Congress and the White House in recent years. Alternative plans for the possible inclusion of mental health benefits into such insurance are often mentioned. The usual issues raised are the cost of such benefits and whether they have any positive impact on the recipients of mental health services. We developed a plan within the American Psychological Association (APA) for evaluation and accountability devices for national health insurance ("Principles for continuing evaluation and accountability controls for a national health insurance program," 1978). It is incredible to me that in spite of the major focus of the issue being on cost and impact of services, we still have difficulty getting both politicians and bureaucrats to seriously consider possible plans for evaluation and accountability, the very heart of the political question.

One underlying problem is that the President and the Congress do not have an institutionalized source for high-level advice on issues for behavioral science. The President's Science Advisor's Office does not include behavioral scientists. Yet one-half of the federal budget is dependent on major assumptions in that field. We need in the White House an Office of Behavioral Science and Policy Review, to advise the President (and the Congress) on federal policies in which assumptions regarding human behavior are critical and central. The President's science advisor does not and never has performed this function. To the extent that scientific knowledge about human behavior has affected federal decisions and policies, it has been through such economic advisors as Walter Heller. Perhaps a behavioral scientist other than an economist would not offer better advice, but at least their behavioral background is more germane to the human questions underlying social policy and social programs.

We desperately need such advice and, more particularly, the systematic study of policy alternatives. Consider a few examples of the interplay between technology and human behavior that will continue to haunt the country unless approached knowledgeably and systemically.

EXAMPLES OF THE INTERPLAY BETWEEN TECHNOLOGY AND HUMAN BEHAVIOR

ENERGY USE

The development of new energy sources and the refinement of techniques of production of energy are clearly problems for the engineering and physical sciences. However, the patterns of use of energy are almost entirely a question of human attitudes and behavior. Here, conservation rests on such simple behaviors as turning a switch on or off, monitoring one's own behavior (as in the use of dishwashers or one's driving habits), turning up the thermostat in the summer and down in the winter, and the acceptance and/or purchase of alternative modes of supply (there is obviously great resistance to conversion to solar energy, for example). The behaviors and attitudes involved are simple and relevant questions easily researchable, and all could have an important impact on the overall use of energy and the patterns of use. It is a good guess that the nation's use of energy could be decreased somewhere on the order of 20%–30% by effective strategy within these behavioral areas (see Pallak's article in this volume, for example). On a theoretical level the change of these simple behaviors is not complex at all. However, translating this theoretical knowledge into large-scale programs would not be a simple task, and would require further programmatic work. We already know a great deal about such issues in psychology and the behavioral sciences, and have the social technology (to use Varela's, 1977, term) to make a considerable contribution.

MEDICAL COMPLIANCE

This issue refers to people taking drugs as prescribed or following medical regimens as recommended. For example, a person may be receiving a drug for an intestinal infection. The medical practitioner might prescribe the drug for seven days. However, it would not be unusual for a patient to quit taking the drug after beginning to feel better. What has been found is that if people do not follow drug regimens as prescribed, it is very likely for the symptoms to reappear, with the consequent costs in medical charges, absenteeism, and the like. Designing a system in which people will follow medical regimens should not be a complex problem for social psychologists. Indeed, compliance is probably one of the most researched topics in social psychology over the last 40 years. A simple problem perhaps, but the costs of medical noncompliance are now alleged to be $30 billion a year in the United States alone (Sackett and Haynes, 1976). This is a clear-cut problem in applied social psychology, but the lack of attention to it is now costing the country $30 billion a year. It is ironic to note that Weisskopf (1972) estimates that the total cost of basic science throughout world history to the present is $30 billion.

PREVENTION

Behavioral science has a good deal to offer in the area of primary prevention, including potential research on dietary habits, exercise, dental habits, and smoking, to name only a few. The current human costs in these areas and the potential savings in human misery are enormous. It is worthwhile to note that some of these topics of research go back 35 years in social psychology, most specifically including the early research of Kurt Lewin and his colleagues on dietary habits.

GENERAL MEDICAL CARE

It is generally acknowledged that 50%– 70% of the cases that medical general practitioners treat are psychological in nature. We know that, but we are giving little thought on how to handle it, except for a few more hours of classroom instruction for medical students. Unfortunately, the whole medical system is designed to funnel these cases to professionals who are probably the least qualified to treat them. Research here must focus on (1) the incentives which lead individuals to seek out general practitioners for what are basically psychological problems and (2) the apparent reluctance of practitioners to refer patients to others in the mental health system better trained to handle the problems. These patients, incidentally, are very high users of the medical system; and their drain on that system prevents it from better dealing with the overall array of problems of physical health.

WELFARE

As mentioned, welfare and social security constitute about half the total federal cost in social programs. To some extent, the nation focuses its attention in the areas of welfare on food (such as food stamps and the like) and income (the negative income tax is a good example, even though it was never really accepted). One could consider both of these activities to, be largely maintenance in character: activities which may directly alleviate human suffering, but which may also tend to freeze the individuals concerned into a particular rung on the social ladder.

The design of the welfare system needs conceptual attention beyond simple maintenance, particularly with reference to the types of welfare activities which could produce cross-generational change. That is to say, the most desired welfare commitment would be one which alleviates human suffering at a given point in time, but allows the children involved in that circumstance to become more effective participants in the society as they mature. In this sense, one would design potential welfare programs to emphasize variables affecting the life alternatives of children: whether they would graduate from high school and go on to technical school, college, or apprenticeship programs. I can remember my own experience as a 16-year-old on welfare and of a social worker trying to prevent me from going to college on the grounds that I should work full-time to support my family and reduce welfare costs. That seemed terribly shortsighted to me then, and it still does. The most effective welfare system would not be self-perpetuating across generations. What is needed is some research into those variables which interfere with or alleviate systemic self-perpetuation.

The above are merely examples of rather large-scale and costly social problems today that desperately need the attention of applied behavioral science. Research is needed both in specific aspects of human behavior (e.g., compliance) and in broader issues related to decisions among alternative policies (factors leading to increased education among children from lower income families).

In summary, psychology and behavioral science need to direct attention to several areas. We need to review federal policies with regard to the potential psychological implications for the people involved; we need to develop and promote an experimenting flavor to program implementation and consideration; we need to crystallize our advice on such issues, if only to show how the right questions can be asked; we need to point to underdeveloped areas such as medical compliance to stimulate and support research; and we need to help fill in the gaps between societal questions and basic research knowledge.

PROBLEMS OF PSYCHOLOGY IN RELATING TO POLICY ISSUES

We have sketched a variety of needs of policy makers for psychological information. The problems with providing that information—with extrapolating from psychology to policy—are many and as varied as the needs. Let us simply touch on a few examples in this section.

PROBLEMS WITH RESEARCH METHOD

There are a number of difficulties in extrapolating from our research in social psychology. For example, in social psychology there is considerable confusion between the generalizability of experimental operations versus that of theoretical variables. The antiexperimental component to the so-called crisis in social psychology rests on just such a confusion. Take an example from dissonance theory. It would be silly to propose offering small rewards to change national smoking habits. It is true that dissonance theory says that small monetary inducements for behavior change are more effective in producing attitude change. However, that is a theoretical variable; and the extent to which the experimental operation of offering small rewards can be extrapolated to less controlled settings is less clear, particularly with regard to important behaviors that are difficult to change. I have no doubt that if people quit smoking for a small reward, they would be more likely to stay off the habit than people who are offered a large reward. I also have no doubt that very few people would change such an important behavior on the basis of a small reward. On the other hand, we can easily understand that an ex-smoker such as Secretary Califano would become more zealously antismoking than someone who had been a nonsmoker all along. The point is that people have been induced to comply with counterattitudinal suggestions in the laboratory setting and with the predicted effect. However, with a less controlled setting, few would comply. The theory is generalizable, but some specific experimental operations are less so.

One must be careful not to confuse the experimental operations used in a laboratory (such as small rewards in a dissonance experiment) with the theoretical process (dissonance reduction or self-justification) that underlies such research. It is not the case that operations under careful control in the laboratory can be extrapolated to uncontrolled conditions outside the laboratory without careful consideration of the environmental context surrounding the individual.

One also often sees confusion between the demonstrated success of an isolated variable and that same variable taken in a larger context. There is no doubt that a Skinnerian token economy can be enormously effective in a variety of circumstances. There is also no doubt that one has to be careful about extrapolating the demonstrated effectiveness of rewards for small isolated behaviors into a larger context. In his graduate class on personality theory, Albert Bandura was fond of the example of trying to use Skinnerian techniques to teach someone to drive a car. His point was clear: The techniques would probably be very effective, but only on the small percentage of the people who physically survived the learning experience. These are only two examples of the many ways in which an uncritical use of basic laboratory findings and settings could lead to silly recommendations in large-scale programs.

SCIENTIFIC CONSENSUS AND CRYSTALLIZED ADVICE

Psychology and the behavioral sciences have not developed techniques and methods of interacting that allow scientists to easily assert a consensual view of particular human problems and possible solutions. The notion of a scientific consensual view is neatly caught by Abt's phrase, "crystallized advice." Our training seems to lead us to critical analysis rather than creative synthesis. "The worlds of the laboratory and of public affairs represent different specializations of function, different sets of intentions, and different complexes of value. One is analytical, operational, realistic, and concerned with rational means to ends; the other is characterized by human feeling and passion, high aims but also manipulation, and the achievement of equilibrium through compromise" (Bevan, 1976: 490). Our analytical training provides us with the ability to tear apart conceptual or empirical issues, but it can also interfere with trying to reassemble our ideas to provide advice to policy makers. However, this is a most important step for policy development. Many outside the behavioral sciences see us as unable to agree on theoretical issues and, therefore, probably not worthy of serious consideration.

This need for crystallized advice on policy issues does not imply that behavioral scientists should suspend their critical faculties in a pragmatic cause. Rather, it suggests two strategies. One, if possible we should be able to summarize a best guess in policy issues based on the state of the art. Two, failing to achieve confidence in critical aspects of a particular judgment, we should be able to offer advice on how to design a system which produces the very information we are unable to provide. The concept of the experimenting society and some creative flair for program evaluation should be very useful tools in this regard.

For example, suppose we were asked how to increase medical compliance. We might not be able to decide from the literature whether Skinnerian or Lewinian techniques would be more effective and cost efficient in a large-scale effort. We could advise that both techniques would work to some degree, but an intermediate stage of applied social research would be preferred, comparing the effectiveness to each technique (and a combination of the two).

SYSTEMS AND SIZES OF PROBLEMS

Social problems and a variety of policy issues are related to large social systems. The possible solutions are fundamentally related to the demographic parameters of the problem and not simply to theoretical issues. The size of the country and its problems determine partially, and often substantially, the array of alternative solutions. Problems in large social systems are particularly perplexing for the behavioral sciences in any event. But we also lose sight of the fact that the size of the problem alone often dictates possible solutions.

Consider one example, the delivery of mental health services in the United States. With some detail we can demonstrate how the size of the problem affects possible solutions. Consider the following statistics. There are now approximately 220 million people in the United States. For this population, approximately 50%– 70% of medical visits are basically psychological in nature, which conceivably could involve as many as 100 million people. Further, estimates of serious psychological disturbance in the population range between 10%– 20%, which would mean that in our country somewhere between 22 million and 44 million people have problems with potentially serious consequences. For example, a study in Great Britain found fundamental and serious characterological problems in 14% of the people coming in for national health visits (B. Brown, 1977). The English percentage would translate in the United States to more than 30 million people with serious and fundamental characterological problems.

Let us assume for the purpose of discussion that these estimates reliably indicate the frequency of mental health problems in the United States. If so, the range of estimates of people needing attention in the United States begins at 22 million, at a minimum, to 100 million or more, at a maximum, at any one time (with the seriousness of the problems and the type of services needed varying across the estimates, of course). The size of these numbers alone severely limits the possible solutions for delivering mental health services to those who need it.

Now let us look at the problems from the perspective of potential services available. We have approximately 45,000 psychologists and psychiatrists delivering mental health services in the United States at the present time. If each of them maintained 30 hours of service delivery a week (an unusually high number because of other requirements such as research, administration, public activities, and the like), then each would be responsible for 1,500 hours of services a year and the 45,000 psychologists and psychiatrists would deliver a total of 67,500 person hours a year of mental health services. This is only a potential capability: We estimate that psychologists deliver 18 million hours of mental health services a year in the United States now (Gottfredson and Dyer, 1978), and probably the total for psychologists and psychiatrists does not much exceed 40 million person hours.

Now let us compare the hours of service available to the range of potential need. Going back to our original statistics, the potential of 67 million hours of service delivery implies somewhere from 3 hours per person needing treatment (at the most optimistic) to 40 minutes per person needing treatment (at the least optimistic) per year. Some obvious implications about possible treatment follow from this derivation. One, we clearly cannot encourage three-times-a-week 50-minute therapy. If everyone in therapy received such treatment, then the whole system of psychologists and psychiatrists could treat only 400,000 people in total, which in turn is less than 2% of the minimum estimate. Phrased a different way, given the human resources of the country, long-term, face-to-face treatment could lead at a maximum to less than one person in 50 who needed services actually receiving them. A somewhat different implication is that we also could not encourage hospitalization of people needing mental health services. Recall that the Great Britain study suggested that up to 14% of the people visiting medical practitioners had serious and fundamental problems sufficient to consider hospitalization. Translating this number into United States statistics would mean that we would consider hospitalizing some 30 million people at a cost of several hundred dollars per day per person, an obviously impossible situation.

The parameters of this problem imply that certain possible alternatives should be concentrated on. One possibility, of course, is that we dramatically increase the number of care givers by, say, quadrupling the number of psychologists and psychiatrists in the country. However, this in itself is a costly proposition and politically unfeasible. A different set of alternatives would be to concentrate our attention on the types of care which have the most effect in short-term circumstances. That is to say, we should concentrate our research and policy effort in areas of short-term therapy and the extrapolation of professional services to supervised paraprofessionals. There is a considerable body of evidence suggesting that both of these techniques can be very effective. If I were called upon to make a comprehensive set of recommendations regarding the policy issues in mental health care in the United States, I would certainly concentrate on issues of short-term care and a coordinated paraprofessional effort. There is a variety of evidence indicating that short-term care can be extremely effective for a broad array of psychological problems (Cummings, 1977), and the parameters of the national problem suggest there may be little alternative. Further, one would encourage effective practices and research regarding ways to avoid hospitalization—a national policy of noninstitutionalization, as it were.

On the other hand, national policy is quite inconsistent with both the data and the parameters of the problem. For example, the most frequent recommendation in consideration of mental health benefits of national insurance is that of catastrophic insurance, insurance that would handle only the most serious and long-term problems. If such a policy were enacted, then that would be the only insurance alternative for mental health practitioners, and it would surely encourage hospitalization of clients with psychological problems. As we have seen from the parameters of the problem described above, logically (even psychologically, I would suggest), a system which encourages hospitalization is impossible as a solution. Counterintuitively, a national system of mental health care would better fit national needs and resources if everyone were given, on demand, a free three hours of care and hospitalization forbidden.

This example is detailed because it is illustrative of the problems of psychology and the behavioral sciences in offering good advice regarding national problems. It is an excellent example of how the parameters of a problem can be so overwhelming that, without extraordinary shifts in other related policies, certain types of solutions are excluded on a priori grounds. An analysis of the overall system can dramatically change the context and complexity of the problem. It is precisely this lack of involvement in and articulation of systems analysis of social problems that prohibits psychology and the behavioral sciences from making good use of their own fundamental knowledge. Indeed, Varela defines social technology as the "systems approach to solving problems in the social area" (1977: 914). Knowledge in depth of human behavior cannot effectively be applied to social problems without detailed knowledge of the context of the behavior in question and the general system in which it occurs.

CHANGES IN PSYCHOLOGY AND THE BEHAVIORAL SCIENCES IN THE NEXT DECADE NECESSARY FOR POLICY INTEGRATION

RESEARCH ON DESCRIPTIVE PARAMETERS

As described in the example of mental health, there is a need for research describing the parameters of the extent and nature of national problems. The lack of sense of the total problem is a major stumbling block against applying psychology to important large-scale problems. Research exists, of course, on the description of national problems. However, a good deal of it is not relevant to psychological considerations, and there is little psychological expertise involved in the accumulation of systems parameters. Economists often find psychologists naive in their discussions of national problems and possible psychological solutions. On the other hand, description of social problems in only economic terms is sufficiently lacking in behavioral information that psychological expertise cannot accurately be employed.

Further, an analysis of a social problem in only economic terms can be seriously misleading. For example, the major analyses of the possible inclusion of mental health care in national health insurance have been economic. There has been a tendency among economists to assume that if mental health care is free, everyone will take advantage of it. That assumption is consistent with the economists' view of "rational man" but inconsistent with the empirical facts Dörken (1977) reviewed the claims experience of the Civilian Health and Medical Program of the Uniformed Services (CHAM-

PUS) in 10 states covering 2.9 million beneficiaries. He found less than 2% used the mental health benefits and that figure was stable across a three-year period. Some further work into motivations and incentives underlying mental health care utilization is needed, but it is clear that the simple assumption that a large segment of people will routinely take advantage of such services is inaccurate and misleading.

CRYSTALLIZED ADVICE

We clearly need to develop in the behavioral sciences more interaction regarding strategies of approaching social problems. It seems to me that to better develop both crystallized advice and some descriptive parameters on which to base it, we need methods and places of focused discussion and reflection. A think tank—a Brookings Institution of Applied Social Psychology, as it were—would be very appropriate at this point to better crystallize psychological knowledge and increase its usability by the public (see also Goodwin, 1971, regarding the need for a National Social Science Institute).

BETTER COMMUNICATION

If we are to provoke greater interest among psychologists in applied research, then we have to make knowledge about specific problem areas more easily accessible. It is now difficult for a psychologist to become knowledgeable about specific social problems and data, particularly since the data are usually not psychological in nature and are widely scattered in the literature across several fields. Some rather systematic attention to developing better scientific communications on social issues is needed. There is no doubt that journals such as the *Journal of Social Issues* do help, but they do not in any way solve the problem. One need is more systematic literature reviews: in a sense, the *Psychological Bulletin* of social problems. In order to better entice psychologists to become involved with various social problems, coordinated statements of the state of the art are necessary. New journals are one such possibility. Coordinated and edited reviews of the literature published in book form are another, this annual being one good example. Great service can be performed in this area by those with editorial skills.

DEVELOPMENT OF COMMUNICATION NETS

In recent years, the Board of Scientific Affairs of APA has coordinated what it calls the NEAR reports: the Newly Emerging Areas of Research. Three such reports have recently appeared on the psychology of women, environmental psychology, and health research. The primary impetus underlying these reports is the assumption of a developing area, with the various people working in relatively isolated circumstances and publishing in relatively far-flung outlets. The purpose is to bring these separately developing areas together, to provide better communication among investigators, and to promote further research. It is noteworthy that both the NEAR report on women and that on health research led to new divisions of APA, and the one on environmental psychology led to a new section of an existing division. These reports have demonstrated the effectiveness of such an approach, but they only whet the appetitite of those of us interested in social policy. Clearly, psychology needs to increase the tempo of this integrative and stimulating approach to the development of better communication nets of researchers on social issues.

More formal communication nets are also possible. It would certainly be useful to develop computer contacts among people in several places working on the same topic, or to assist widely scattered people to share grants in several places at the same time. I understand that the sharing of grants among researchers at several universities is not at all unusual in economics, for example, particularly when the problem is very large. Perhaps such an approach of sharing a grant would demand a little more ego submersion than psychologists are accustomed to, but it might be very effective in promoting new solutions to problems in which psychologists should be involved.

DEEPER INVOLVEMENT WITH PROBLEM-ORIENTED RESEARCH

Over the course of their history, psychologists have emphasized theoretically oriented laboratory research. Such an approach has been very effective in the development of psychology as a scientific enterprise. As we have discussed, however, it has also led to a lack of involvement with problem-oriented research, and our contacts with broad problems often seem to be superficial compared with, say, economists. I have often heard a colleague describe a developing research interest as "doing a little on police community relations and some on population." With the degree of complexity of those problems, that approach could only be superficial and tangential. Such a statement implies an orientation more toward the overlap of psychology with the problem, with little attention to the problem as a whole. As Sarason eloquently puts it, "Science has learned a lot about problem solving, but when it looks beyond its confines to the areas of social problems, it has tended not to ask what the 'basic' problems are but rather to seek problems that fit its problem-solving style: clear problems that have unambiguously correct solutions" (1978: 73).

We have seen in the case of mental health how misleading a problem analysis can be if it does not take account of the whole system. Of course, this is not to denigrate the sort of research described, except to say that it cannot be·our only, or even typical, way of doing applied research. We will never collectively be able to offer good advice or to develop anything other than shallow approaches to complex social problems unless we have a grasp of the whole problem whether or not it is specifically relevant to psychology. "The social sciences have a hard time recognizing what other sciences have long known: problems are solved around problem-centered synthesis rather than by further theory-oriented analysis" (Varela, 1974: 469).

I have described some of the changes that will be necessary in psychology (and the behavioral sciences) if it is to be applied more effectively to issues of large-scale social problems. The strength in psychology is the quality of our laboratory research and the fundamental soundness of our theory. These strengths, however, are not easily translated to systematic and worthwhile advice on large-scale social problems. Several changes will have to be necessary in order to involve the science of psychology in larger and more complex problems. It is important to note that these changes are additions to our basic field, rather than substitutes for basic research or sound theory. These notions make more difficult some of the changes in training that are appropriate to the broadening of psychology for the future.

POSSIBLE FUTURE CHANGES IN GRADUATE TRAINING IN PSYCHOLOGY IN THE AREAS OF APPLIED RESEARCH

Glazer (1978) has termed these various trends described in this article as "increased professionalization" in the social sciences. This term is not easily used in psychology because we have a special alternate meaning for "professional." I do not have an alternative term to suggest, except that I think of these trends as suggesting merely the continuing maturation of psychology leading to a better public use of the field.

Whatever one calls these trends, they do create problems in training and in career definition. Graduate training in psychology has become relatively standardized in psychological science, and developing careers are typically built on issues and research related to broad theory. Perhaps the future will appreciate more specialized theory. As Glazer puts it in sociology, "now theory in the sociology of health will more typically arise directly from issues in the field of health." One can already see that happening in psychology, in the field of mental health, for example, or in the relationship of psychology and the law. The major question is, How do we approach this problem collectively and will we collectively nurture the broadening of psychology through our publishing channels, our construction of introductory books, and the like?

These processes lead to complicated and time-consuming trade-offs in training. They lead, on the one hand, to increasing specialization in specific human problems and, on the other, to potentially detrimental effects on breadth and depth within the field of psychology per se. At a minimum, we do not help by ignoring the problem, and we need to approach it directly and explicitly plan for the possible trade-offs.

We need to deliberately and actively preserve and nurture basic research in psychology, particularly the training in basic research that occurs in graduate schools. Various federal agencies are already developing more "targeted" areas of training, more applied funds in research and training, and more problem-oriented influence at the federal and state level. The funds available for research and training in essentially all areas of applied psychology exceed those for basic research and training. There is a significant danger that the basic scientific psychology will be swamped at the departmental level through competition for funds alone. Indeed, one can see such problems happening now in some of our more applied departments around the country. But traditionally, the major strength of psychologists has been their core training and their constant involvement in basic research during graduate training. Its preservation in light of other trends will surely take our collective efforts.

There are various ways that one could develop the added training needed. For example, graduate students could easily have access to needed courses from other fields, courses such as demography, survey research, large-scale statistics, design of natural experiments, and the like. Psychologists have been involved over the years in providing service courses to a variety of other fields. It should not wound us now to let them return the favor. Indeed, many content courses in such areas as population, welfare, health policy, and the like could be provided by other departments without disturbing the basic departmental staffing requirements internally. In other words, it is not necessary for departments to hire batches of new faculty to implement many of these training changes, but it certainly does take some spirit of cooperation and tolerance of ambiguity on the part of the departmental powers that be.

To expand the uses of psychology, we need to expand training in graduate schools. As a result, we probably also need to encourage graduate students to defer a crystallized career and help them to see the Ph.D. as a stepping stone to other and more specialized training. Fortunately, postdoctoral opportunities are expanding, but psychologists have yet to pay much attention to nonpsychologist positions that are available, too. For example, it seems to me that for a new Ph.D. to be coordinator of mental health services in a particular region of the country could be a very useful and educational experience in the long run for someone interested in mental health as a career, including a career in research in mental health.

I personally would like to see more psychologists taking short-term professional positions involving policy making or policy review. This concept I call the "scientist-administrator": people who alternately are involved with the production of knowledge and its application and use. Certainly this approach has a long and distinguished history in such areas as physics, but little sympathy in psychology yet. It is my impression that psychology could benefit immensely from the nurturance of this concept.

Graduate students receiving basic science training in psychology have yet to see many of the possible scientific roles that are available outside the traditional university laboratory and the ever rarer tenure-track position. Bevan has drawn our attention to three such roles which have gone unfilled and undeveloped but which are badly needed to be filled in the service of psychology:

> One is that of the skillful integrator and interpreter of science. In the arts and the humanities this is a highly esteemed role, as evidenced by the respect shown great musical performers, great literary critics, great legal scholars, and authors of leading textbooks in history, economics, political science, and the law. A second is that of the scientifically or technically knowledgeable legislative staff officer. One can virtually count on the fingers of both hands the number of scientists who serve as members of Congress and congressional staff or committee professionals. And a third neglected role is that of the scientist qualified to work with large-scale, multifaceted social systems. Systems analysis is a young, not yet exact science, and one not yet taken with universal seriousness . . . . If the need for these and other new roles for scientists is going to be fulfilled successfully, then we in the scientific community are going to have to submit ourselves . . . to a revolutionary change in attitude about the significance of such roles as career opportunities for able young scientists. [1976: 490].

The field of psychology is at a critical decision point regarding what it will be in the future, how useful it will be, and how much it gives back to the broader society that has supported it. There are significant problems in sharpening psychology's utility in social policy, but there are significant benefits as well, both for the field and for society.

REFERENCES

ABT, C. (1976) "Toward the benefit/cost evaluation of U.S. government applied social research and social programs, and the marginal productivity of their components, 1965-1975." Presented at the International Economics Association Conference on "Econometric Contributions to Public Policy," Urbino, Italy.

BEVAN, W. (1976) "The sound of the wind that's blowing." American Psychologist 31: 481-491.

BROWN, B. (1977) Personal communication.

CAMPBELL, D. (1969) "Reforms as experiments." American Psychologist 24: 409-429.

CUMMINGS, N. (1977) "The anatomy of psychotherapy under national health insurance." American Psychologist 32: 711-718.

DORKEN, H. (1977) "CHAMPUS ten-state claim experience for mental disorder: fiscal year 1975." American Psychologist 32: 697-710.

GLAZER, N. (1978) "Theory and practice in the social sciences." Chronicle of Higher Education 16(21): 28.

GOODWIN, L. (1971) "On making social research relevant to public policy and national problem solving." American Psychologist 26: 431-442.

GOTTFREDSON, G.D. and S.E. DYER (1978) "Health service providers in psychology." American Psychologist 33: 314-338.

"Principles for continuing evaluation and accountability controls for a national health insurance program" (1978) American Psychologist 33: 305-313.

SACKETT, D. and R. HAYNES [eds.] (1976) Compliance with therapeutic regimens. Baltimore, MD: Johns Hopkins University Press.

SARASON, S.B. (1978) "The nature of problem solving in social action." American Psychologist 33: 370-380.

VARELA, J.A. (1977) "Social technology." American Psychologist 32: 914-923.

_____(1974) "Giving psychology away?" Contemporary Psychology 19: 468-469.

WEISSKOPF, V.F. (1972) "The significance of science." Science 176: 138-146.

Methodology
and
Analysis

LEONARD SAXE
MICHELLE FINE

4

REORIENTING SOCIAL PSYCHOLOGY
TOWARD APPLICATION:
A Methodological Analysis

Increasingly, applied problems have become the focus of social psychological research and theorizing. The present volume devoted to applied social psychology is but one indicator of this trend (see, also, Deutsch and Hornstein, 1975; Kidd and Saks, forthcoming). Social psychology's movement toward application and the study of actual social problems has developed over a number of years. In part, this movement toward application simply reflects the social concern of the members of the discipline; in part, the movement is the result of shifts in government research funding and the application of new ethical guidelines to certain kinds of research. Whatever the reasons, we think that social psychology, as well as society, has much to gain from this explicit change in orientation.

Applied problems can provide social psychology with the basis for fulfilling its promise of a discipline that contributes both to the theoretical understanding of social behavior and the amelioration of social problems. Unfortunately, contributing to theory and contributing to the solution of social problems have often been viewed as two separate tasks. As Katz (1978)'has noted, a division exists in the field of social psychology such that there are two social psychologies. One social psychology is laboratory based, while the other is field based and, as Mayo and LaFrance (forthcoming) have noted, this division has led to a bifurcation in social psychology between basic and applied research. It is difficult to refute, at least during the past two decades, the preeminence of laboratory-oriented social psychology (Hendrick, 1978).

However, a fundamental shift seems to be taking place, both in terms of

AUTHORS' NOTE: We would like to express our appreciation to Len Bickman, Susan Green, and Alan Gross who provided useful comments on an earlier version of this chapter. The support of the U.S. Congress, Office of Technology Assessment, where the first author worked during the final stages of preparing this manuscript, is also gratefully acknowledged.

how social psychologists think about their work and the research that they conduct. Social psychologists are beginning to recognize the legitimacy and theory relevance of applied research. A parallel change involves the greater use of experimental methods, traditionally confined to theoretical laboratory research, to understanding social problems. This chapter will explore some aspects of these shifts in thinking. Our goal will be to promote an expanded view of social psychological research; a view that incorporates the scientific study of real-world problems with the development of theory about social behavior.

Our focus in this exploration of social psychological research will be methodological. Although a variety of other perspectives could be employed, a methodological focus seems most appropriate because of our concern with the process of "applied" research. Our view is that there is no fundamental incompatibility between traditional social psychology and a social psychology concerned with application. In fact, we think that both types of social psychology are necessary in order to achieve the kind of social problem relevance and theory development subscribed to by most social psychologists (see also, Hamsher and Sigall, 1973). This seems most clear when the methods social psychologists use to generate knowledge are examined. Our methodological consideration of social psychology will lead us to promote a view of the field that blurs distinctions between basic and applied research and attempts an integrated view of how social psychologists might collect data and integrate them theoretically.

AN APPLIED PROBLEMS FOCUS

Perhaps the easiest way to illustrate the importance of expanding views of social psychology is to recount McGuire's well-known parable, offered in 1961, illustrating his opposition to a social problem-oriented discipline of social psychology. The parable involved two students: one was interested in social psychology because "he thinks the field has something to offer the problem of 'international tensions'"; the other was interested in social psychology because "he thinks he might be able to do some neat things by using a little matrix algebra and difference equations" (1965: 139). McGuire advises the student interested in international tensions to consider entering the law or the ministry; in contrast, he encourages the student interested in applying mathematics to pursue social psychology. According to McGuire's formulation, hypotheses for research should not be derived because of their relevance to social action; rather, they should develop because of their relevance to theory. Thus, McGuire condoned the now-questioned incompatibility assumed to divide social action and social theorizing (cf. O'Donnell, 1979). A student interested in social action, McGuire presumed, would be frustrated by the orientation of social psychology.

While this view of social psychology seems no longer tenable, an important question is the *degree* to which a change in views about social psychology has occurred. Clearly, as McGuire (1969, 1973) and other prominent theorists have noted (e.g., Hendrick, 1978), the discipline has changed markedly both theoretically and methodologically during the past 15 years. Social psychology has gone through over a decade of both unparalleled growth and, also, crisis (Elms, 1975; Gergen, 1973; Harré and Secord, 1973). As a consequence of the "crisis" in social psychology and the resulting transformation of social psychology, the discipline is shifting, at least in some sectors, toward a social problem focus.

In part, a problem-based focus would be nothing new to social psychologists since, ostensibly, the discipline has always been devoted to the study of human behavior in its social context. Paradoxically, however, social psychology's interest in studying universal social processes has backed us into the laboratory. In the laboratory, it is assumed that we can conduct research that is "theoretically pure," if often lacking in mundane realism and applicability (cf. Aronson and Carlsmith, 1969). Social psychology, historically and in particular response to the cries of "crisis," has evolved toward a discipline able and willing to apply scientific rigor to social problems. Yet, social psychologists seem to have gotten trapped, at least psychologically, by methodological rigidity (Lachenmeyer, 1970). Somehow, experimental control, theoretical sophistication, and scientific rigor have come to be associated exclusively with laboratory research that is divorced from applied issues. Such bifurcation is spurious. In this chapter we will demonstrate the commonalities and challenge some of the assumed divisions between applied and basic research.

The central principle that distinguishes social psychology as a discipline is the commitment of both so-called basic and applied social psychologists to empirical verification of psychological constructs. Although there is certainly controversy over the use of empiricism, to some extent all social psychologists are committed to a form of positivist logic. Unlike novelists— to use an extreme example—who conceptualize (and symbolize) social behavior without use of a formal logical system, social psychologists—for the most part—are unwilling to accept ideas as concrete without empirical evidence. Although there are probably clear limitations to what is knowable using a logical positivist orientation (Gergen, 1976), it nevertheless represents a part of the shared perspective of social psychology. We're suggesting that the process of inquiry in social psychology (i.e., our methodology), rather than the issues addressed by social psychologists, defines the field. As social psychologists, we share a commitment to a logic of inquiry based on empiricism. We have developed many distinct operationalizations of this logic, yet most social psychologists share a common grounding in empiricism. Now, as we consider a more applied model of research, we ask ourselves what will be different about an applicable social psychology? The answer is far less than we fear. In fact, it appears as though the opportunity to apply social psychology to social problems is the opportunity to extend our methods and test the durability of our social theories.

Methodologically, the opportunity to test hypotheses in the real world will help us to strengthen the external and construct validities of our theoretical formulations. As well, problem-based research will promote creativity; it will force social psychologists to test the boundaries of our old theories while generating new ones (Gergen, 1978). Our academic notions about human behavior, when put to the real-world test, will inevitably be modified to accommodate the complexities of social problems. In problem-based research, social psychological theories, as well as methods, will contribute and profit.

VALIDITY AS YARDSTICK

The applied problem model casts our discipline in a new light. Characterization of research will no longer be whether it is basic or applied, but rather the extent to which it can demonstrate the unequivocal relationship between variables. This issue, commonly referred to as validity, is the yardstick for assessing the quality and utilizability of social psychological research. As we move toward an applied problem research discipline, in which we apply our theories and methods to problems, and develop our theories and methods as a result, we need to adopt a way to conceptualize research which is concerned with the validity of results. As described by Campbell and his colleagues, the concept of validity refers to the degree to which one is confident in stating causality between variables (cf. Campbell, 1957; Campbell and Stanley, 1966; Cook and Campbell, 1979). Causality involves an understanding that X causes Y. This is substantiated if X and Y occur at the same time, if X is followed by the onset of Y, and if no third variable can account for the cooccurrence of X and Y. Validity is the standard by which we can securely assume causality between two (or more) variables. Alternative explanations, different ways of explaining the occurrence of Y, are proved insufficient when the X-Y relationship is deemed valid.

The presence of plausible alternative explanations interferes with a determination of validity. A definite and valid statement of causality requires that alternative explanations be demonstrated incorrect. Validity is dependent on the quality of the research design and the efforts taken to demonstrate alternative explanations invalid. Valid research is not the exclusive province of "basic" research. Conceptually, validity may be achieved by any category of research. Validity problems, therefore, are shared by all types of research; and each type of research can be improved methodologically to yield better validity. There are four separate validity criteria: three of these are of particular concern to us. A brief discussion of these types of validity follow (see Cook and Campbell, 1979, for an extended discussion). We discuss how to best achieve high validity in so-called basic and applied research.

INTERNAL VALIDITY

Usually considered the most basic form of validity, internal validity specifies the degree to which one is confident that a relationship exists between two or more variables. In basic research conducted in laboratory settings, this criterion is rather easily satisfied. In these settings, the investigator has essentially total control over the situation and can randomly assign subjects to treatment conditions. With full randomization, differences obtained between conditions can be attributed to treatment differences, reducing to some extent the number of possible alternative explanations. Internal validity has been more troublesome, however, for applied research because investigators have typically assumed it difficult or impossible to control assignment of individuals to conditions. This popular assumption that random assignment is hard to achieve in applied research has been challenged, as we will describe later in this chapter. New methodological procedures have been developed to fit the requirements of random assignment with the needs of applied research programs (Boruch, 1976; Cook and Campbell, 1979; Saxe and Fine, forthcoming). It is important to recognize, therefore, that there is nothing inherent in either basic or applied research that makes internal validity easier or harder to achieve. It is that we have simply gotten trapped into assuming that randomization is possible only in a laboratory—not achievable in the real world.

EXTERNAL VALIDITY

External validity is no less important, in some respects, than internal validity. External validity is the degree to which the findings of a particular study can be generalized to other settings and populations. As such, external validity is a problem for both basic and applied research. Basic research studies often use one type of subjects, for example, college students (cf. Higbee et al., 1976). A homogeneous subject pool limits the generalizability of the research because populations may respond differently to treatments.

For applied research, the problem of external validity is similar in that results are often too closely tied to a single setting. What is true about how an income maintenance program works in suburban New Jersey and Pennsylvania may not be true of how it would work in other areas (Rossi and Lyall, 1976). While in many cases, for both applied and basic research, the restriction in subjects/settings makes *no* difference, this needs to be empirically demonstrated before it can be accepted.

CONSTRUCT VALIDITY

A more complex type of validity is construct validity. It has to do with the appropriate labeling of the independent (i.e., treatment) variable. In basic research studies this is a problem of knowing the relationship between the operationalization of the construct and the construct itself. The problem is similar in applied research, although the difficulty is often one of backtracking from an existing social intervention to the idea or theory that underlies the intervention. Although it is perhaps easier to establish construct validity when one begins with the construct (as is typical in theory-derived basic research), this is not necessarily the only way to achieve construct validity. The critical factor is one's ability to understand the relationship between the construct and its operationalization. If the operationalization only weakly represents the construct, validity will be low and/or one should redefine the construct.

VALIDITY AND PROBLEM-BASED RESEARCH

Problem-based research, like any other form of research, needs to have its validity demonstrated. Depending on the design of the research—for example, how participants are assigned to condition—it may be difficult to demonstrate internal validity. Because so many variables are free to "float" in problem-based research, a clear statement of causality (i.e., internal validity) is often difficult to achieve. Problem-based research, however, will often enhance the construct validity of theoretical formulations. Construct validity, for problem-based research, is easily achieved because the research, as we have noted, will be designed in such a way that it is guided by theory rather than politics or whim; the independent variables will accurately reflect the constructs.

For example, a program designed to test student versus teacher motivation might involve randomly assigning classrooms to conditions so that in condition A, teachers receive monetary incentives to improve students' scores while in condition B, students receive incentives to improve their own scores. Hughes (1979) suggests the use of a true experiment to determine how best to resolve the problem of high school illiteracy. In this case, the validity of the construct "incentive" would be quite high. The operationalization is clear and adequately represents the construct. The nature of the treatment is explicit and true to the concept, not trivialized like many social psychological variables (Ring, 1967).

Indeed, such a study would not only have high construct validity but also if true experimental conditions were maintained (that is, if classrooms were stringently assigned to condition) high internal validity could be achieved. If classrooms were randomly assigned to incentive conditions, the influence of student and teacher incentive on learning could be scientifically determined. If many different kinds of classrooms were used—for example, racially segregated and racially integrated, older and younger, and open classes and traditional classes—external validity concerns could also be addressed. The external validity problem is as difficult (or easy) for problem-based research as it is for any other kind of research. The most effective remedy, of course, is to conduct research at various sites, with numerous populations, and at different times, to determine generalizable laws of human behavior.

Problem-based research, therefore, introduces no new validity concerns; in fact it may lessen a few. The issue of whether basic or applied research is more valid or produces better data is, in this framework, a moot issue. The mythology around "pure and clean" basic research versus "contaminated and fuzzy" applied research should be dispelled. Validity can be insured in design, not in context, and can be achieved in problem-based research.

TOWARD GREATER VALIDITY

Improving the validity of any research study involves the application of a variety of methodological strategies. Perhaps most important is the systematic use of what Cook and Campbell have called "true experiments": randomized control group tests of hypotheses. Although such studies most directly improve internal validity, if appropriately conducted they can also lead to improved external and construct validity. Such studies, referred to as social experiments when conducted for social policy purposes, are becoming a significant part of social research (cf. Riecken and Boruch, 1974; Saxe and Fine, forthcoming). If social psychology is to produce the better and more meaningful information about the nature of and potential remedies for social problems, we need to generate information that is scientifically credible and policy relevant. To insure this end, we need to retain a problem focus while respecting the criteria for internal, external, and construct validity. One method to achieve this is through the social experiment. We will next describe the nature and logic of social experimentation.

SOCIAL EXPERIMENTATION

Social experimentation, as a methodology, involves the systematic application and manipulation of social variables in natural settings. These social variables can range from a human relationship seminar, to a novel medical technology, to an income subsidy program. In some respects, social experimentation represents the direct extension of basic research methods to applied problems; after all, the sine qua non of social psychology has been the experiment (Festinger, 1953; Hendrick, 1978; Mills, 1971). In other respects, though, social experimentation represents for social psychology a wholly different approach to research. In a social experiment the independent variable is a social action program, rather than a discrete conceptual variable. Manipulation refers to making a social program available to randomly selected groups.

Discussion about the use of experimental methods to study social problems has a relatively long history. Chapin (e.g., 1947), a sociologist, advocated the use of experimental methods to study social problems over 60 years ago. He conducted a variety of experiments on problems such as housing and delinquency. In social psychology the idea for social experiments has also existed for some time, although not very explicitly. Social experimentation seems to be imbedded in Lewin's theorizing about the nature of research. Lewin (1947, 1951; see also, Marrow, 1969; Sanford, 1970) believed that in order to understand social processes, one must study social behavior in context and must observe the effects of systematic change. The idea of systematically intervening in social processes and studying outcomes underlies most current views of social experimentation.

ILLUSTRATIONS

In a social experiment a construct about social behavior is tested by trying out an intervention in a way that reflects the logic of science. In essence, social interventions are treated as independent variables which are "manipulated" in much the way of the laboratory experiment. The design for the experiment creates, for comparison purposes, treatment and control groups. Social experiments, through their careful design, allow one to maximize all of the types of validity.

During the past decade, a variety of social experiments have been conducted (cf. Boruch et al., 1978; Riecken and Boruch, 1978) within the justice, education, health, and welfare systems. These experiments vary greatly, not only in terms of their scope and substance but also in terms of their success at solving particular problems and contributing to general knowledge. None of these experiments focuses entirely on social psychological variables; nevertheless, each has implications for the knowledge base of social psychology. A few illustrations of social experiments may clarify their potential.

"*Sesame Street.*" One example of social experimentation is the educational research conducted on the development of the "Sesame Street" television program. "Sesame Street" is perhaps the most successful educational television program. It was developed in the late 1960s to stimulate learning in disadvantaged children. An experimental evaluation was conducted of the initial efforts to develop the program (Ball and Bogatz, 1971) and the evaluation data were reanalyzed by Cook et al. (1975). Ball and Bogatz's initial experiment with "Sesame Street" involved encouraging a randomly selected group of children, in at least four different areas, to watch "Sesame Street" on a regular basis. Children in the encouraged group were visited and through a variety of means (including discussion with parents) were made aware of "Sesame Street" and encouraged to view it. Encouragement to view, rather than viewing, was used as the intervention because of the difficulty of providing such a television show on a random basis and because the program's developers believed that the show would not be very popular.

A variety of cognitive measures were used to assess the effects of "Sesame Street." As Ball and Bogatz reported, disadvantaged children in the encouraged-to-view group improved—relatively dramatically—on most cognitive tests. Children (age 2-5) who viewed "Sesame Street" scored higher on tests of letter and number recognition and on tests of simple cognitive processes. The conclusion—based also on the fact that almost 50% of the children to whom the program was aimed were regular viewers—was that the program was successful and was able to provide disadvantaged children with important learning skills.

Cook et al. (1975), in a reanalysis of Ball and Bogatz's data, agreed that the experimental program had had very positive effects; however, Cook et al. placed a very different emphasis on the interpretation of the data. Most important, the reanalysis suggested that the process of encouraging children to view "Sesame Street" had effects over and above those provided by the program. When analyses were conducted of children who were supposedly voluntary viewers, the positive effects of the program were not as strong as with the encouraged-to-view group. In addition, some of Cook et al.'s analyses suggested that the program, although aimed at disadvantaged children, actually served to improve disproportionately the educational skills of middle-class children and to widen the achievement gap between so-called advantaged and disadvantaged children.

The applied problem represented by "Sesame Street" is clear: How can educational opportunities be improved? The results of the initial "Sesame Street" experiments hint at the complexity of the problem and the need for a variety of carefully conducted and evaluated educational programs. The theoretical issues—related to education, learning theory, social development, and social processes—are no less complex (cf. Bar-Tal and Saxe, 1978).

The "Sesame Street" research demonstrates some interesting validity issues. First, internal validity appears well documented. Whatever the treatment, be it the program or the encouragement to view, it did seem to produce rather dramatic cognitive advances in the children. However, the external and construct validity of the study are problematic. The external validity question asks "For whom is 'Sesame Street' effective?" Does it really work equally across socioeconomic lines? The construct validity question, which may be more crucial, asks "Is it the program or the encouragement to view it that is effective? The Cook et al. secondary analysis suggests that the encouragement to view was more effective than the program itself. This is a critical, and obvious, policy concern. If encouragement to view is the important variable, one might be unwilling to make "Sesame Street" more widely available without built-in encouragement to view.

Police practices. One of the best known of recent social experiments is the Kansas City Police Patrol experiment (Kelling et al., 1976). Although this experiment is not social psychological in nature, it has interesting social psychological implications, both substantive and methodological. The experimenters, with the assistance of police officials in Kansas City, tested a well-accepted principle of policing: Crime is deterred by creating an impression of police omnipresence. The goal of the experiment was to determine the consequences of changes in police patrolling patterns. While the researchers were concerned with the pragmatic question of how to deploy police personnel, they were interested in a more fundamental question of how community perceptions of police, as well as criminal perceptions of police, affect community and criminal behavior.

As part of the experiment, several police patrol beats of Kansas city were matched and then randomly divided into *reactive, control,* and *proactive* beats. In the reactive patrol areas, police entered the area only in response to a specific request for police assistance; in the control beats, patrols were maintained as normal; in the proactive beats, the number of police on patrol was doubled or tripled. The investigators collected data on the resulting changes in crime rates, community perceptions of police, and police reaction. The results indicated few differences between the patrol areas. Across the different beat areas, there were approximately equal rates of criminal activity and similar perceptions of the police.

While the obvious implication of this study is that police should discontinue wasteful patrolling practices, there are a number of methodological and validity problems with the study. Probably most important is the fact that the experimental manipulations may not have been carried out as intended (Larson, 1976). Because of the way that the Kansas City police organized its patrol forces, there may not have been a very great difference in actual police presence across districts. For example, specialized police units were not restricted and, as well, the volume of calls from the reactive districts was such that there were always police passing through these areas. In essence, this is a construct validity problem and the experiment, as carried out, did not adequately test the underlying idea.

These are also external validity problems with the Kansas City study. Kansas City has a uniquely trained police department, as well as unique geographical and socioeconomic conditions. To what extent similar findings would be obtained in other cities is an empirical question. At the very least, it should be clear that one needs information about such differences in order to interpret adequately the results of such an experiment.

As with the "Sesame Street" experiment, the issues involved in the Kansas City study are undoubtedly complex. It should also be clear that no study provides unequivocal answers and that alternative explanations will always be present. At the heart of the matter is a basic research problem for social psychology of how perceptions (of citizens, criminals, police) affect behavior. While it is difficult to assess whether the Kansas City study provided an adequate test of any theoretical ideas about perception, it is certainly possible that future research of this kind could do so. At the very least, further experiments with police practices should contribute to more efficient use of police.

A HETEROMETHODOLOGICAL APPROACH

It should be obvious that there are situations in which true experiments cannot be conducted. Despite the fact that it is probably more often a problem of not seeing the *potential* for conducting experiments (Boruch, 1976; Cook and Campbell, 1979), there are times when social experimentation is not feasible. A variety of pragmatic problems, as well as ethical problems (cf. Rivlin and Timpane, 1975; Warwick, 1978), may make it unfeasible to conduct an experiment. In these cases, the costs of doing an experiment (both in terms of monetary and human resources) are not worth the foreseen benefits.

Conceptually, one can also argue against the exclusive use of social experimentation; simply stated, the kind of independent variables manipulated in such studies may include too complex a set of variables. No one experiment or series of experiments can yield an adequate enough test of such complex variables; even if internal validity were obtained, external and construct validity would be elusive. In a social experiment such as "Sesame Street," the independent variable is much more complex than an educational intervention. In fact, a variety of other variables were manipulated, including important social conditions. It is difficult, in such a large-scale study, to determine the role of these factors with any great degree of validity. Cook and Campbell (1979) call this the "kitchen sink" problem. It is essentially the problem of sorting out, from among all the treatments involved in any social intervention, the factors responsible for particular effects.

For these reasons, laboratorylike tests of hypotheses about applied problems are still necessary and desirable. At some stage in the understanding of any social problem, it is going to be necessary to isolate components of a phenomenon; this can be done in a field setting (one in which no program is being established, but one in which participants are aware of being studied) or in a laboratory (a place where the individuals being studied know that they are being studied). Perhaps the best strategy is to conduct studies of a particular construct in many settings, under a variety of conditions.

Unfortunately, heteromethodical approaches to "hypothesis" testing have received only scant attention. Boruch (1975), in the context of discussing the complexity of randomized social experiments with other research, has promoted component-wise testing. In Boruch's scheme, the central hypotheses of large-scale social experiments are tested in small-scale studies. Understanding the components leads to a better understanding of how the program works as a whole.

Saxe and Fine (1979) have proposed a similar approach which we refer to as macro-micro evaluation. The macro-micro approach was developed to solve some of the problems of doing large-scale evaluative tests of new programs. While it is often not possible to conduct evaluative studies of on-going social programs in an experimental way, it is often possible to conduct two levels of research: the macro level and the micro level. Macro studies are conducted to collect descriptive (and quasi-experimental) data about a program in operation. Such macro studies have no assumptions of random assignment or experimental control, although they can, certainly, be well-designed experiments. Micro studies, on the other hand, are conducted, in parallel, to test rigorously central hypotheses about the construct(s) which underlies the intervention. Micro studies are conducted with assumptions of random assignment of participants to condition and experimental control.

The example of a macro-micro analysis provided by Saxe and Fine involved a test of a communication system for health professionals who practice in isolated rural settings. The communication system used interactive television to provide two-way face-to-face contact for health professionals who might otherwise have little professional contact. A macro study of user reactions to the system (using a quasi-experimental design) was proposed, coupled with a series of microexperiments to test the communication capability of two-way television. These latter studies resemble laboratory studies of nonverbal communication. They differ, though from usual studies in that they were designed specifically to test components of the actual operating system.

A macro-micro approach to the "Sesame Street" research might clarify some of the interpretation problems of the original data. Despite the true experimental design of the "Sesame Street" study, too many components were included within the treatment (i.e., the program plus encouragement to view). Small laboratory studies of various program components, such as encouragement to view, might provide information to distinguish the effects of encouragement to view from the effects of the education program.

The thrust of these suggestions is that no single set of methodologies can yield a comprehensive picture of a social problem. We are suggesting, in part, a return to early notions in social psychology of the interplay between the laboratory and the field (cf. Lewin, 1947). By coupling the conduct of basic and applied research, the full range of available methodologies can be utilized in social psychology. The experimental method is the basic tool but, as has been described above, it can be used in a variety of ways and in many contexts (Lachenmeyer, 1970). It is only when these many ways are used together that we can maximize the development of valid and useful new knowledge.

IMPLICATIONS

The burgeoning application of experimental methods to understand and ameliorate social problems should have major effects on the field of social psychology. It should blunt the critics of applied work in social psychology and help us better develop valid and relevant knowledge about social behavior. It should also result in social psychology's having a positive impact on society and provide a mechanism for society to deal with the myriad of social problems. Below, we suggest some of these changes.

EXPERIMENTING SOCIETY

Increased opportunities for conducting real-world experimental tests of important social hypotheses is part of what Campbell (1969, 1971) has called the "experimenting society" (see also, Riecken and Boruch, 1974; Saxe and Fine, forthcoming). In the experimenting society, social research and social policy formation are interdependent processes. Policy makers use experimental tests of policy options to verify theories about social functioning and to ameliorate specific social problems. Social researchers work closely with policy makers to design, implement, and analyze these experiments.

Social experimentation, although it is the application of well-used experimental design principles, represents something more than an extension of the basic research model. It suggests a different basis for deriving research problems in social psychology and results in the study of independent variables that are very different than those of traditional social psychological research. The experimenting society is one in which problem-based research is conducted with basic experimental procedures applied to social concerns. The idea of the experimenting society evolves as the traditional distinctions between basic and applied research blur. In the experimenting society, social problems are approached from a scientific perspective grounded in validity concerns.

A variety of circumstances have arisen to make the experimenting society more than wishful thinking on the part of social scientists. For one, societal organizations (i.e., governments) are increasingly being asked to solve complex social problems. As interdependence between members of our society increases (e.g., because of the complexity of modern technology), it becomes more necessary to adopt more formal processes, such as scientific logic, to understand social problems. While this is certainly not a revolutionary concept for social psychologists, it is somewhat radical for policy makers. Policy makers seem willing to adopt these methods, with guidance, and to utilize whatever social concepts are available to solve social problems (Rivlin, 1971).

ROLE IMPLICATIONS

Our view is that social experimentation offers social psychology a new framework. As such, it creates a need for social psychologists to take on different roles. In some cases, their roles will parallel activities common to social psychologists; in other cases, it requires adapting to a new research environment.

One central role for the social psychologist involved in social experimentation will be to serve as methodological and design consultants. In this role, social psychologists will assist policy makers and administrators in operationalizing policies into treatment variables, as well as in the development of appropriate control and comparison groups. The social psychologist in this role is "protector of validity," responsible for assuring construct and internal validity. Another role appropriate to the social psychologist is to develop ways of measuring social behavior, that is, the outcomes of social experiments. This is probably the most traditional role for psychologists in applying their skills to social problems, although in this context it will require a different (and more intense) kind of collaboration with those involved in social policy. Social psychologists should also have a role in developing the programs involved in social experimentation. The discipline has much to offer the actual development of conceptualization of social interventions (see Saks, 1978) and this expertise will be helpful to the developers of social experiments.

Rather than being independent researchers isolated in academic settings, these new role descriptions necessary for problem-based research require that social psychologists collaborate with a variety of other individuals. Implicit in each of the above role descriptions for social psychologists is collaboration between social psychologists, policy makers, and others in the social science community.

Problem-based research falls at the intersection of many disciplines. For example, if research on the recent decline in Scholastic Aptitude Test scores is conducted, it would require input from educators, social psychologists, sociologists, and family specialists (College Entrance Examination Board, 1977). If nutritional deficiencies would appear to play a role in the test score decline, one would have to introduce a nutritionist to the research team. If employment demands interfered with the students' abilities to study, an economist might have to be invited. If the score decline were possible due to an influx of non-English-speaking students taking the exam, an English-as-second-language specialist might be helpful.

One interpretation of the current situation is that we are at a crossroad. In effect, the need to improve the process of social policy formation and the methods of social research can be brought together. Social science methods, based on the principles of experimentation, can be used to understand and solve social problems. Social science, in turn, needs the real world as a laboratory to test better conceptions about social behavior. Social experiments may be the tool which allows both groups to meet their needs.

DISCIPLINE IMPLICATIONS

The field of social psychology, in addition to role changes, will be affected in a number of ways by greater involvement in large-scale tests of social programs. Probably the most important change is that problem-based application, rather than being a step child of social psychology, will become a more primary focus. As such, theories will not be accepted until they are tested in real-world settings and social psychologists will not have to struggle to make their abstract theorizing relevant to the real world. The processes of theorizing and application will become much more closely linked.

Social psychology, representing the expanded use of social experimental methods, will be a field in which scientific rigor, measured in terms of validity, is an accepted principle across all subfields. As has been emphasized, the applied study of social problems does not have to involve less valid or singular methodologies. Rigor will take on a new meaning, having more to do with the validity of the data developed from the research than with the settings where research is conducted or the particular methodological tools that are employed.

There is an important tradition in social psychology of using natural settings to test social psychological ideas. A central difference between field experiments and the type of research that we are advocating is that field experiments have typically derived their hypotheses from abstract theoretical ideas. In contrast, ideas for social experiments develop from practical problems; treatments represent proposed solutions to problems. While this difference has often resulted in social experiments being poorer theoretical tests, it has other advantages. Most important, it insures that the operationalization of the construct will represent an ecologically valid manipulation (cf. Brunswick, 1955). As recent discussions of applied social psychology have indicated (e.g., Helmreich, 1975; McGuire, 1973), one of the failures of social psychology has been its concentration on simple models of causality. In the real world, causality is multifaceted. The isolation of a few variables at a particular time may yield a distorted or inaccurate view of the problem. Problem-derived variables, which are difficult to conceptualize because of this complexity, may force investigators to develop better and more sophisticated causal models.

Along with development of social experimentation, then, will come the opportunity to develop more meaningful theories of social behavior. To the extent that relatively invariable laws about human social behavior exist, they should be discernible in large-scale tests of programs. Theory will be viewed as a constantly evolving set of concepts; no one experiment will be expected to resolve any critical theoretical problem. Theories will be tested through experiments that use multiple methodologies both for the manipulation of independent variables and the assessment of dependent variables. Social psychological theories will also benefit from comparison and scrutiny with other social science theories. Social experiments—which will bring social psychologists together with sociologists, economists, political scientists, and others—will provide the setting for the development of more unified principles of social behavior.

It should be noted that while the emphasis here is on research and its role in verifying ideas about social processes, that does not preclude other activities for social psychology. In particular, there may be a need for social psychological "clinicians" (Saxe, 1977) who deal with the practice of social intervention. In terms of research, while social experimentation represents a potentially important methodology, social psychological research does not have to involve social experimentation. Social experiments cannot always be conducted and they may not yield the kinds of specific information about social processes necessary for understanding social problems. In fact, our view of a heteromethodological approach includes, when necessary, components of both traditional basic and applied research. As such, the research process in social psychology should include various forms of laboratory and field experimentation as well as other forms of research.

Of course, we think that social psychologists will increasingly want to incorporate social experimentation procedures in their research. Because of ethical concerns (e.g., Kelman, 1972), it may become more difficult to conduct laboratory experiments with the provision of "informed consent." At the same time, it may become easier to conduct social experiments. In the latter case, the researchers do not necessarily have responsibility for the "ethicality" of the intervention, although other ethical considerations may apply (Rivlin and Timpane, 1975).

Social experimentation, it should be understood, is not a panacea. In fact, there are of number of critiques of the social experimentation model. Most prominent has been Guttentag's (1977) position that social experimentation is not viable because it is unresponsive to program decision needs. Others have suggested that the requirements of experimental design are too rigid, constrain change in a program, and that experimental designs are too difficult to carry out. Although these criticisms may be applicable to some social experiments, our view is that social experiments are much more flexible than portrayed in these criticisms.

The emergence of social experimentation will not instigate a major breakthrough for our discipline, and it will not induce a Kuhnian (1970) paradigmatic shift. The introduction of social experimentation will, however, have significant consequences for the field. If nothing else, it will allow social psychologists to develop a more valid knowledge base with greater applicability (Mayo and LaFrance, forthcoming) to current social problems. Perhaps the most important change is that social psychologists will be able to close the gap that exists between the professional aspiration to create a useful discipline and to function as social activists and social scientists. In part, this change will represent the emergence of social psychology from its crisis (cf. Elms, 1975).

SOCIETAL IMPLICATIONS

The widespread development of experimental methods should also have a major impact on society. Decision-making processes, as well as lay understanding of social psychology, should greatly benefit. As illustrated by Senator Proxmire's Golden Fleece awards (Shaffer, 1977), social psychology is often viewed as irrelevant to societal problems as well as societal interests. The joining of social psychological research methods with social problems will put our research in a more understandable framework. Although it may be pollyannaish, this should lead to improved social policy formulation.

It is hoped as the experimental ethic becomes more widespread, that society will come to appreciate the logic, as well as to better appreciate the substance of social psychology. While this may appear to be an idiosyncratic view, it may be that the most enduring and stable of social psychology's contribution to society is our methodological perspective. In a world which is everchanging and whose rate of change is ever increasing (Toffler, 1970), the value of a perspective which aids in developing solutions and understandings of problems becomes even more evident.

CONCLUSIONS

The present discussion has emphasized the role of methodology in deriving a social psychology oriented to application. Along with some philosophers of science (e.g., Kaplan, 1964), we have viewed methodology rather broadly. The starting point for our discussion was the assumption that basic research and applied research in social psychology were not fundamentally different or incompatible. From a methodological perspective, we have tried to show how social psychology and society can benefit from a better integration of research approaches.

This chapter has presented one view of the development of a problem-based social psychology—a view that maintains high standards of validity and incorporates widespread utilization of experimental methods. While this bias is clear, it should not obscure the fact that the basic premise is that the widest range of methods and conceptual tools must be applied to studying and understanding social behavior. This is the only way that social psychology will prosper as a field of study and that we will have any chance of influencing social policy and improving our shared societal goals.

REFERENCES

ARONSON, E. and J.M. CARLSMITH (1969) "Experimentation in social psychology" in G. Lindzey and E. Aronson (eds.), The Handbook of Social Psychology (vol. 2). Reading, MA: Addison-Wesley.

BALL, S. and G.A. BOGATZ (1971) The First Year of Sesame Street: An Evaluation. Princeton, NJ: Educational Testing Service.

BAR-TAL, D. and L. SAXE [eds.] (1978) The Social Psychology of Education: Theory and Research. Washington, DC: Hemisphere.

BORUCH, R.F. (1976) "On common contentions about randomized field experiments" in G.V. Glass (ed.), Evaluation Studies Review Annual 1: 158-194.

_____ (1975) "Coupling randomized experiments and opportunities to conduct experiments in social program evaluation." Sociological Methods and Research 4: 35-57.

_____ A.J. McSWEENY, and E.J. SODERSTROM (1978) "Randomized field experiments for program planning, development, and evaluation: an illustrative bibliography." Evaluation Quarterly 4: 655-695.

BRUNSWICK, E. (1955) The Conceptual Framework of Psychology. Chicago: University of Chicago Press.

CAMPBELL, D.T. (1971) "Methods for the experimenting society." Presented at the meeting of the American Psychological Association, Washington, DC.

_____ (1969) "Reforms as experiments." American Psychologist 24: 409-429.

_____ (1957) "Factors relevant to the validity of experiments in social settings." Psychological Bulletin 54: 297-312.

_____ and J.C. STANLEY (1966) Experimental and Quasi-Experimental Designs for Research. Skokie, IL: Rand McNally.

CHAPIN, F.S. (1947) Experimental Designs in Sociological Research. New York: Harper & Row.

College Entrance Examination Board (1977) On Further Examination: Report of the Advisory Panel on the Scholastic Aptitude Test Score Decline. Princeton, NJ: Author.

COOK, T.D., H. APPLETON, R.F. CONNER, A. SHAFFER, G. TOMKIN, and S.J. WEBER (1975) "Sesame Street" revisited. New York: Russell Sage Foundation.

_____ and D.T. CAMPBELL (1979) "Quasi-experimentation: design and analysis issues for field settings" in M.D. Dunnette (ed.), Handbook of Industrial and Organizational Psychology. Skokie, IL: Rand McNally.

DEUTSCH, M. and H. HORNSTEIN (1975) Applying Social Psychology. Hillsdale, NJ: Lawrence Erlbaum Associates.

ELMS, A.C. (1975) "The crisis of confidence in social psychology." American Psychologist 30: 967-976.

FESTINGER, L. (1953) "Laboratory experiments" in L. Festinger and D. Katz (eds.), Research methods in the behavioral sciences. New York: Holt, Rinehart & Winston.

FINE, M. and L. SAXE (1978) "Evaluation research and psychology: toward synthesis." Presented at the meeting of the American Psychological Association.

GERGEN, K.J. (1978) "Toward generative theory." Journal of Personality and Social Psychology 36: 1344-1356.

————(1976) "Social psychology, science and history." Personality and Social Psychology Bulletin 2: 373-383.

————(1973) "Social psychology as history." Journal of Personality and Social Psychology 26: 309-320.

GUTTENTAG, M. (1977) "Evaluation and society." Personality and Social Psychology Bulletin 3: 31-40.

HAMSHER, H.J. and H. SIGALL (1973) "Introduction" in H.J. Hamsher and H. Sigall (eds.), Psychology and Social Issues. New York: Macmillan.

HARRE, R. and P. SECORD (1973) The Explanation of Social Behaviour. Totowa, NJ: Littlefield, Adams.

HELMREICH, R. (1975) "Applied social psychology: the unfulfilled promise." Personality and Social Psychology Bulletin 1: 548-560.

HENDRICK, C. (1978) "Social psychology as an experimental science" in C. Hendrick (ed.), Perspectives on Social Psychology. Hillsdale, NJ: Lawrence Erlbaum Associates.

———— (1976) "Social psychology as history and as traditional science: an appraisal." Personality and Social Psychology Bulletin 2: 392-403.

HIGBEE, K., W.J. LOTT, and J.P. GRAVES (1976) "Experimentation and college students in social psychology research." Personality and Social Psychology Bulletin 2: 239-241.

HUGHES, R. (1979) "Education could pay." New York Times (March 15): A23.

KAPLAN, A. (1964) The Conduct of Inquiry: Methodology for Behavioral Science. Scranton, PA: Chandler.

KATZ, D. (1978) "Social psychology in relation to the social sciences: the second social psychology." American Behavioral Scientist 21: 779-792.

KELLING, G.L., T. PATE, D. DIECKMAN, and C.E. BROWN (1976) "The Kansas City Preventive Patrol Experiment: A Summary Report" in G.V. Glass (ed.), Evaluation Studies Review Annual (vol. 1). Beverly Hills, CA: Sage Publications.

KELMAN, H.C. (1972) "The rights of the subject is social research: an analysis in terms of relative power and legitimacy." American Psychologist 27: 989-1016.

KIDD, R.F. and M.J. SAKS [eds.] (forthcoming) Advances in Applied Social Psychology. Hillsdale, NJ: Lawrence Erlbaum Associates.

KUHN, T. (1970) The Structure of Scientific Revolutions. Chicago: University of Chicago Press.

LACHENMEYER, C.W. (1970) "Experimentation—a misunderstood methodology in psychological and socio-psychological research." American Psychologist 25: 617-624.

LARSON, R.C. (1976) "What happened to patrol operations in Kansas City?" Journal of Criminal Justice 3.

LEWIN, K. (1951) Field Theory in Social Science. New York: Harper & Row.

———— (1948) Resolving Social Conflicts. New York: Harper & Row.

———— (1947) "Group decision and social change" in T.M. Newcomb and E.L. Hartley (eds.), Readings in Social Psychology. New York: Holt, Rinehart & Winston.

MARROW, A.J. (1969) The Practical Theorist: The Life and Work of Kurt Lewin. New York: Basic Books.

MAYO, C. and M. LaFRANCE (forthcoming) "Toward an applicable social psychology" in R.E. Kidd and M.J. Saks (eds.) Advances in Applied Social Psychology: Conceptual Issues. Hillsdale, NJ: Lawrence Erlbaum Associates.

McGUIRE, W.J. (1973) "The yin and yang of progress in social psychology." Journal of Personality and Social Psychology 26: 446-456.

_____ (1969) "Theory-oriented research in natural settings: the best of both worlds for social psychology" in M. Sherif and C.W. Sherif (eds.), Interdisciplinary Relationships in the Social Sciences. Chicago: AVC.

_____ (1965) "Discussion of William N. Schoenfield's paper" in O. Klineberg and R. Christie (eds.), Perspectives in Social Psychology. New York: Holt, Rinehart & Winston.

MILLS, J. (1971) "The experimental method" in J. Mills (ed.), Experimental Social Psychology. New York: Macmillan.

O'DONNELL, J.M. (1979) "The crisis of experimentalism in the 1920's: E.G. Boring and his uses of history." American Psychologist 34: 289-295.

RIECKEN, H.W. and R.F. BORUCH (1978) "Social experiments." Annual Review of Sociology 4: 511-532.

_____ [eds.] (1974) Social Experimentation: A Method for Planning and Evaluating Social Intervention. New York: Academic Press.

RING, K. (1967) "Experimental social psychology: some sober questions about some frivolous values." Journal of Experimental Social Psychology 3: 113-123.

RIVLIN, A.M. (1971) Systematic Thinking for Social Action. Washington, DC: Brookings Institution.

_____ and P.M. TIMPANE [eds.] (1975) Ethical and Legal Issues of Social Experimentation. Washington, DC: Brookings Institution.

ROSSI, P. and K. LYALL (1976) Reforming Public Welfare: A Critique of the Negative Income Tax Experiment. New York: Russell Sage Foundation.

SAKS, M. (1978) "Social psychological contributions to a legislative subcommittee on organ and tissue transplants." American Psychologist 33: 680-689.

SANFORD, N. (1970) "Whatever happened to action research?" Journal of Social Issues 26: 3-23.

SAXE, L. (1977) "Clinical social psychology." Newsletter of the Society for the Advancement of Social Psychology 4: 12.

_____ and M. FINE (forthcoming) Toward the Experimenting Society: Methods for the Design and Evaluation of Social Experiments. Belmont, CA: Brooks/Cole.

_____ (1979) "Expanding our view of control groups in evaluation groups" in L. Datta and R. Perloff (eds.), Improving Evaluations. Beverly Hills, CA: Sage Publications.

SCHLENKER, B.R. (1976) "Social psychology and science: another look." Personality and Social Psychology Bulletin 2: 384-390.

_____ (1974) "Social psychology and science." Journal of Personality and Social Psychology 29: 1-15.

SHAFFER, L.S. (1977) "The golden fleece: anti-intellectualism and social science." American Psychologist 32: 814-823.

TOFFLER, A. (1970) Future Shock. New York: Random House.

WARWICK, D.P. (1978) "Ethical guidelines for social experiments" in G. Bermant et al. (eds.), The Ethics of Social Intervention. Washington, DC: Hemisphere.

WEISS, C.H. (1977) "Introduction" in C.H. Weiss (ed.), Using Social Research in Public Policy Making. Lexington, MA: Lexington Books.

THOMAS D. COOK
LEONARD DINTZER
MELVIN M. MARK

5

THE CAUSAL ANALYSIS OF
CONCOMITANT TIME SERIES

INTRODUCTION

THE CASE FOR CATHOLICISM

For the past decade, critics within and outside of social psychology have called for change in the methods and questions that characterize the subdiscipline. In particular, calls have been made to reduce the heavy dependence on theory testing rather than theory generation and to reduce reliance on short-term, contrived laboratory experiments which use respondents who are somewhat homogeneous with respect to many social characteristics and who are very homogeneous with respect to age. The proposed methodological alternatives include passive observational studies in "natural settings" and field experiments with longer-lasting treatments and broader classes of respondents. The proposed substantive alternatives generally focus on "relevance," a concern which might involve asking largely atheoretical questions (as evaluation research at first appears to do), or using social psychological theory for the major purpose of planning and implementing social changes rather than for further developing theory.

We do not wish to take a stand on the relative merits of any particular methodological or substantive approach for social psychologists. We are convinced, first, that researchers should wrestle with *personally* exciting questions, which might or might not be the traditional questions of a particular subdiscipline; and, second, that some methods, while essential for answering one type of research question, may be of little use in answering other types. However, we do advocate that social psychologists have easy access to a wide range of social science methods; otherwise, they may be inadvertently restricted in the research questions they ask by the limitations of the particular methods with which they are most acquainted.

different at each moment even when the observed variables do not appear to change in how they are measured. "If only we could understand the phenomena operating at different times and could formulate our theoretical proposition in terms of these phenomena," claim scholars interested in explanation, "then we would have no need of the concept of 'time' and could have an ahistorical, 'field-theoretic' science." Scholars with such a bent would consider the concern of Gergen and most of the concerns of Rosnow to be irrelevant to the development of a science, and would not expect most phenomena to be stable across time since time locates unstable explanatory processes.

To more pragmatic scholars who are interested in theory and explanation in senses other than the essentialist sense of the foregoing paragraph (Cook and Campbell, 1979), time is a useful construct even though it is not theoretically meaningful. There are two basic reasons for usefulness over and above the probing of generalizability. First, the failure to replicate a reliable finding at different times (or in different settings or with different types of persons) suggests that the theoretical proposition under investigation needs a contingency statement. That is, one must attempt to discover the conditions under which a relationship holds and the nature of the different times associated with the different outcomes will be one clue as to the nature of the contingency conditions. Increasingly in social psychology, programs of research result in contingency theories, whether they be explicitly labeled as such (e.g., Fiedler's contingency theory of leadership effectiveness) or not (e.g., dissonance theory, the discounting cue hypothesis, and such). While we hope that such contingency theories will someday be respecified with novel constructs in less contingent form, it is nonetheless more accurate in the short term to work with a contingency theory rather than a global-appearing theory whose hidden conditionality still remains to be elucidated.

A second way in which time is of great importance is for testing *causal* propositions. Most (but not all) philosophical considerations of "cause" include the requirement that the cause precede the effect in time. Moreover, some discussions add the requirement that there be no plausible alternative interpretations of a relationship other than that A caused B. Temporal data can help satisfy both requirements, the first more obviously than the second. With respect to the second requirement, if a relationship holds across a sufficiently heterogeneous sample of times, then any alternative interpretation is ruled out that did not operate at all the times when the relationship occurred. It is precisely the unreliable nature of time that permits this advantage, for in longitudinal field research different irrelevancies will inevitably occur at different times. The "irrelevancies" that include plausible alternative interpretations are "irrelevancies" of particular inferential importance.

Most of the interest manifested by social psychologists in using time data to test causal propositions has centered around the use of interrupted time series methods (ITS). Briefly, these methods are used to assess whether a shift occurs in the level, slope, variance, or seasonal pattern of some time series immediately after a treatment was administered. The focus is to describe any shifts, to estimate their magnitude and the associated level of statistical significance, and to rule out any alternative interpretations of the observed shifts. In the past, ITS methods have proven useful in both theoretical and applied contexts, in both laboratory and field settings.

Our focus in this article is on a different type of time-series analysis that we shall call the analysis of concomitant time series (CTS). Unlike ITS, CTS does not require a designated intervention point. Rather, the aim is to assess whether the fluctuations in one series are associated with fluctuations in another series and to examine which series's fluctuations precede the fluctuations in the other. To achieve these aims means meeting two of the most frequently stated assumptions for inferring cause—association and temporal precedence. Moreover, it is possible *under some conditions* to assess whether the third major assumption is met—that no other explanation is plausible other than that the fluctuations in one series cause fluctuations in the other. At issue, then, is estimating the magnitude of the association between the fluctuations in two or more time series, identifying the pattern of temporal precedence between these fluctuations, and assessing the plausibility of other interpretations of the link between fluctuations.

WHY STUDY CONCOMITANT TIME SERIES?

It is not demeaning to social psychology to claim that it is a borrower of social science methods rather than a significant contributor to new methods. Merely to note that concomitant time-series methods are widely used in economics and are being increasingly used in sociology, political science, and developmental psychology is enough, we suspect, to lead one to believe that social psychologists will begin to use such methods more extensively.

However, the use of such methods has more justification than mere imitation. Clearly, scholars who are persuaded by Gergen or Rosnow, or scholars who want to "refute" Gergen empirically, must resort to concomitant time-series data. Without them, historical generalizability and reciprocal causal relationships cannot be easily assessed. In addition, as more social psychologists develop interests in applied questions, the more likely it is that they will use archival data. This is because national and local archives in the United States contain data for monitoring the economic, social, and subjective social level of welfare of the nation, and most of the ameliorative efforts of applied social scientists are aimed at modifying the supposed problems that the indicators are meant to measure. Since archives have been growing at a tremendous pace particularly in the 1970's, data will be increasingly available for CTS analysis. (It must be stressed, though, that current archives are more comprehensive for addressing economic and social questions than for issues relating to psychological mediating processes.)

Also, it is worth noting that some CTS studies have gained considerable visibility among social scientists and policy makers. One need only point to the work of Brenner (1973, 1975) in relating unemployment rates to such social variables as alcoholism or first-time admissions to mental hospitals and to his attempts to explain the relationships he believed he discovered in terms of role theory. Vigderhaus (1978) did something similar, trying to relate unemployment and suicide rates. In the field of public policy, other crucial questions have been addressed using CTS methods—the effects of the money supply on inflation, for instance. In the private sector, CTS methods have also been used, as when Helmer and Johansson (1977) investigated whether fluctuations in marketing expenditures affect subsequent sales. Even among psychologists the use of CTS methods can be observed, as in Simonton's (1975) work on creativity and Bakeman and Brown's (1977) and Thomas and Martin's (1976) work on mother-child interactions.

It is worth noting that some of these last instances involved investigator-collected data rather than archival data. Most CTS analyses to date have used archival data, often covering many decades, but an investigator can sometimes collect his or her own data on preferred measures over time. Thus, investigators can tailor their measurement to their research questions in a way that archives rarely permit for social psychologists; and they can also collect data at the preferred time intervals rather than using those that are in the record. Sometimes the use of archived data hinders detecting reliable effects in which the cause affects its change in a period shorter than the measurement interval.

The justification for understanding CTS methods, then, is that they are becoming more widely used in all the social sciences, particularly for answering more applied questions dealing with aggregate level hypotheses which involve in some way the construct of time. While CTS is still more rarely used than more established methods—including more established time-series methods such as forecasting and ITS analysis—CTS analyses are nonetheless on the increase. More important for social psychologists, perhaps, the purported benefits of CTS studies overlap to some extent with changes that some commentators call for in the conduct of social psychological research. More emphasis has been called for on applied issues, on transhistorical questions, on reciprocal causal chains, and on aggregate level theory. CTS analysis *promises* to achieve these ends; and it also *promises* to be a useful tool for any investigator who collects his or her own multivariate data over time. Though most CTS analyses to date have been with archival data covering long time spans, this is not a necessary restriction of the methods; also possible is the use of shorter, investigator-collected series to probe inter- and intrapersonal issues of obvious theoretical relevance.

THE PURPOSE OF THIS CHAPTER

This chapter aims to introduce five of the principal methods currently used in CTS analyses. The presentation will stress conceptual issues rather than computational procedures and will especially emphasize the threats to internal validity that are typically associated with each method. To give the reader an intuitive understanding of the very different causal conclusions that can result when different modes of CTS analysis are applied to the same data, we shall use each of the five methods to analyze a set of data dealing with the state of the economy and suicides. We shall not explain in operational detail *how* the analyses were conducted; rather we want to use the example to illustrate the conceptual underpinnings of the mode of analysis and to demonstrate the extent to which "answers" about cause depend on how the data are analyzed. The data sets we have chosen deal with employment or the gross national product (GNP) and suicide, an example where the direction of causality—if there is any—is considerably more likely to be from the level of employment or GNP to the level of suicides than vice versa. Such an example makes many matters simpler, though whatever small excitement might have resulted from the reader exploring issues of reciprocal causality is lost.

The five methods we shall discuss are simple ordinary least-squares regression; traditional generalized least-squares regression; cross-correlation analysis with nonprewhitened data; cross-correlation analysis with "prewhitening" by the assumed cause; and cross-correlation analysis with independent prewhitening. We do not have the time to explore other methods, many of which are described by Pierce and Haugh (1977) and Haugh (1976).

In particular, we shall not concentrate on spectral analysis. The procedures we will present focus on the time domain, e.g., is X at time t correlated with X at time $t+k$ or with Y at time $t+k$. In contrast, spectral analysis focuses on the frequency domain, e.g., how much does a given frequency contribute to the variance of a series or to the covariance of two series? Bloomfield (1976), Gottman (1979), and Mayer and Arney (1974) provide an introduction to spectral analysis; and more mathematically sophisticated presentations are given by Granger (1969), Granger and Hatanaka (1964), and

Jenkins and Watts (1968). We feel that spectral analysis provides a most useful adjunct to the time domain analysis procedures described in the present article, and we recommend its further study to the reader.

Other specialized topics of importance with which we cannot deal include: the pooling of cross-sectional and time-series data (see, e.g., Hannon and Young, 1977; Nerlove, 1971); CTS analysis when some observations are missing; interrupted time series or intervention analysis (Box and Tiao, 1975; Hibbs, 1977; McCain and McCleary, 1979); combining ITS and CTS methods to estimate and remove the effects of interruptions in one or more series prior to causal analysis; the fitting of transfer function models to a bivariate relationship (Box and Jenkins, 1976; Haugh and Box, 1977); and time-series procedures specifically designed for categorical or nominal variables (Gottman and Notarius, 1978). Further, in some instances, causal hypothesis can be probed via shared growth patterns, i.e., trend (cf. Rogosa, 1978) or shared seasonal patterns (e.g., lunar cycles and homicide rates, menstrual cycles and depression). We will not discuss these issues here.

SIMPLE ORDINARY LEAST-SQUARES REGRESSION

The simplest statistical model commonly applied to CTS analysis is the ordinary least-squares (OLS) regression model. As commonly applied, OLS regression assesses the synchronous linear relationship between two time-series variables, X and Y. That is, simple OLS regression addresses the question: When X is large, does Y at the same time tend to be large (positive relationship) or small (negative relationship)?

Readers will be familiar with two expressions of the OLS model—the simple correlation coefficient (r) and regression analysis where Y is regressed on X, with X being the presumed cause of Y. These approaches identically estimate the statistical significance of the covariation between two series. Their major difference is that only regression analysis provides an estimate of β, the expected increase in Y given a unit increase in X. However, the causal analysis of time-series data usually focuses upon statistical significance, so the correlation and regression approaches will be discussed interchangeably below.

OLS REGRESSION WHEN TREND
OR SEASONALITY IS PRESENT

Trends or seasonal patterns frequently inflate the correlation between two untransformed time series. A series has a trend when it consistently increases or decreases for a long period of time. One cannot meaningfully describe a trended series in terms of a mean value, because the mean apparently changes over time. For example, in Figure 1 observations in either series tend to be larger, on the average, the later they occur. Thus, no mean value can meaningfully be attached to either series.

Trend can obscure the true causal relationship between two time series. As an example, consider the relationship between the number of suicides and the number of employed persons in the United States, illustrated in Figure 1. The correlation between these series is .83 (p < .001). From this, one might erroneously infer that high levels of employment cause increased suicides, particularly since the opposite causal connection—that suicides increase employment—seems so implausible. However, Figure 1 warrants no causal interpretation, since the large positive correlation may result from increases in each series caused by expanding population. The obtained relationship may, therefore, be due to a third variable, population growth,

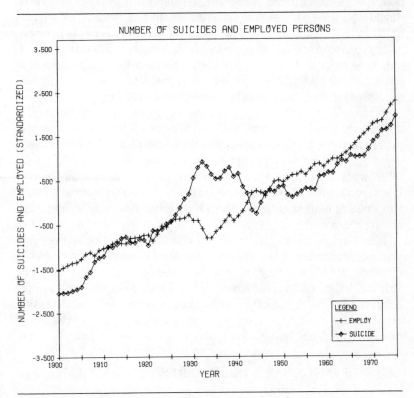

FIGURE 1   Number of Employed Persons and Number of Suicides, 1900-1975

which affects each series similarly. For this reason, the trends in Figure 1 should be removed prior to causal analysis, i.e., population growth should be "controlled for."

Trends can have many causes. For instance, inflation would create long-term increases in most indicators of economic expenditures, even when population increases are controlled for. This is why expenditures are sometimes expressed as per-capita outlays *in constant dollars*. In other cases, the rationale for detrending may be less clear. We may ask: Is detrending necessary whenever trend is present? *Our* answer to this is almost always yes. First, trends normally can be accounted for by plausible historical explanations other than the causal relationship between the two variables under study, e.g., by population growth or inflation. Second, observable trends must be removed to meet the analytic requirement of stationarity,[1] which is assumed in most types of CTS analysis. Third, we and others (Haugh and Box, 1977; Granger, 1969; Pierce, 1977a) believe that tests of covariation should determine whether past and current values of series X add significantly in predicting future values of series Y *over and above the predictability arising from Y's own past orderly behavior.* Trend is a type of orderly behavior that allows one to partially predict the current value of a series based on past regularities in the series. To meet our proposed criterion of covariation, then, trend must be removed prior to testing for covariation.

Seasonality sometimes occurs in time-series data, particularly monthly or quarterly data. The hallmark of a seasonal process is that the same general pattern repeats every *period* (which is the length of the seasonal process, e.g., 12 months for monthly data and four quarters for quarterly data). In other words, seasonality is present when the expected value of an observation depends on which part of the period it is. For example, average monthly temperatures in most of the Northern Hemisphere rise in summer months and decline in winter months.[2]

Like trend, seasonality can spuriously affect the correlation between two variables. For instance, two variables, measured monthly, might be highly correlated not because they are causally related but because they are similarly affected by weather conditions. Alternatively, a true causal relationship might be obscured if, in addition to the causal relationship between the two variables, one variable has a seasonal pattern affected by weather while the other does not. Thus, seasonality should be removed prior to causal analysis.

OLS REGRESSION WHEN TREND AND SEASONALITY ARE ABSENT OR REMOVED

Let us now demonstrate the importance of removing trends by continuing our example with detrended data—the employment *rate* and the suicide *rate*. The rated series plotted in Figure 2 presents a picture dramatically different than the simple frequency series displayed in Figure 1. In contrast to our analysis of the trended series, Figure 2 suggests a strong negative relationship between the rated series and this is confirmed statistically, $r = -.59$ ($p < .001$; $\beta = -.229$; $t = -6.32$). Thus, one might conclude that decreases in the employment rate cause increases in the rate of suicide. Contrast this conclusion with the inference one might reach based on the trended frequency series—that employment and suicide are positively related.

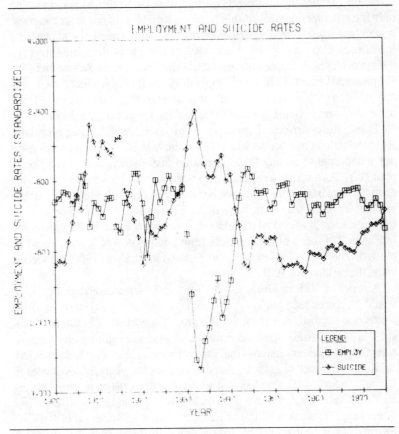

FIGURE 2   Employment Rate and Suicide Rate, 1900-1975

OLS ASSESSED

Though it might be tempting to accept these new results, an OLS regression with untrended data still has at least three shortcomings. First, attempts to remove a trend or seasonal pattern may not be completely satisfactory. If trends or seasonal patterns are not completely removed, they may still spuriously affect the correlation. On the other hand, detrending and deseasonalization procedures, especially those based on "best fit" estimations, will sometimes overadjust and remove from a series variation not truly attributable to the underlying cause(s) of trend or seasonality. To protect against over- or underadjustments, one should cross-check transformations, using several methods to detect the presence of the trends and seasonality.[3]

Second, *in practice,* researchers usually use OLS regression to examine only the synchronous relationship between variables. In our example, most researchers would only determine whether the employment rate at one time (notationally, X_t) is associated with the suicide rate at the same time (Y_t). This provides no evidence concerning whether the presumed cause precedes the presumed effect (Cook and Campbell, 1979). It is ironic that time-series analysts commonly investigate only synchronous relationships, since time-series data are particularly suitable for probing temporal precedence.

Third, *autocorrelated error* frequently renders OLS inappropriate. Autocorrelated error occurs when the residuals from an OLS regression are not independent.[4] In any OLS regression analysis, X_t will not perfectly predict Y_t. As a result, a residual, also referred to as the error, ϵ_t, exists for each X_t, Y_t pair. ϵ_t is the difference between the observed value of Y_t and the value of Y_t predicted on the basis of X_t. These residuals can be ordered by time, resulting in a residual (time) series. For instance, for the data presented in Figure 2, a series of the residuals from a regression of Y on X could be plotted. The first value would be the residual for the year 1900, the second value the residual for 1901, and so on.

A series of such residuals is very likely to be autocorrelated; that is, ϵ_t would be correlated with ϵ_{t+1}, and perhaps with ϵ_{t+2}, and so on. In other words one residual, ϵ_t, can be used to predict a portion of future residuals, ϵ_{t+1}, ϵ_{t+2} . . . . Autocorrelated error violates an important underlying assumption of OLS regression—that the errors are independently distributed. While the presence of autocorrelated error does not bias OLS estimates of the regression coefficient (β), it does have serious negative implications. First, the estimates of β are not efficient or asymptotically efficient (see Kmenta, 1971, section 8.2); that is, the sampling distribution of the OLS estimate of β is unduly large compared with the sampling distribution associated with different methods of estimation. Second, and more important, estimates of the standard error of β are biased, consequently biasing any associated tests of significance. When the autocorrelation is positive (as it usually is), the bias acts to underestimate the standard error of β. Type I errors thus occur: t statistics for regression coefficients are inflated, as are values of r and R^2 (see Hibbs, 1974).

TRADITIONAL GENERALIZED LEAST-SQUARES REGRESSION

The inferential problems associated with autocorrelated error are widely recognized in the econometrics literature, though they are often disregarded in practice. When analysts make adjustments for autocorrelated error, they usually employ some variation of generalized least-squares (GLS) regression. Unfortunately, these procedures do not always adequately account for autocorrelated error.

As we have seen, the OLS model assumes that the errors are independent. The OLS model also assumes that errors are homoscedastic.[5] These assumptions are not required in the GLS model, which is called "generalized" because it subsumes other models, including the more restrictive OLS model.

In theory, to conduct a GLS regression one must know how the errors are autocorrelated; or more precisely, one must know the variance-covariance matrix of the errors. Practically speaking, knowing how the errors are autocorrelated requires knowing: (1) the *structure* of the autocorrelation, which involves the general form of the relationship between residuals, e.g., is ϵ_t directly related only to ϵ_{t+1}, or is it also directly related to ϵ_{t+2} and (2) the *parameter values* for the appropriate model of the error structure, e.g., what is the magnitude of the direct relationship between ϵ_t and ϵ_{t+1}.

Prior knowledge of these details is almost never available in practice. Nonetheless, researchers have frequently made assumptions about both of them in an attempt to reduce the problem of autocorrelated error. Most often when both autocorrelation structure and parameter values have been assumed a priori, the method of first differences has been applied to remove the autocorrelation (see Kmenta, 1971, 289-292; also see below for a definition of differencing). In other cases, more complicated types of autocorrelated error have been assumed a priori (e.g., Sims, 1972).

More frequently in recent empirical work, a restrictive assumption is made about the structure of the autocorrelated error, and the parameters of the assumed error model are estimated empirically. Many such procedures have been devised (e.g., Cochrane and Orcutt, 1949; Durbin, 1960; Hildreth and Lu, 1960). Nearly all of them assume that the autocorrelated error is described by a first-order autoregressive model.

The first-order autoregressive model assumes that each residual equals a portion of the preceding residual plus a current random effect represented by a_t:

$$\epsilon_t = \phi_1 \epsilon_{t-1} + a_t.$$

The ϕ_1 parameter is a correlation coefficient which describes how much each error, ϵ_t, depends on the previous error, ϵ_{t-1}. Traditional GLS procedures assume in practice this first-order autoregressive error structure. We can characterize a GLS analysis in the following terms: (1) conduct an OLS regression; (2) estimate the degree of correlation between immediately adjacent points in the residual series, i.e., estimate ϕ_1 in Equation 1; and (3) conduct another regression(s) adjusting for the estimated autocorrelation. Some GLS procedures follow exactly these three steps, while others involve equivalent operations. Most analysts who rely on traditional GLS procedures do not apply them unless some diagnostic, usually the Durbin-Watson d statistic, indicates that OLS is inappropriate; thus, determining that OLS is inappropriate usually comprises a prior step. For greater detail on such procedures than given here, the reader can consult nearly any standard econometrics text (e.g., Johnston, 1972; Kmenta, 1971).

Traditional GLS procedures can be illustrated with our employment and suicide rate example. For the OLS regression of the employment and suicide rates, the Durbin-Watson d equals .1628. Comparison with tabled values of d indicates that the residuals are autocorrelated and that OLS is therefore inappropriate. Given that GLS regression is indicated, we need to estimate the degree of autocorrelation. By two different estimation procedures (Cochrane and Orcutt, 1949; Hildreth and Lu, 1960), we find the coefficient of first-order autogression, the ϕ_1 in Equation 1, to be equal to one. This estimated coefficient can then be used to transform the original series so that the errors are independent. Following the appropriate data transformation,[6] we obtain an r of $-.60$ (p $<$ .001; $\beta = -.19$, t $= -6.44$). The value of the Durbin-Watson d statistic obtained for this traditional GLS procedure indicates that the error series (barely) satisfies the requirements of independence.

The estimated correlation obtained with the traditional GLS methods is somewhat surprising given our earlier comments on the consequences of autocorrelation. We indicated that, in the presence of positive autocorrelation, r and R^2 are usually inflated. Yet, when we compare the OLS regression of the employment and suicide rates (r $= -.59$) with the GLS regression (r $= -.60$), the obtained correlation coefficients are virtually identical. This is because the GLS statistics and the OLS statistics cannot be directly compared, a fact ignored by many authors (cf. Hibbs, 1974; see also Buse, 1973).

The r of $-.60$ estimated by traditional GLS procedures refers to the correlation of transformed employment and suicide rates (see Note 6), not to the untransformed rates employed in OLS regression.[7]

TRADITIONAL GLS ASSESSED

At least three serious problems beset traditional GLS procedures. First, since they assume *in practice* a first-order autoregressive error structure, they may not be satisfactory when the residuals follow some other model of autocorrelation. To the extent that autocorrelation remains in the error series after adjustment, estimates will be inefficient and significance tests will be biased, usually in the direction of false positives (see Engle, 1974).

Second, GLS procedures *in practice* almost always assume the direction of cause and usually examine only the synchronous relationship. That is, the researcher usually begins with an a priori supposition that variable X is the cause of variable Y, and does not consider the opposite direction of causality, from Y to X. Yet, establishing the temporal precedence of the causal variable is a commonly accepted requirement for making causal inferences.[8]

Third, while autocorrelated error (i.e., autocorrelation in the ϵ_t series) will sometimes be accounted for, autocorrelation will often remain in the X_t and Y_t series themselves. This can have negative consequences, as we see when we consider simple cross-correlation analysis.

SIMPLE CROSS-CORRELATION ANALYSIS
(WITH NONPREWHITENED DATA)

The preceding methods of CTS analysis, as they are generally practiced, do not probe the temporal precedence of the causal variable. In contrast, the cross-correlation function has been suggested as a means of examining temporal precedence. To explain this procedure, we must first introduce the complementary concepts of *lead* and *lag*. When one series, Y, lags K units behind another series, X, or equivalently when X leads Y by K units, Y is displaced relative to X: Current observations of X (X_t) are paired with observations of Y that fall K units later (Y_{t+k}).

The *cross-correlation coefficient* describes the correlation between two variables at some specified lag, where the values entering into the computation are all values of X that are separated from values of Y by the lag interval, K, irrespective of the time in history when X and Y are separated. Thus the cross-correlation between X and Y, where X leads Y one year, would involve values of X in 1910 and Y in 1911, as well as X in 1930 and Y in 1931, and X in 1955 and Y in 1956. We refer to the correlation between two variables at a specified lag as the *cross*-correlation. The cross-correlation coefficient, $r_{xy}(K)$, gives the estimated correlation between the two subscripted variables, X and Y, when the first subscripted variable, X, leads the second subscripted variable, Y, by K units. For instance, $r_{xy}(1)$ gives the cross-correlation when X leads Y by one time unit. On the other hand, $r_{yx}(1)$ gives the cross-correlation when Y leads X by one time unit.

The *simple cross-correlation function* is defined as the cross-correlation coefficient $r_{xy}(K)$ for lags $K = 0, \pm 1, \pm 2, \pm 3$. That is, the cross-correlation function gives the value of the cross-correlation coefficient for many values of K, with X leading Y in some cases and Y leading X in others. The simple cross-correlation function involves nothing more than applying the simple OLS regression model (r) to a range of lagged relationships. Thus, the synchronous cross-correlation coefficient, $r_{xy}(0)$, is the equivalent of r in the simple OLS regression model.

The cross-correlation function need not be symmetrical, e.g., $r_{xy}(1)$ need not equal $r_{yx}(1)$. This potential asymmetry has led some to suggest that the cross-correlation function provides a unique aid in inferring causality from time-series data. Hooker (1901) initially proposed that, if X causes Y, cross-correlations should be greater when X leads Y than when Y leads X. Since Hooker, inspection of the cross-correlation function has been generally neglected until recent attention by Campbell (1976; see also Lee, 1977). Campbell's previous support of studying the simple cross-correlation function was based on the same logic previously used to support the cross-lagged panel correlation (Campbell and Stanley, 1966; Cook and Campbell, 1976; for a more recent position, see Cook and Campbell, 1979).

Hooker and Campbell focus on the asymmetry in the cross-correlation function. They recognize that autocorrelated error and any third-variable cause can spuriously affect cross-correlations. But they also believe that these spurious effects should be distributed symmetrically across the cross-correlation function: If autocorrelated error inflates $r_{xy}(1)$, should it not also inflate $r_{yx}(1)$ equally? If this were true, the expected value of the cross-correlations would be unknown; but in the absence of any causal relationship between the two series, $r_{xy}(K)$ and $r_{yx}(K)$ would be equal. As a result, asymmetry in the cross-correlation function would suggest a causal connection between the two series. For instance, if all the cross-correlations are positive, and $r_{xy}(1) > r_{yx}(1)$, $r_{xy}(2) > r_{yx}(2)$, and so on, the asymmetry would apparently indicate that X is the predominant cause. That is, X would be taken to be a stronger cause of Y than Y is of X. Or, as Rogosa (1979) has vividly expressed in a discussion of the cross-lagged panel correlation, X would be taken to be the "causal winner."

SIMPLE CROSS-CORRELATION ANALYSIS ASSESSED

By focusing on the causal winner, the simple cross-correlation function approach neglects other more important aspects of the relationship between two variables. Generally, we are interested in the strength of a causal relationship and not just in whether one causal direction is apparently stronger than the other. Additionally, we are often interested in detecting reciprocal causal relationships, or feedback, and this is not possible in the simple cross-correlation function approach. Focusing on the causal winner would lead us to reformulate the classical chicken-and-egg question—accurately characterized as a feedback system—as: Are chickens a stronger cause of eggs than eggs are a cause of chickens?

However, more serious problems beset simple cross-correlation analysis than the focus on the causal winner. Most important, the autocorrelation in the two series, X_t and Y_t, can obscure their underlying causal relationship to the point of suggesting the wrong series as the causal winner.

Table 1 presents an empirical example of the cross-correlation function. That table lists the cross-correlation between the employment and suicide rates, with each series leading the other up to 10 lags. The synchronous (or lag zero) cross-correlation equals the simple OLS correlation presented earlier: $r_{xy}(0) = -.59$.

The cross-correlation function in Table 1 is asymmetrical. The pattern of asymmetry would seem to suggest strongly that changes in the suicide rate precede changes in the employment rate. The largest cross-correlation coefficient occurs when the suicide rate leads one year, and nearly all the negative coefficients are larger for suicide leading employment than vice versa. For example, when the suicide rate leads the employment rate by three years, the cross-correlation equals $-.51$, while for the employment rate leading three years, the cross-correlation equals only $-.22$. This is precisely the kind of pattern that would have led Hooker (1901) and Campbell (1976) to declare the suicide rate the causal winner.

This interpretation is not consistent with expectations, however. Previous researchers have explained obtained (usually synchronous) correlations between the suicide rate and the employment rate or related economic indicators (e.g., the unemployment rate) in terms of employment—or whatever aspects of the economy it stands for—causally affecting the likelihood of suicide. In addition, we would not expect enough suicides in one year to reduce the overall employment rate in the next year.

Our expectations about the nature of the causal relationship between the employment and suicide rates may remain intact, though. The asymmetry in the cross-correlation function of Table 1 may be spurious. Certain patterns

TABLE 1 Simple Cross-Correlations Between the Employment and Suicide Rates

.05	−.06	−.14	−.25	−.32	−.36	−.42	−.51	−.56	−.59	−.59	−.47	−.32	−.22	−.15	−.08	−.04	.02	.10	.16	.19
10	9	8	7	6	5	4	3	2	1	0	1	2	3	4	5	6	7	8	9	10

Suicide Leads Employment — Lag (in years) — Employment Leads Suicide

110

of autocorrelation in the two series being studied will lead to spurious, asymmetrical cross-correlations. That is, the dependencies within series (autocorrelation) are likely to obscure the dependencies between series (cross-correlation). Note that the problem is not the same as autocorrelated error, or autocorrelation in the ϵ_t series, but refers to autocorrelation in X_t and Y_t themselves.

Figure 3 illustrates the problem that can arise because of autocorrelation in X_t and Y_t. The X and Y represent real, observed time series, and the a_x and a_y represent unobserved random shock components, or white noise processes, which cause changes in the values of X and Y. (We use the convention that uppercase letters represent observed variables, while lowercase letters represent unobserved variables in the remainder of the article.) Figure 3 gives hypothetical causal parameters, which, as we shall soon see, do not equal the expected correlations. In this hypothetical example and in all similar examples which follow, we make the simplifying assumption that the white noise processes (from which X_t and Y_t are here generated) are of the mean zero and variance one.

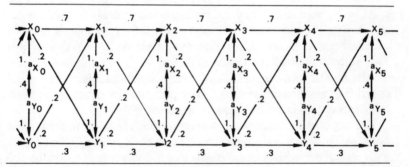

FIGURE 3   Hypothetical Causal Parameters for
Counterexample to Simple Cross-Correlation Function
Analysis

Disregarding for the moment the diagonal paths from $X_t \rightarrow Y_{t+1}$ and $Y_t \rightarrow X_{t+1}$, the variables X and Y are both first-order autoregressive:

$$X_t = .7\,X_{t-1} + a_{X_t};$$

$$Y_t = .3\,Y_{t-1} + a_{Y_t}.$$

The variable X is more strongly autocorrelated than Y (.7 versus .3). The white noise processes a_{X_t} and a_{Y_t} are of mean zero and variance one. The a_X

and a_Y processes are synchronously related, with the synchronous covariation equal to .4. As a result, X and Y will be synchronously cross-correlated. In addition, feedback occurs between X and Y; that is, a causal path connects X_1 to Y_2, X_2 to Y_3, and so on; and a causal path also connects Y_1 to X_2, Y_2 to X_3, and so on. Note that these lagged causal paths (the diagonal paths in Figure 3) are both equal to .2.

Table 2 lists the theoretical cross-correlations for the hypothetical model presented in Figure 3, which we computed according to the system of equations provided by Jenkins and Watts (1968, p. 332). Two points are especially noteworthy. First, many cross-correlations clearly differ from zero. (For example, assuming $N = 100$, 10 cross-correlation coefficients are statistically significant.) This occurs even though X and Y are causally linked only at the synchronous and ± 1 lags in Figure 3, and corresponds to our earlier comment that, as Hooker and Campbell recognized, the expected value of simple cross-correlation coefficients is unknown. A second, more troubling finding is that the cross-correlation function shows a clear asymmetry. Cross-correlations are larger when Y leads X than when X leads Y. For instance, $r_{yx}(1) = .56$, while $r_{xy}(1)$ is only .46. Similarly, $r_{yx}(2) = .46$ and $r_{xy}(2) = .36$. Such an asymmetrical pattern would probably have led Hooker and Campbell to conclude (tentatively) that Y is the predominant cause, or causal winner. This conclusion is disturbing since the $X_t \rightarrow Y_{t+1}$ and $Y_t \rightarrow X_{t+1}$ paths in Figure 3 both equal .2; that is, no *true* causal winner exists. Similar results, with unequal lagged cross-correlations arising from equal underlying causal parameters, have been pointed to by critics of the cross-lagged panel correlation technique (Rogosa, 1979).

But why does such spurious asymmetry occur? The key to understanding lies in recognizing that (1) indirect routes connect X_t with Y_{t+1} and Y_t with X_{t+1} and (2) the indirect routes connecting Y_t to X_{t+1} tend to run through the stronger $X_t \rightarrow X_{t+1}$ path, while the indirect paths connecting X_t to Y_{t+1} tend to run through the weaker $Y_t \rightarrow Y_{t+1}$.

Let us illustrate. The theoretical cross-correlation coefficients listed in Table 2 could be generated using the causal paths shown in Figure 3. We can estimate an approximate lagged cross-correlation, say between X_t and Y_{t+1}, by (1) identifying every route joining X_t and Y_{t+1}, (2) determining how much each route contributes to the total correlation, and (3) summing the contributions of each route. The contribution of each route equals the product of the path coefficients of all the individual paths involved in the route.

For instance, let us consider the relationship between X_t and Y_{t+1} (based on the pairs X_0 and Y_1, X_1 and Y_2, and so on), from which $r_{xy}(1)$ is computed. Let us also consider the relationship between Y_t and X_{t+1} (based on the pairs Y_0 and X_1, Y_1 and X_2, and so on), from which $r_{yx}(1)$ is

TABLE 2   Theoretical Cross-Correlation Coefficients Corresponding to the Hypothetical Causal Model in Figure 3.

.06	.08	.10	.13	.17	.22	.28	.36	.46	.56	.60	.46	.36	.31	.23	.18	.14	.10	.08	.06	.05
10	9	8	7	6	5	4	3	2	1	0	1	2	3	4	5	6	7	8	9	10

Y Leads X   X Leads Y

Lag
(in years)

computed. A direct route links X_t and Y_{t+1}. The associated path coefficient is .2, contributing .20 units of correlation to $r_{xy}(1)$. A direct route likewise links Y_t and X_{t+1}, contributing .20 units of correlation to $r_{yx}(1)$. Indirect routes also link X_t to Y_{t+1} and Y_t to X_{t+1}. We can illustrate the first indirect route between X_t and Y_{t+1} by looking at X_2, Y_2, and Y_3:

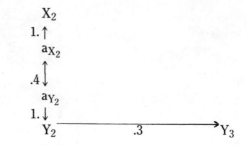

This route contributes .12 to the correlation coefficient, $r_{xy}(1)(.12=1.\times.4 \times 1. \times .3)$. Now consider the corresponding route linking Y_t to X_{t+1}:

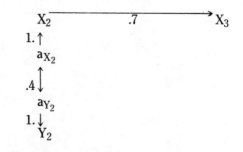

This route contributes .28 to the correlation coefficient, $r_{yx}(1)(.28=1.\times .4 \times 1 \times .7)$. While the direct routes contribute equally to $r_{xy}(1)$ and $r_{yx}(1)$, the indirect routes contribute unequally. Other indirect routes, not shown here, for the most part also contribute unequally to $r_{xy}(1)$ and $r_{yx}(1)$. As a result, $r_{yx}(1) > r_{xy}(1)$. Again, this occurs because routes contributing to $r_{yx}(1)$ tend to run through the larger $X_t \rightarrow X_{t+1}$ path (.7) while the indirect routes contributing to $r_{xy}(1)$ tend to run through the smaller $Y_t \rightarrow Y_{t+1}$ path (.3). For the same reason, $r_{yx}(2) > r_{xy}(2)$, and $r_{yx}(3) > r_{xy}(3)$, and so on. These differences decrease as the lag (K) increases because the inequality-causing routes are less direct.

The major point of the previous example is that, under conditions which may characterize much social science data, the dependencies within series (auto-correlation) will obscure the dependencies between series (cross-correlation). This problem should be contrasted with that of autocorrelated error, described above. Autocorrelated error, or autocorrelation in the ϵ_t series of residuals from an OLS regression, biases the estimated significance between two variables, X_t and Y_t, usually in the direction of overestimating the strength of their relationship. The problem just described is that autocorrelation in X_t and Y_t, the time-series variables of interest, biases their lagged cross-correlations, and this bias will *not* be constant or symmetrical across different lags. If we were interested only in the *synchronous* correlation between two variables, an unbiased estimate could be achieved by reducing the unnecessary restrictions usually assumed in traditional GLS procedures. However, if we wish to establish temporal precedence, such a *pseudo-GLS* approach (Hibbs, 1974) may not prove satisfactory. Even when autocorrelated error is well accounted for, autocorrelation can remain in (transformed) X_t and Y_t, and this remaining autocorrelation will differentially bias the lagged cross-correlations. This could easily result in drawing incorrect conclusions about temporal precedence.

Only recently has the econometrics literature widely recognized the inferential ambiguity created by autocorrelation in X_t and Y_t themselves, and not all observers have been persuaded (e.g., Sims, 1977). It is noteworthy, however, that even authors frequently cited as advocates of GLS have described the limitations of that method and now advocate alternatives such as those described below (e.g., Granger, 1977).

Given that autocorrelation in time-series data can create spurious asymmetry in the cross-correlation function, it would seem desirable if we could somehow estimate and remove the autocorrelation from a series. Fortunately, procedures exist for doing just this. One major procedure for doing so involves applying *ARIMA modeling* to individual time series to remove their autocorrelation, so that the lagged cross-correlations between series will not be biased by autocorrelation.

CROSS-CORRELATION ANALYSIS WITH "PREWHITENING" BY THE ASSUMED CAUSE (THE BOX-JENKINS PROCEDURE)

The next two modes of analysis presume an aquaintance with identifying, estimating, and diagnosing the extent of autocorrelation between observations in a time series. The ARIMA models that have been developed for achieving these goals are widely discussed in textbooks (see McCain and McCleary, 1979; Hibbs, 1974; Glass et al., 1975; and, for a more mathematically sophisticated presentation, Box and Jenkins, 1976). We do not want to repeat these past discussions here since our aim is not to illustrate how to do

ARIMA modeling. Rather, it is to illustrate the major inferential pitfalls in using time-series data to draw causal inferences. Nonetheless, we shall have to define the major concepts of ARIMA modeling so that the following discussion is comprehensible to readers unfamiliar with ARIMA models.

ARIMA MODELING

The general ARIMA(p,d,q) model is actually a consolidation of different mathematical formulations which might plausibly describe a time series, and it is most easily understood by considering its components individually. These components assume that each observation in a time series consists of a "random shock,"[9] which is uncorrelated with other random shocks, and a portion of preceding observation(s) or random shock(s). The first component, the *autoregressive model* or AR(p), assumes that an observation is directly dependent on preceding observations. Figure 4 represents the simplest, or first-order, autoregressive process [AR(1)] schematically. Each observation of the series $(X_1, X_2, X_3, \ldots)$ equals the current random shock $(a_1, a_2, a_3, \ldots)$ plus a portion (ϕ_1) of the immediately preceding observation. For the simple autoregressive model of Figure 4, the ϕ_1 parameter is like a correlation coefficient describing the extent to which the current value of the series can be predicted from the previous value. More complicated autoregressive models could be constructed. For instance, we could modify Figure 4 by adding an arrow directly from X_1 to X_3, from X_2 to X_4, and so on, and the result would be called a second-order autoregressive model, or AR(2).

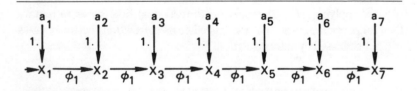

FIGURE 4   Diagram of a First-Order Autoregressive Model

The second component of the general ARIMA(p,d,q) model is called *integration* or I(d), which is actually a misnomer (Box and Jenkins, 1976, p. 12).[10] This component assumes a model like that shown in Figure 4, except that it additionally assumes that $\phi_1 = 1$. The integration component of the ARIMA(p,d,q) model is usually applied to a time series in conjunction with one of the other components. Normally, it is applied when a series has a trend (see section on OLS Regression When Trend or Seasonality Is Present, above) and no theoretical or commonsense transformation, such as correcting for population growth, is available for detrending the series. When the integration component of the ARIMA model is judged appropriate for a real-time series, the series is *differenced* to remove that component of autocorrelations, i.e., one subtracts from each observation the value of the preceding observaton.

The third component of the general ARIMA(p,d,q) model, the *moving average model* or MA(q), assumes that the current observation consists of a current random shock plus a portion (ϕ_1) of the preceding random shock(s). The simplest, or first-order, moving average model, MA(1), is represented schematically in Figure 5. Higher order moving average models could be constructed with the addition of other set(s) of diagonal lines, as from a_1 to X_3, a_2 to X_4, and so on.

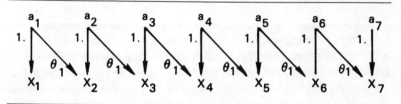

FIGURE 5   Diagram of a First-Order Moving Average Process

In practice, one tests empirically whether a real time series is best described by an autoregressive, integrated, or moving average model, or by some combination of these, as well as what order the apparent model should be. Two key tests in doing so are the autocorrelation function and partial autocorrelation function. The *autocorrelation function*, or ACF, describes the correlation between a series and that same series lagged one, two, three, . . . units. Thus, we might speak of the lag one autocorrelation coefficient, which is often quite large because immediately adjacent observations tend to be highly similar. We might also speak of the lag two autocorrelation coefficient, which will usually be smaller, sometimes strikingly so, and so on. The *partial autocorrelation function*, or PACF, is akin to a partial autocorrelation coefficient between a series and its lagged self; and essentially, the autocorrelation at smaller lags is partialed out. For instance, the lag two partial autocorrelation is the autocorrelation at lag two partialing out the autocorrelation at lag one. See Glass et al. (1975) and Box and Jenkins (1976) for greater detail. Different kinds of ARIMA(p,d,q) models are associated with different patterns in the ACF and the PACF.[11]

Through a multistaged procedure we will not describe (see Box and Jenkins, 1976), one can determine which ARIMA(p,d,q) model best describes a time series. This information can further be used to transform the observations so they are not autocorrelated, a procedure known as prewhitening. Note that this is equivalent to estimating the random shocks, or a_t series, illustrated in Figures 4 and 5; and that obtaining uncorrelated series in this way may allow us to establish temporal precedence better and to reduce the number of alternative causes. In some cases though, one cannot easily determine which of two or three ARIMA models better describes a time series. In these cases, we advocate prewhitening with all reasonable ARIMA(p,d,q) models. A more serious concern is that a small number of time series, particularly those with fewer observations, will not be satisfactorily described by *any* ARIMA(p,d,q) model.

THE BOX-JENKINS PROCEDURE

The Box-Jenkins (1976) approach has as its ultimate goal identifying and estimating a particular kind of (transfer function) model of the relationship between two series. Describing this class of bivariate models is beyond the scope of the present article, and the interested reader should consult Box and Jenkins (1976). We focus here on the simpler use of Box-Jenkins procedures: identifying whether X is the apparent cause of Y, or Y of X, or both. While the approach was developed and illustrated primarily in engineering contexts, Box-Jenkins procedures have gained the attention of, and have been used by, social scientists (e.g., Helmer and Johansson, 1977; Vigderhaus, 1978).

Box and Jenkins were concerned primarily with situations where a researcher believes a priori that X causes Y and wants to estimate the strength and the duration of X's causal impact on Y. Given this focus, Box and Jenkins proposed a multistage procedure which we will illustrate using their example: X_t, the input series or independent variable, is the measured rate of methane gas feed into a gas furnace, and Y_t, the output series or dependent variable, is the percent concentration of CO_2 in the outlet gas.

In the first stage of the Box-Jenkins procedure, one determines the ARIMA(p,d,q) model of the presumed causal series, X_t. To do so, one uses the ARIMA identification-estimation-diagnosis modeling procedures described in many texts. Using these procedures, Box and Jenkins found the methane gas feed rate was well described by an ARIMA(3,0,0) model. (Higher order ARIMA processes are apparently more common in the natural sciences than in the social sciences.)

In stage two of the Box-Jenkins procedure, one prewhitens both the X_t

and Y_t series according to the ARIMA model estimated in stage one for the X series. (Because both series are transformed using the same ARIMA model, we refer to the Box-Jenkins procedure as involving *"joint* prewhitening.") From the X_t series we obtain the estimated white noise process: $\hat{a}_t$, which are the residuals from the estimated ARIMA model of X_t. For example, Box and Jenkins, using the estimated ARIMA(3,0,0) model of methane gas feed rate series, transformed the original autocorrelated series into a series of white noise residuals. On the other hand, because the Y_t series is transformed by the ARIMA model of X_t, the residuals from Y_t, which we will call α_t, will only be white noise when the ARIMA model of Y_t is sufficiently similar to that of X_t. Box and Jenkins transformed their output series, percent CO_2 concentration, according to the ARIMA(3,0,0) model of the methane gas rate estimated in stage one. Not surprisingly, perhaps, Box and Jenkins found that the residual series α_t was autocorrelated. Thus, we might refer to the transformation of the Y_t series into α_t as "pseudo-prewhitening."

In stage three of the Box-Jenkins procedure, one cross-correlates the two prewhitened residual series, $\hat{a}_t$ and α_t, obtained in stage two. For instance, Box and Jenkins (1976) cross-correlated the transformed methane feed rate, $\hat{a}_t$, and the transformed percent CO_2 concentration, α_t. However, they only present cross-correlations for $\hat{a}_t$ leading α_t, perhaps because they initially assumed that the methane feed rate causes the percent CO_2 concentration, and not vice versa. Box and Jenkins find that after near-zero coefficients at lags 0, 1, 2, $\hat{a}$ and α are negatively cross-correlated at lags three through seven.

The Box-Jenkins procedure has several further steps, in which one identifies, estimates, and diagnoses what is called a transfer function model. However, we are not concerned with describing transfer function models here, and the interested reader should consult Box and Jenkins (1976). Our concern is with the more basic use of the Box-Jenkins approach—*identifying* whether two series are related in a way that is consistent with a causal hypothesis.

AN ASSESMENT OF THE PROCEDURE

Box and Jenkins present two major justifications for their joint prewhitening strategy. First, with nonprewhitened data, the estimates of the cross-correlation function are generally inefficient. Second, and more important, the autocorrelation in the series X_t and Y_t differentially biases the lagged cross-correlations, as we illustrated earlier. While these two points argue convincingly against relying on the simple cross-correlation function, they do not exclusively and convincingly justify the Box-Jenkins approach of *joint* prewhitening and cross-correlating.

The major shortcoming of the Box-Jenkins approach occurs because the prewhitening model of X_t often does not transform the presumed outcome variable, Y_t, into uncorrelated white noise. We will illustrate this by considering the relationship between the GNP in constant dollars and the suicide rate rather than by examining the earlier example of employment and suicide rates. We substitute GNP for the employment series because, for our purposes, the suicide rate and GNP have sufficiently different ARIMA models while employment and suicide are both best described by an ARIMA(2,0,0) model. Since it is difficult to discriminate which of three ARIMA models of GNP is superior, in what follows we shall employ all three different models, each of which meets the normal criteria for an adequate model. None of them, however, is identical with the ARIMA model for suicide rate.

The Box-Jenkins approach, as we have noted, assumes a priori knowledge of which is the causal variable, and this assumption determines which series's ARIMA model is used for prewhitening. Let us assume as many past researchers have that the economy, here represented by the GNP, causally affects the suicide rate. Given our three alternative ARIMA models of GNP, we can conduct three separate Box-Jenkins analyses. In each instance we transform both the GNP and the suicide rate by one of the ARIMA models of GNP and then cross-correlate the resulting two residual series.

Table 3 contains the results of such a Box-Jenkins analysis of the GNP-suicide rate relationship. The first, second, and third rows of Table 3 present the results of the Box-Jenkins procedure using the alternative GNP models. These three analyses reveal remarkably similar patterns of cross-correlations. For all three GNP models, the Box-Jenkins approach shows the strongest negative correlation to be at the synchronous lag. But the analyses also show negative cross-correlations when GNP leads suicides by one or two lags, though not all are reliable. The analyses further show the cross-correlations to be near zero when the suicide rate precedes GNP (and the few exceptions may be spuriously caused by unremoved cyclicality in the GNP models which do not explicitly account for a seven-year cycle which is suggested in the ACF and PACF of GNP). Thus, when the analyses are all considered together they tend to support the hypothesis that GNP—or whatever aspect of the economy it represents—causally affects the suicide rate.

We might ask, however, whether this conclusion would change if we changed the a priori assumption that GNP causes the suicide rate. That is, if we had transformed both series according to the ARIMA model of the suicide rate, would increases in GNP still appear to precede decreases in the suicide rate? The cross-correlations listed in the fourth row of Table 3 address this question. These cross-correlations were obtained with the Box-

TABLE 3 Box-Jenkins Cross-Correlations of Gross National Product and the Suicide Rate

Series Presented by:

	GNP Leads Suicide											Suicide Leads GNP									
Lag (in years)	10	9	8	7	6	5	4	3	2	1	0	1	2	3	4	5	6	7	8	9	10
GNP (1,1,0) Prewhitening Model	−.06	−.04	−.08	−.13	−.04	−.04	−.14	−.05	−.18	−.21†	−.29*	.01	−.02	.01	.01	−.07	−.17	−.09	−.04	−.13	.11
GNP (1,1,0) with (θ_0) Trend Parameter Prewhitening Model	−.09	−.08	−.12	−.16	−.10	−.10	−.19†	−.14	−.24*	−.27*	−.31*	−.08	−.08	−.05	−.05	−.11	−.19	−.15	−.10	−.13	.04
GNP (1,1,0) X (1,0,0)$_7$ Prewhitening Model	−.03	−.02	−.03	−.05	−.03	−.03	−.16	−.08	−.19	−.17	−.26*	.01	.01	.01	.01	−.01	−.11	−.03	.01	−.04	.13
Suicide (2,0,0) Prewhitening Model	.24*	−.18	.06	−.01	−.15	−.01	.07	.05	−.01	.22†	−.31*	−.03	−.09	−.14	−.14	.09	.07	−.12	.01	.04	−.03

*p≤.05 †p<.10

121

Jenkins procedure, using the identified ARIMA(2,0,0) model of suicide for joint prewhitening. As we would expect, the largest coefficient in Row 4 is the negative synchronous cross-correlation. Also, the coefficients for the suicide rate leading the GNP are generally near zero, which is consistent with the results in Rows 1– 3. Surprisingly, the cross-correlation for GNP leading one year is positive and marginally significant ($r = .22$), implying that high values of GNP one year are associated with high rates of suicide the next, in direct contrast to the negative lagged relationship implied in Rows 1– 3.

Thus, we find that: (1) when GNP and the suicide rate are jointly prewhitened according to one of the alternative ARIMA models of GNP, GNP is *negatively* correlated with the suicide rate when GNP leads one or two years and (2) when GNP and the suicide rate are transformed according to the ARIMA model of the *suicide rate*, GNP is *positively* correlated with the suicide rate when GNP leads one year. This discrepancy apparently arises because, when two series, X_t and Y_t, are jointly prewhitened using the ARIMA model of X_t, Y_t will not necessarily be transformed to pure white noise. The autocorrelation remaining in Y_t can then cause spurious patterns in the cross-correlation function, in a manner described earlier (see section on Simple Cross-Correlation Analysis Assessed, above). For instance, when both GNP and the suicide rate are transformed using the ARIMA model of GNP, the suicide rate is not transformed into white noise. The autocorrelation that remains in the suicide rate then complicates the cross-correlation between the two transformed series.

Spurious complication of the cross-correlation function by autocorrelation in the pseudo-prewhitened Y_t is the most serious shortcoming of the Box-Jenkins approach. Such spurious complication will not occur in the Box-Jenkins approach if the two series, X_t and Y_t, share very similar ARIMA models, because each would become white noise when transformed according to the ARIMA model of the other series. Unfortunately, we cannot at present specify what degree of dissimilarity is unacceptable.

In most instances one can learn whether unremoved autocorrelation is spuriously affecting the cross-correlation function by conducting independent Box-Jenkins analyses. In one analysis, joint prewhitening would use the ARIMA model of X_t; in the other analysis, the ARIMA model of Y_t (e.g., Rows 1– 3 versus Row 4 of Table 3). However, this approach is not completely satisfactory. For instance, one cannot readily interpret the analyses summarized in Table 3, and even more troublesome results can arise. Fortunately, an alternative procedure exists.

CROSS-CORRELATION ANALYSIS WITH INDEPENDENT
PREWHITENING (THE HAUGH-BOX PROCEDURE)

Haugh and Box (1977; Haugh, 1976) recently proposed a revision of the Box-Jenkins joint prewhitening and cross-correlation procedure (this revision was earlier suggested by others, e.g., Granger and Newbold, 1974). One reason they did so is to avoid the spurious asymmetry which can arise in the Box-Jenkins cross-correlation function due to the autocorrelation in α_t, the pseudo-prewhitened Y_t series. Thus, the Haugh-Box procedure involves prewhitening both series independently, *using their own ARIMA models*. According to the Haugh-Box procedure, one: (1) determines the ARIMA(p,d,q) model of X_t, using the customary indentification-estimation-diagnosis procedures and then prewhitens X_t by its own ARIMA model to obtain the estimated white noise series, $\hat{a}_{X_t}$; (2) likewise determines the ARIMA(p,d,q) model of Y_t and prewhitens Y_t by its own ARIMA model to obtain the estimated white noise series $\hat{a}_{Y_t}$; and (3) cross-correlates the residual series, $\hat{a}_X$ and $\hat{a}_Y$. We refer to this strategy as "independent prewhitening and cross-correlation" because one prewhitens each series independently, according to its *own* ARIMA model, before cross-correlating the series.

In the Haugh-Box procedure, one bases causal inference on the pattern of cross-correlations between $\hat{a}_X$ and $\hat{a}_Y$. According to its proponents, one interprets this cross-correlation function as follows: When the cross-correlation is significant for $\hat{a}_X$ leading $\hat{a}_Y$, but not for $\hat{a}_Y$ leading $\hat{a}_X$, there is unidirectional causation from X to Y; when the cross-correlation is significant for $\hat{a}_Y$ leading $\hat{a}_X$, but not for $\hat{a}_X$ to $\hat{a}_Y$, there is unidirectional causation from Y to X; when the cross-correlation is significant both for $\hat{a}_X$ leading $\hat{a}_Y$ and for $\hat{a}_Y$ leading $\hat{a}_X$, there is feedback, or reciprocal causality; when only the synchronous correlation is significant, temporal precedence is not established, so no causal inference is warranted; and when no cross-correlation is significant, X and Y are causally independent. We suggest these rules be exercised cautiously, first, because $\hat{a}_X$ and $\hat{a}_Y$ may be significantly cross-correlated through the influence of some third variable, as we discuss below, and, second, because insufficient ARIMA model fits, or chance alone, can create totally spurious cross-correlations between $\hat{a}_X$ and $\hat{a}_Y$.

Haugh and Box present several reasons for preferring independent prewhitening to its alternatives: joint prewhitening or no prewhitening. The following five reasons are paramount. First, independent prewhitening should minimize the spurious cross-correlations which may arise because of autocorrelation in X_t and Y_t. Second, feedback effects (in which X_t affects later values of Y, and Y_t also affects later values of X) should be easier to detect following independent prewhitening. Third, in the Haugh-Box approach one need not specify a priori which is the causal series. Fourth, Haugh (1976) has shown that when X and Y are independent (i.e., unrelated), the cross-correlations between $\hat{a}_X$ and $\hat{a}_Y$ are normally and independently distributed with a mean of zero and standard deviation of $1/\sqrt{N}$. Thus, the significance of Haugh-Box cross-correlations can be judged against this standard error.[12] Fifth, the Haugh-Box approach satisfies our—and Haugh and Box's—favorite criterion for assessing covariation in time series: Covariation should be inferred only when X adds to the predictability of Y over and above the predictability arising from the orderly behavior of Y itself (Granger, 1969). When we transform a series into white noise, we remove that part of the current observation which could be predicted from past observations. Thus, when the prewhitened series, $\hat{a}_X$, is significantly correlated with lagged values of the prewhitened series, $\hat{a}_Y$, $\hat{a}_X$ is predicting part of Y that could not be predicted by past values of Y alone. To Haugh and Box's list, we might add a sixth reason for preferring the Haugh-Box approach: It is simpler in practice to conduct the Haugh-Box procedure than it is to conduct two separate Box-Jenkins analyses, prewhitening both series first by the ARIMA model of X_t and then by the ARIMA model of Y_t.

THE HAUGH-BOX PROCEDURE ASSESSED

Table 4 presents the results of a Haugh-Box analysis of the GNP and the suicide rate. Rows 1-3 list results from separate analyses using the three alternative ARIMA models of GNP. All three analyses show a large synchronous cross-correlation and lagged cross-correlations which do not differ from zero. Thus, we do not obtain the anomalous findings which occurred in the Box-Jenkins analysis and in the simple cross-correlation analysis. However, only the synchronous cross-correlation is significant, so temporal precedence is not established. Since one might suspect that a causal flow exists from the economic variable to the suicide rate, one can wonder whether independent prewhitening decreases the sensitivity for detecting any lagged effect.

Indeed, one of the most serious shortcomings of the Haugh-Box approach is that it apparently underestimates causal parameters under some conditions. Consider the unidirectional causal system illustrated in Figure 6. In this figure, the autoregressive process X_t causes the variable Y_t. No causal parameter directly links adjacent observations of Y. Nevertheless, observed values of Y_t will be autocorrelated because adjacent values of Y_t are indirectly linked through the autocorrelated, causal variable X_t. As a result, when one prewhitens the observed variable Y_t according to its estimated

TABLE 4   Haugh-Box Cross Correlations of the Suicide Rate [ARIMA (2,0,0)] with the Gross National Product and with the Employment Rate.

GNP Prewhitened by:

	Suicide Leads GNP (Employment Rate)											GNP (Employment Rate) Leads Suicide									
Lag (in years)	10	9	8	7	6	5	4	3	2	1	0	1	2	3	4	5	6	7	8	9	10
ARIMA (1,0,0)	.14	−.23*	.01	−.10	−.14	.05	.08	.03	−.03	.04	−.41*	−.06	.11	−.11	.09	.01	−.13	.02	.03	−.03	
ARIMA (1,0,0) Trend	.10	.25*	−.02	−.11	−.13	.06	.07	.01	−.07	−.04	−.42*	−.07	−.05	.10	−.10	.09	−.01	−.13	.02	.02	−.03
ARIMA (1,0,0)X(1,0,0)$_7$	.14	−.24	−.01	.04	−.15	.10	.08	.07	−.10	.02	−.33*	−.06	−.09	.18	−.09	.09	.07	−.13	−.05	.05	−.01
Employment Prewhitened by ARIMA (2,0,0)	−.03	−.14	.10	−.18	−.28*	.15	.09	−.29*	.01	.00	−.59*	−.01	.15	.15	−.11	.17	−.02	−.20	.16	.14	−.06

*p <.05

ARIMA model, autocorrelation will be removed; but the variation in Y_t attributed to its own autocorrelation should really be attributed to the causal influence of X_t. For this reason, the causal parameter, ω, will be somewhat underestimated by the Haugh-Box procedure. On the other hand, the ω in Figure 6 should be better estimated using the Box-Jenkins approach. We believe, however, that researchers rarely study a relationship like that illustrated in Figure 6, in which an outcome series is autocorrelated only because it is caused by some other autocorrelated variable. Nevertheless, the Haugh-Box approach will underestimate causal parameters under some conditions. Further work is required before we can specify the magnitude and delineating conditions of this underestimation. We believe that the bias will most often lead to underestimation of the causal parameter, but not to complete attenuation. Even with the possibility of underestimation, we prefer the Haugh-Box approach to its alternatives. We would rather underestimate a relationship than base causal inference on spuriously inflated cross-correlations.

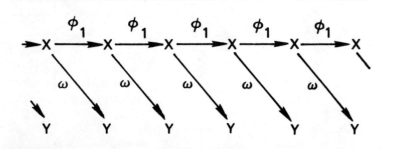

FIGURE 6   Hypothetical Causal System, Illustrating
Haugh-Box Underestimation of Causal Parameters

A second shortcoming of the Haugh-Box approach, shared by Box-Jenkins, is that it relies on ARIMA modeling procedures. Several decision points exist in ARIMA modeling where the researcher must exercise his or her own judgment. Indeed, one might ask whether ARIMA modeling is as much art as science. Our judgment is that this reliance on ARIMA modeling procedures is not too serious a problem. First, one can conduct multiple Haugh-Box analyses, using alternative ARIMA models whenever some question exists as to which model is "best." Second, our experience suggests that with adequate training, a high degree of reliability across analysts can be obtained. Finally, the alternative ARIMA models that might be chosen usually lead to similar results because the alternative models are mathematically similar (compare, e.g., Rows 1-3 of Table 4).

A third problem of the Haugh-Box approach, also shared by Box-Jenkins, is that some series are not well described by any ARIMA model. As an example, we independently prewhitened the employment and suicide rates, and the resulting cross-correlations are shown in Row 4 of Table 4. The synchronous cross-correlation is large, and at lags ± 1 and ± 2 the coefficients are near zero. This is consistent with the Haugh-Box analysis of GNP and the suicide rate. However, several other cross-correlations are large (most notable are the significant coefficients obtained when employment leads suicide three and six years). These isolated cross-correlations apparently occur primarily because the employment rate is not well described by its ARIMA(2,0,0) model. As a result, the attempted prewhitening does not adequately transform the employment rate into a white noise process, and the remaining autocorrelation creates spurious spikes in the cross-correlation function.

Two other shortcomings derive from the Haugh-Box procedures' reliance on prewhitening. First, to the extent a series is completely regular, it will be fully predicted on the basis of its own past—and therefore detecting its covariation with other series will be impossible. Second, the transformed white noise processes, $\hat{a}_{X_t}$ and $\hat{a}_{Y_t}$, presumably contain a higher proportion of measurement error than the original series, X_t and Y_t. We expect this to occur because $\hat{a}_{X_t}$ and $\hat{a}_{Y_t}$ consist of that part of X_t and Y_t which could not be predicted from each series's own past regularities; and random measurement error should not be predictable, while much of the systematic, "true score" component of X_t and Y_t will be. The consequence of this relative preponderance of measurement error should of course be to attenuate the relationship between $\hat{a}_{X_t}$ and $\hat{a}_{Y_t}$. We anticipate further work on both the consequences of measurement error and on methods for dealing with measurement error in the context of Haugh-Box and related CTS procedures.

Several other shortcomings beset the Haugh-Box approach. We believe these shortcomings to be inherent in CTS analysis, and we will discuss them next.

CONCLUDING REMARKS

SOME GENERIC PROBLEMS

CTS analysis is only a special case of "passive observational" or "nonexperimental" methods (Cook and Campbell, 1979). As we have seen, a carefully conducted CTS analysis can establish the temporal ordering of variables, unlike most other types of correlational studies. In other respects, CTS studies share the classical inferential ambiguities associated with correlational research. Most notably, an obtained relationship between X_t and Y_t (whether synchronous or lagged or both) might alternatively be explained in terms of a third variable, Z_t, which causes both X and Y. One can sometimes reduce the plausibility of third-variable causation by directly examining a measure of the third variable or by examining indirect evidence, such as how a presumed causal series is related to patterns of "outcomes" across many variables or how the cause affects different subgroups of respondents. Nonetheless, the possibility of third-variable causation can never be logically ruled out in CTS studies. Consequently, specification errors are always a problem (see, e.g., Kmenta, 1971, section 10.4).

The nature of the data sometimes limits one's ability to draw causal inferences from a CTS analysis. Such shortcomings most often occur when one analyzes archival data. With archival data, questions of construct validity—which concerns the fit between the theoretical construct being discussed and its operational measure—become paramount (Cook and Campbell, 1979) because the researcher cannot tailor his or her measures to the constructs of interest. Moreover, archives rarely contain measures of psychological or "small group" processes. As a result, it is usually difficult to study the process which mediates an observed relationship between two variables. For example, one cannot readily study the psychological mechanism which mediates the relationship between economic indicators and the suicide rate.

Archival data are often not available in the preferred form. Generally, we prefer to obtain data collected at small measurement intervals (e.g., months) about different subgroups (e.g., black males or white females and so on or Nebraskans versus Marylanders and so on). Unfortunately, such finely detailed information often is not recorded. Additionally, in some instances only a small number of observations is available. Having few observations reduces statistical power and may make more sophisticated CTS analysis impractical. For instance, with only a few observations, the ARIMA model of a series usually cannot be determined.

Another data-related problem is that the meaning of a particular nominal variable can change over time. As a result, a variable with the same name may have a different factorial structure at different time points, making it unrealistic to expect the same relationships between variables across the whole length of two time series. Sometimes, these shifts in factorial composition result from changes in official definitions and in data collection procedures. For example, numerous changes have occurred in how cost-of-living indices are computed (U.S. Department of Labor, 1966). Further, even given constant measurement procedures, the underlying meaning of a variable can change. For instance, the unemployment rate probably means something different in the modern industrial welfare state than in an earlier, more agrarian society. Such shifts in the meaning of a variable over time (called either changing factorial structure or autocovariance nonstationarity) commonly will result in changes in relationships between variables. Therefore, we suggest that when changes in factor structure are identified, supplementary analyses be conducted with various segments of a series in which the structural changes are least. Of course, the number of observations must be sufficiently large to permit this.

While we have argued that the cross-correlation of independently prewhitened series should be examined, we have not addressed the question: What pattern of cross-correlations allows the analyst to infer temporal precedence? Is a single, lag one cross-correlation sufficient? What about marginally significant coefficients at lag three and four? Or what should one conclude about causation if there is synchronous cross-correlation only? Unfortunately, no single criterion is appropriate for assessing the temporal ordering necessary for drawing causal attributions. Indeed, the relevant criteria vary with the nature of the research question and depend primarily on the nature of the presumed causal process—for instance, with birth control issues a delay of at least nine months is expected—and on the length of the measurement interval—rapid causal onsets may appear as synchronous correlations with, say, annual data. We can, however, suggest some general guidelines. The temporal precedence required for causal inference is most readily inferred when one finds a pattern of contiguous cross-correlations which occurs near the lag corresponding to the length of the presumed causal process, and when the correlations at increasing lags show a pattern of relative increase and/or decrease that is consistent with theory and common sense.

A pervasive problem with Haugh-Box type analyses is that they often show synchronous, but not lagged relationships (Pierce, 1977a). This is especially likely when a large measurement interval (e.g., annual observations) is used. In some cases, we might attempt to draw causal inferences from a synchronous cross-correlation alone, using logic and outside evidence to render implausible both one direction of cause (e.g., $Y \rightarrow X$) and the most likely third-variable cause explanations. In such a case, however, the use of CTS has not increased one's ability to draw a causal inference over the inferential strength associated with other correlational methods.

A PERSPECTIVE ON THE LIMITS OF CTS ANALYSES

We have tried in this chapter to be critical and explicit about the limitations of different types of CTS analyses. We have judged such analyses by criteria of internal validity and by the relevance of the available time-series data for testing theories about interpersonal and intrapersonal processes. Our critical presentation should not be misinterpreted, and we would be distressed if readers concluded from this chapter that CTS analyses are so problem-riddled as not to be worth learning or applying.

A minor reason for this distress is that much basic research is now being conducted on CTS analysis, and new methods are being proposed by both statisticians and social scientists at a rapid rate. We therefore expect some of the internal validity problem to be resolved in this decade. Also, more archives with psychological measures are being collected, and more investigators are gathering their own longitudinal data to examine questions concerning the sequencing and consequences of human interaction.

More important than these reasons, however, is that *all* the methods available to social psychologists have warts when considered from a broad enough perspective on the validity requirements of social research. When in the past our self-conscious and critical examination of causality-probing with CTS was presented to social psychologists, a number responded, "Boy, those methods have so many problems I'm glad I stick to the lab and the experiment." We then bit our lips and refrained from the retort: "But if we opened up a wide enough range of validity issues and also considered, for instance, 'relevance,' external validity, and the construct validity of effects, then the laboratory experiment would appear as problem-riddled as CTS analysis appears from an internal validity and theory-testing perspective. It is only by limiting the criteria by which research is evaluated that the laboratory experiment seems superior to CTS analysis."

It is our enervating task as applied social psychologists who aspire to a catholic science to perform our work under conditions of inevitable uncertainty—not just in a philosophical sense in which all absolute knowledge is called into question but also in a more practical craftman's sense which stresses that our methods are so fallible that we cannot exhaustively probe most questions about the nature and consequences of important social events and about the processes that mediate these events and perhaps explain them. Responsible and self-critical CTS analyses have an important role to play, first, in testing causal hypotheses that cannot be investigated in other ways, e.g., how unemployment affects suicides at an aggregate level; second, in probing reciprocal causal relationships; and, third, in describing and attempting to explain interpersonal acts, especially in small groups.

That the methods are not infallible should not prevent us from being able to choose the best of the available CTS methods, from being explicitly self-critical in applying these methods, and from relating the tentative conclusions drawn from the CTS research to other observations and theories.

NOTES

1. *Stationarity* is a characteristic of time series which refers to the properties of the series being invariant over time. For most purposes, we can depict stationarity in terms of stationarity in the mean. Stationarity in the mean occurs when different segments of a series can all be described by the same mean, regardless of when the segment occurs. For more technical treatments of stationarity, see, e.g., Dhrymes (1974, p. 385), Malinvaud (1970, section 11.1), and Granger and Newbold (1977, section 1.2).

2. Some authors distinguish *seasonality,* in which the period is a year or less, from *cyclicality,* in which the period is greater than a year. Though this distinction sometimes proves useful, we do not generally hold to it in the present article.

3. In Figure 2, trend apparently remains in the suicide series despite our use of rates. This trend is demonstrated when other cross-checking procedures are used, as when the series is regressed on a linear index of time ($R^2 = .21$). We could present additional analyses which show that a strong negative relationship holds between the employment and the suicide rates when the latter is detrended using a variety of detrending procedures. We do not so because this would require a comparison of alternative deseasonalization and detrending procedures, which is beyond the scope of the present article.

4. OLS regression assumes that the residuals are independent:

$$E(\epsilon_t \epsilon_{t+k}) = 0,$$

i.e., the expected value of the covariance of the errors at one time, ϵ_t, and the errors at some other time, ϵ_{t+k}, is zero. When errors are autocorrelated, this assumption is violated, i.e.:

$$E(\epsilon_t \epsilon_{t+k}) \neq 0.$$

5. Homoscedasticity refers to the variance of the disturbance, ϵ_t, being constant for different values of X. When the variance of ϵ differs for difference values of X (e.g., the variance of consumption probably increases with income), the errors are called heteroscedastic.

6. These transformations for the OLS equation

$$Y_t = \alpha + \beta X_t + \epsilon_t$$
are
$$(Y_t - \phi_1 Y_{t-1}) = \alpha^* + \beta (X_t - \phi_1 X_{t-1}) + V_t,$$

where α^*, the transformed constant or intercept, is equal to $\alpha(1 - \phi_1)$, and V_t, the transformed residual, equals $(\epsilon_t - \phi_1 \epsilon_{t-1})$. In the present case, where $\phi_1 = 1$, this approach is equivalent to the method of first differences, and thus violates usual assumptions concerning autoregressive error (see Johnston, 1972: 244).

7. The transformations applied to achieve independent errors involve transforming the

OLS residuals, ϵ_t, into V_t, where $V_t = \epsilon_t - \phi_1 \epsilon_{t-1}$ (see Note 6). As a result, the residual variance of the traditional GLS model estimates $\sigma_{\tilde{V}}^2$, the variance of the transformed residuals V_t, rather than $\sigma_{\underset{\epsilon}{}}^2$, the variance of the OLS residuals, ϵ_t.

The GLS estimate of R^2 is thus based on the transformed residual variance, $\sigma_{\tilde{V}}^2$, and so is not directly comparable to the OLS estimate of R^2. Buse (1973) discussed such problems with commonly used GLS goodness-of-fit estimates. In general, transformations can be applied to the GLS estimates to determine the OLS overestimation of R^2. In our particular case, this cannot readily be done because $\phi_1 = 1$.

8. A special class of instances in which nonsynchronous relationships are investigated, usually by traditional GLS regression, are the distributed lag models, with which some readers may be familiar. In a distributed lag model, the dependent variable is predicted simultaneously by synchronous and lagged X:

$$Y_t = \alpha + \beta_1 X_1 + \beta_2 X_{t-1} + \beta_3 X_{t-3} + \ldots \beta_{k+1} X_{t-k} + \epsilon_t.$$

Very often some restriction is placed on the β coefficients. In practice, the restriction is either (a) that the β's should decline geometrically (if we expect the effects of X_t to decay for increasing values K in Y_{t+k}) or (b) that the β's should first increase and then decrease (if we expect the effects of X on Y to "build up" for a few lags and then decay, e.g., as in polynomial lag models).

Because synchronous and nonsynchronous lags are investigated in a distributed lag model, one might expect that useful information will be obtained about temporal precedence. Generally, this will not occur. First, in practice the causal variable is usually specified a priori, so Y is regressed on X but X is not regressed on Y. Second, the restrictions usually placed on the β coefficients obscure the precise relationship of X to Y at the different lags. Third, as with other traditional GLS approaches, autocorrelation can remain in the X_t and Y_t series and obscure their relationship. Finally, if a similar distributed lag model were computed for Y on X and for X on Y, the relative reliability of X and Y will partially determine whether the X→Y or Y→X model is stronger.

9. The random shock, $a_t \sim$ NID $(0,\sigma^2)$, i.e., a_t is a sequence of independently and identically distributed random normal variates with zero mean and fixed variance. For the sake of simplicity, we will assume throughout that the random shock has variance one. If the original series X', has a nonzero mean, it is transformed to mean zero as

$$X_t' = X_t - \overline{X}'.$$

10. The reason for including the term *integrated* in the ARIMA title is as follows. If we have a differenced series:

$$\Delta X_t = X_t - X_{t-1}$$
then
$$\Delta X_1 = X_1$$
(because no previous value exists to be subtracted)
$$\Delta X_2 = X_2 - X_1$$
$$\Delta X_3 = X_3 - X_2$$
$$\Delta X_4 = X_4 \times X_3$$

and so on.

To retrieve the original series from the differenced series, we must perform the procedure:

$$X_t = \Delta X_t + \Delta X_{t-1} + \Delta X_{t-2} + \dots$$
For instance
$$X_3 = \Delta X_3 + \Delta X_2 + \Delta X_1$$
$$= (X_3 - X_2) + (X_2 - X_1) + (X_1)$$
$$= X_3.$$

This procedure of summing the series of all previous ΔX's to obtain X_t has widely been called integration, though it would perhaps more appropriately be called summation (Box and Jenkins, 1976).

11. For an autoregressive process of order p, AR(p), the ACF decays approximately as an exponent or as a sine wave of decreasing amplitude (a "damped sine wave"). The PACF is nonzero for the first p lags and zero thereafter.

For a moving average model of order q, MA(q), the ACF has q nonzero spikes and equals zero for lags greater than q. The PACF of an MA model decays roughly as an exponential or damped sine wave.

For nonstationary series which need differencing, i.e., which have an "integration" component, the ACF fails to die out. Rather, it dies off slowly and very nearly linearly.

Models with both autoregressive and moving average components are called "mixed models." For stationary mixed models, both the ACF and PACF either decay exponentially or as a damped sine wave. Further information on all of these models, and their identification from the ACF and PACF, is available from several sources cited in the text.

12. Further investigation is required to determine the distribution of $r_{\hat{a}_x \hat{a}_y}$ (K) when the series X and Y are not independent. That is, it has not yet been demonstrated conclusively that the standard deviation is still $1/\sqrt{N}$ and that the $r_{\hat{a}_x \hat{a}_y}$ is equal to zero at lags other than the true causal lag (e.g., lag 1 when $X_t \rightarrow Y_{t+1}$), when X and Y are not independent.

REFERENCES

BAKEMAN, R. and J.V. BROWN (1977) "Behavioral dialogues: an approach to the assessment of the mother-infant interaction." Child Development 48: 195-203.

BLOOMFIELD, P. (1976) Fourier Analysis of Time Series: An Introduction. New York: John Wiley.

BOX, G.E.P. and G.M. JENKINS (1976) Time Series Analysis: Forecasting and Control. San Francisco: Holden-Day.

BOX, G.E.P. and G.C. TIAO (1975) "Intervention analysis with applications to economic and environmental problems." Journal of the American Statistical Association 70: 70-92.

BRENNER, M.H. (1975) "Trends in alcohol consumption and associated illness." American Journal of Public Health 65: 1279-1292.

————— (1973) Mental Illness and the Economy. Cambridge, MA: Harvard University Press.

BUSE, A. (1973) "Goodness of fit generalized least squares estimation." American Statistician 27: 106-108.

CAMPBELL, D.T. (1976) "Theory of social experimentation, measurement, and program evaluation." (Research proposal to the National Science Foundation)

————— and J.C. STANLEY (1966) Experimental and Quasi-Experimental Designs for Research. Skokie, IL: Rand McNally.

COCHRANE, D. and G.H. ORCUTT (1949) "Application of least squares regression to relationships containing auto-correlated error terms." Journal of the American Statistical Association 44: 32-61.

COOK, T.D. and D.T. CAMPBELL (1979) Quasi-Experimentation: Design and Analysis Issues for Field Settings. Skokie, IL: Rand McNally.

_____ (1976) "The design and conduct of quasi-experiments and true experiments in field settings," in M.D. Dunnette (ed.), Handbook of Industrial and Organizational Psychology. Skokie, IL: Rand McNally.

DHRYMES, P.J. (1974) Econometrics. New York: Springer-Verlag.

DURBIN, J. (1960) "Estimation of parameters in time series regression models." Journal of the Royal Statistical Society Series B 22: 139-153.

ENGLE, R.F. (1974) "Specification of the disturbance for efficient estimation." Econometrica 42.

GERGEN, K.J. (1978) "Toward generative theory." Journal of Personality and Social Psychology 36: 1344-1360.

GLASS, G.V., V.L. WILLSON, and J.M. GOTTMAN (1975) Design and Analysis of Time Series Experiments. Boulder: Colorado Associated University Press.

GOTTMAN, J.M. (1979) "Detecting cyclicality in social interaction." Psychological Bulletin 86: 338-348.

_____ and C. NOTARIUS (1978) "Sequential analysis of observational data using Markov chains" in T.R. Kratochwill (ed.), Single Subject Research: Strategies for Assessing Change. New York: Academic Press.

GRANGER, C.W.J. (1977) "Comment on Pierce." Journal of the American Statistical Association 72: 22-23.

_____ (1969) "Investigating causal relations by econometric models and cross-spectral methods." Econometrica 37: 424-438.

_____ and M. HATANAKA (1964) Spectral Analysis of Economic Time Series. Princeton, NJ: Princeton University Press.

GRANGER, C.W.J. and P. NEWBOLD (1977) Forecasting Economic Time Series. New York: Academic Press.

_____ (1974) "Spurious regression in econometrics." Journal of Economics 2: 111-120.

HANNON, M.T. and A.A. YOUNG (1977) "Estimation in panel models: results on pooling cross-sections and time series" in D.R. Heise (ed.), Sociological Methodology. San Francisco: Jossey-Bass.

HAUGH, L.D. (1976) "Checking the independence of two covariance-stationary time series: a univariate residual cross-correlation approach." Journal of the American Statistical Association 71: 378-385.

_____ and G.E.P. BOX (1977) "Identification of dynamic regression (distributed lag) models connecting two time series." Journal of the American Statistical Association 72: 121-130.

HELMER, R.M. and J.K. JOHANSSON (1977) "An exposition of the Box-Jenkins transfer function analysis with an application to the advertising-sales relationship." Journal of Marketing Research 14: 227-239.

HIBBS, D.A. (1977) "On analyzing the effects of policy intervention: Box-Jenkins vs. structural equation models" in D.R. Heise (ed.), Sociological Methodology 1977. San Francisco: Jossey-Bass.

_____ (1974) "Problems of statistical estimation and causal inference in time-series regression models" in H.L. Costner (ed.), Sociological Methodology 1973-1974. San Francisco: Jossey-Bass.

HILDRETH, C. and J.Y. LU (1960) Demand Relations with Autocorrelated Disturbances (Technical Bulletin 276). Michigan State University Agricultural Experiment Station.

HOOKER, R.H. (1901) "Correlation of the marriage-rate with trade." Journal of the Royal Statistical Society 64: 485-492.

JENKINS, G.M. and D.G. WATTS (1968) Spectral Analysis and Its Applications. San Francisco: Holden-Day.

JOHNSTON, J. (1972) Econometric Methods. New York: McGraw-Hill.

KMENTA, J. (1971) Elements of Econometrics. New York: Macmillan.

LEE, S.H. "Cross-correlogram and the causal structure between two time series. Northwestern University. (unpublished)

MALINVAUD, E. (1970) Statistical Methods of Econometrics. Amsterdam: North Holland.

MAYER, T.F. and W.R. ARNEY (1974) "Spectral analysis and the study of social change" in H.L. Costner (ed.), Sociological Methodology 1973-1974. San Francisco: Jossey-Ball.

McCAIN, L.J. and R. McCLEARY (1979) "The statistical analysis of the simple interrupted time-series quasi-experiment" in T.D. Cook and D.T. Campbell, Quasi-Experimentation: Design and Analysis Issues for Field Settings. Skokie, IL: Rand McNally.

NERLOVE, M. (1971) "Further evidence on the estimation of dynamic economic relations from a time series of cross-sections." Econometrica 39: 359-382.

PIERCE, D.A. (1977a) "Relationships—and the lack thereof—between economic time series, with special reference to money, reserves, and interest rates (with discussion)." Journal of the American Statistical Association 72: 11-22.

———— (1977b) "R² measures for time series." Special Studies Paper. Washington, DC: Federal Reserve Board.

———— and L.D. HAUGH (1977) "Causality in temporal systems: characterizations and a survey." Journal of Econometrics 5: 265-293.

REPP, A.C. and S.M. DEITZ (1974) "Reducing aggressive and self-injurious behavior of institutionalized retarded children through reinforcement of other behaviors." Journal of Applied Behavior Analysis 7: 313-325.

ROGOSA, D. (1979) "Causal models in longitudinal research: rationale, formulation, and interpretation" in J.R. Nesselroade and P.B. Baltes (eds.), Longitudinal Research in Human Development: Design and Analysis. New York: Academic Press.

———— (1978) "Time and time again: some analysis problems in longitudinal research." University of Chicago. (unpublished)

ROSNOW, R.L. (1978) "The prophetic vision of Giambattista Vico: implications for the state of social psychological theory." Journal of Personality and Social Psychology 36: 1322-1331.

SIMONTON, D.K. (1975) "Sociocultural context of individual creativity: a transhistorical time-series analysis." Journal of Personality and Social Psychology 32: 1119-1133.

SIMS, C.A. (1977) "Comment on Pierce." Journal of the American Statistical Association 72: 23-24.

————(1972) "Money, income, and causality." American Economic Review 62: 540-552.

THOMAS, E.A.C. and J.A. MARTIN (1976) "Analyses of parent-infant interaction." Psychological Review 83: 141-156.

U.S. Department of Labor, Bureau of Labor Statistics (1966) The Consumer Price Index: History and Techniques (Bulletin 1517). Washington, DC: Government Printing Office.

VIGDERHAUS, G. (1978) "Forecasting sociological phenomena: application of Box-Jenkins methodology to suicide rates" in K.F. Schuessler (ed.), Sociological Methodology 1978. San Francisco: Jossey-Bass.

PART

III

**Areas
of
Application**

JOHN S. CARROLL
DAN COATES

6

PAROLE DECISIONS:
Social Psychological Research
in Applied Settings

This is a story about social psychological research in the criminal justice
system. It is a "story" rather than an "article" because we will tell it in
historical sequence, the way it happened. Although this research has been
published in previous articles, those reports do not tell the story because
they present the most current state of ideas as if these ideas had always been
known and merely had to be checked out (theory testing). The problem with
such a presentation is that it misrepresents how the research got done. One
can read those articles and learn what ideas we now have, but one cannot
learn how we did the research (which is much more than a methods section
can express). The goal, then, is to tell a story that could help a social
psychologist learn about doing research in an applied setting.

In the interests of brevity and coherence, only the major lines of research
that are more clearly relevant to applied social psychology have been discussed. The reader interested in our other parole research can look at Carroll
(1979a, 1979b), Carroll and Ruback (1980), and Payne et al. (1978).

THE DEVELOPMENT OF IDEAS

SETTING THE STAGE

In 1974, I[1] was in my first year as an Assistant Professor at Carnegie-
Mellon University in Pittsburgh. My training included a fairly traditional set
of social psychology courses with a couple of courses in my minor, cognitive
psychology. I had completed two research projects in graduate school. The

AUTHORS' NOTE: Support for the writing of this article was provided by National Institute of
Mental Health grant MH 32855-02. We would like to thank the Pennsylvania Board of Proba-
tion and Parole for their support and cooperation.

first had dealt with sex-role stereotypes and had required undergraduates to evaluate descriptions of stereotypic and less-stereotypic undergraduate women on trait rating scales. The second, my dissertation, had investigated implicit personality theory using a variety of tasks such as trait sorting and trait ratings with undergraduates. In short, as a social psychologist, my research experience consisted of getting undergraduates to make paper-and-pencil judgments about people that were known to them only through brief written descriptions.

GETTING AN IDEA

In the spring of 1974, I took my introductory social psychology class on a tour of the State Correctional Institution (Western Penitentiary) in Pittsburgh. The tour was part of a unit on prisons that I had introduced into the course, prompted by having seen Zimbardo present the Stanford prison experiment at the convention of the American Psychological Association in 1973. It was very easy to arrange such a tour, requiring only a phone call to the prison where the word *tour* routed me to the right administrator and a brief follow-up letter to him (all official bureaucratic acts require paperwork).

Western Penitentiary is a maximum security prison, the largest in Pennsylvania, housing over 1000 inmates behind a 30-foot wall. The buildings and grounds are partitioned by doors and fences into isolatable segments (in case of trouble). The inmates were predominantly black; the guards mostly white. We were accompanied by a guard wherever we went. We looked at the inmates; they looked at us. I think we were much more painfully self-aware than they, particularly the women on the tour, since the male inmates were staring, whistling, talking about, and talking at the women.

Many of the staff we met talked to us about their jobs, about prison life, and about criminals. What was most remarkable to me was that they readily characterized offenders into types and clearly felt the need to treat different people differently. Thus, they would talk about passive types, passive aggressives, overt aggressives, sociopaths, psychopaths, weak and vulnerable young or smaller men, and so forth, using several different lexicons drawn from various sources.

My training in implicit personality theory, impression formation, stereotyping, and clinical judgment all suggested that this pigeonholing of inmates was likely to have profound effects on how inmates were treated, and hence on how they behaved. Whether formal diagnostic categories assigned by a psychologist or social worker, or informal labels by staff, these typifications were likely to have a life of their own apart from their objective validity (which I assumed would be a modest level of validity at best). Surely, if my training was worth anything at all, I should be able to use it to study the perception of crime and criminals.

A PLACE ON WHICH TO STAND

I left the prison with my head buzzing and a sense of excitement. The way I get my ideas together is to talk things out with a knowledgeable colleague. My best friend at Carnegie-Mellon was a postdoctoral student in psychology named John Payne whose expertise was in risky decision making. Just to give an example of his training, a typical study might find him asking a college student to choose among gambles which varied in the probabilities of winning and losing and the amounts to win and lose. We had been looking for a way to do collaborative research on a mutually interesting topic.

John and I sat down to explore how we might together pursue the issues that had emerged from my prison visit. We decided to focus on a formal decision made about criminals, in order to capitalize on John's expertise. We considered things like juries, judges, and parole boards, and I spent a few days looking up just what the various entities in the criminal justice system really do. We settled on the parole decision as a place to begin investigating the perceptions of crime and criminals.

The parole decision looked like a particularly good choice for several reasons. First, the parole decision is structured similarly to laboratory tasks. Typically, the parole board spends just a few minutes reading case information, interviewing the parole applicant, and making the decision. Thus, the decision is brief, repetitive, most of the information is in written form, and in Pennsylvania the decision is made by one person rather than by a group. Thus, it was easy to envision studies providing case materials to decision makers containing systematic manipulations of certain cues. Second, collecting data from parole boards seemed relatively easy. Interviews take place on specified days at specified places. The law does not limit access as is the case with juries. The board for an entire state is easier to monitor than the activities of dozens of judges in dozens of counties. Third, parole boards are an important part of the criminal justice system. Nearly all incarcerated serious criminals come up for parole. Parole boards determine when to release people from prison and how to supervise or treat them in society. Their discretion over time in prison can be even greater than that of the sentencing judge (Genego et al., 1975). Fourth, descriptions of parole board functioning and the major factors considered by parole boards existed, particularly in what was then a new series of studies by Gottfredson et al. (1973). However, no social psychological research using parole boards was evident, in contrast to the abundance of simulated jury studies.

FINDING OUT ABOUT PAROLE

Our next step was based on the assumption that we already knew enough psychology but we knew next to nothing about parole. We raided the library and relied heavily on the reports from the Gottfredson studies and a law review article by Kastenmeier and Eglit (1973). The image of the parole decision we developed in 1974 was summarized in Carroll and Payne (1976).

An incarcerated criminal is usually subject to a set of parole procedures, governing his time of release from prison and supervision in the community. These procedures begin when the judge sets bounds on the sentence (e.g., two to six years) without specifying the exact time to serve. An administrative entity, the parole board, reviews the case periodically and decides exactly when to release the offender. A person paroled before the maximum sentence is on conditional release, supervised by the paroling authority, and subject to special rules (e.g., must hold a job, must not use alcohol) to which he must adhere or face a revocation of parole and return to prison. Conditional release ends when the maximum sentence expires or after a specified period of time on parole.

Research investigating the factors influencing parole decisions has revealed, not surprisingly, that different parole boards appear to value different goals (Stanley, 1976). Some boards focus on punishment by assigning prison terms according to crime seriousness, while others try to incapacitate so-called dangerous offenders by denying parole when they judge the probability that the offender will commit a future crime is high. There are boards primarily concerned with institutional discipline, and boards balancing combinations of goals. There are boards that have displayed little of a consistent pattern in their decisions. However, there are some similarities among boards. The Gottfredson studies (Hoffman, 1973) and Kastenmeier and Eglit (1973) agree that the parole decision is primarily based upon two factors: punishment and risk.

ANALYZING THE PAROLE DECISION

Our first approach to bringing psychology to bear on parole decisions was based on two major ideas. First, we felt that the parole board in evaluating a parole applicant would try to understand *why* the person had committed the crime(s). Thus, the evaluations, predictions, and recommendations for release and treatment would depend not only upon the crime but also upon causal attributions made about the offender. Our approach to parole decisions thus drew upon social psychological research in the area called attribution theory, which investigates how people perceive the causes of events and the behavioral and judgmental consequences of these perceptions. Second, we felt that the parole decision maker could be conceptualized as an information processor. Since the case information is voluminous and complex and the time is short, the board member must be selective in what he examines. Clearly, decision makers would of necessity develop short-cut strategies or heuristics for searching through the case information, forming hypotheses, making predictions, and so forth. These two ideas made the parole decision an ideal place to apply and develop ideas from attribution theory and information processing psychology.

By the summer of 1974, our goals became the development of a plan of research and access to expert decision makers. We organized our interim goals as the creation of a grant proposal. This was partly to get funds, but partly just to have a format within which to arrange ideas and plans. Even were the grant not funded, we felt that the writing would be valuable as a step toward carrying out and presenting later research.

Our review of the literature on parole and the application of psychological research to parole is presented in Carroll and Payne (1976). This is nearly identical to the parts of our grant proposal dealing with background and theory. What characterizes this article is a cafeteria style approach to linking psychology with parole. Each of the major attribution theories—Kelley (1967, 1971, 1972), Jones and Davis (1965), and Weiner (1974)—is operationalized in the context of parole and hypotheses are drawn. For example, Kelley (1967) proposed that a person who performs some behavior frequently (high consistency), in many kinds of settings (low distinctiveness), and that other people do not perform (low consensus) will be considered as the cause of that behavior. It is rather simple to predict that frequency of crime or prior record will therefore induce dispositional attributions about criminal behavior (i.e., crime is due to a personality disposition such as aggressiveness). Jones and Davis (1965) propose that observers make more dispositional judgments when behaviors affect them personally (hedonic relevance), which translates into a relationship between the degree of fear of crime and degree of dispositional attributions.

In similar fashion, hypotheses were drawn from research on information processing in decisions. Using Tversky and Kahneman's (1974) representativeness and availability heuristics, we hypothesized that parole decision makers would base their predictions of risk of subsequent crime on how similar a parole applicant was to the stereotypical "hardened criminal," that objective base-rate information would be underutilized, and that risk might be judged by how easily the parole decision maker can imagine this person committing another crime or think of persons with similar characteristics who have recidivated. We also predicted that decision makers would inappropriately prefer redundant cues to independent cues (see Wilkins, 1973).

We began by running some exploratory studies with college students (Carroll and Payne, 1976), while also seeking funding for what we felt would be a major long-term research project. Simultaneously, we were trying to make contacts that would allow us to study actual parole decision makers. The following sections describe these efforts.

GETTING A GRANT

Our research proposal stated as its goal the testing and development of psychological theory with application to the parole decision. Six studies were proposed to be carried out over a two-year period, using college students and expert parole decision makers as subjects.

We prepared a preliminary version of the grant proposal and sent it to the Law Enforcement Assistance Administration (LEAA). They replied that the proposal was much too theoretical and lacked useful application to the pressing problems of parole. We then sent the same preproposal to the Division Heads or Section Chiefs of Social Sciences, Personality and Cognition, and Crime and Delinquency at the National Institute of Mental Health (NIMH), and to Social Psychology and Law and Social Sciences at the National Science Foundation (NSF). We received some moderately encouraging feedback and went to Washington and talked with each of these people.

In the process we learned quite a bit about grant agencies and about our grant. Getting one's grant proposal to the right agency can be very tricky. There is a big difference between mission-oriented funding sources which are trying to solve problems (such as LEAA) and basic research funding sources which are trying to increase knowledge (such as NSF). A proposal dealing with parole decisions could slip through the cracks, being too theoretical for one group but too applied for the other. The particular substantive interests and priorities of different agencies and parts of agencies differ markedly. We decided that our proposal primarily addressed theory and accordingly submitted it to Personality and Cognition at NIMH and Social Psychology at NSF. NSF approved funding at the requested level and I cancelled the NIMH application before they finished processing the grant. So, beginning September 1975, we had the money.

GETTING ACCESS

Although our first studies were directed at understanding parole decisions using college students, we naturally realized that eventually we would have to study actual parole experts. Our first step was to send a version of our research proposal, in April 1975, to the Pennsylvania Parole Board in Harrisburg requesting their cooperation. Their staff looked it over and referred it to the Governor's Justice Commission, the state channel for LEAA funds. I received a letter from the Justice Commission indicating that the research was too theoretical and lacked any perceptible payoff to the board to warrant their spending time on it. They would, however, fully support a study aimed at developing a decision model useful for guideline development (more about this later) if theory would take a back seat. We decided not to revise our proposal in this fashion, so at the time we submitted our grant proposal to NSF and NIMH in 1975, we had no notion of how we actually would find experts to do what we proposed.

A second abortive search for experts was directed at a different kind of population. We felt that ex-offenders would have substantial direct knowledge about crime and provide a useful intermediate subject population (between students and parole board members). I contacted two halfway house community centers with the request to use their clients as subjects. One center flatly refused to allow me near their clients, on the grounds that these people had enough problems already. The other was very cooperative, and I made a lengthy presentation of my interests to an assembled group of ex-offenders. I handed out the same questionnaires that college students had filled out, dealing with ratings of crime categories, and offered payment upon completion of the questionnaire. Only four questionnaires came back, and my embarrassment and disappointment made that the last contact with this group. Lest you think this problem stemmed from an uncooperative group of subjects, let me state that the questionnaire must have been the most boring, repetitive, and irrelevant document they had ever encountered. For example, the main part consisted of 190 similarity judgments among all pairs of 20 crimes.

My big break came in the summer of 1975. Debbie Malafa, an undergraduate at a small college north of Pittsburgh, arranged a readings course with me in order to expand her psychology background, specifically regarding the criminal justice system. She did some readings, and then I directed her to set up interviews with local criminal justice experts regarding their attitudes about crime and criminals. We developed an interview schedule and she set up and conducted the interviews. I went along on several of these.

The list of interviewees provided me with my first contacts with experts in parole decisions. It was at this local level that I first arranged to sit in on parole hearings. At this point, in August of 1975, the Pittsburgh parole staff told me that my involvement had reached a level where they needed official approval from the board to continue. I sent another letter to the Pennsylvania Parole Board seeking their cooperation in our research.

This time, our efforts met with a very different response for several reasons. First, we had been awarded a grant which gave us credibility, importance, and our own resources. Second, the fact that we had already worked with the Pittsburgh parole staff added more credibility and reduced the risks associated with our request. After all, the Pittsburgh people had been able to work with us and it was therefore apparent that we were doing reasonable things and not making inappropriate demands. Third, we were able to specify in some detail exactly what we wanted from the board. This meant whom we would interview, to whom we would give questionnaires, what we would observe, and how much time these procedures would take. Since parole personnel are very pressed for time, a more specific request poses less risk to them. Further, our request showed our sensitivity to their problems and presented our wishes as flexible. Finally, and most important of all, in the months following our previous unsuccessful request, the board itself had developed a more supportive attitude toward research. The board had recently initiated research aimed at making their policy (the factors taken into account in the parole decision) explicit and structuring discretion to make parole decisions more consistent with policy through the creation of guidelines similar to the Gottfredson work with the U.S. Board of Parole (Gottfredson et at., 1975). However, their efforts were "stymied by resource constraints." The new Director of their in-house Research and Statistical Division, Jim Alibrio, was able to see the potential value of our research to the Board. We could cooperate so as to collect and analyze data useful for our scientific goals and their practical goals as well. I communicated directly with him in September and October, and he presented our project at board meetings. In November, our project was formally approved. Since that time, Jim has acted as liaison and informal consultant to the project.

SYSTEMATIC RESEARCH

THE FIRST MAJOR STUDY

The most crucial of the six studies proposed in the grant addressed the effects of causal attributions upon parole decisions. It seemed unnecessary to study how parole boards make attributions unless we knew with certainty that attributions were implicated in the parole decision. Accordingly, this was the earliest study to be implemented. This study (Carroll and Payne, 1977a, 1977b) adapted Weiner's (1974) model describing the effects of attributions upon evaluations and expectations in achievement settings. This model specifies that, given some achievement behavior (e.g., getting an A or a D on a test), attributing the behavior to internal causes, particularly internal-intentional causes (e.g., the person did or did not study hard), leads to more praise for success and more blame for failure than does attributing the behavior to external causes (e.g., an easy or difficult test). To the extent that the attributed cause is stable and enduring over time, future behavior will be expected to resemble past behavior.

It seemed both parsimonious and elegant to propose that the punishment aspects of parole decisions were related to blame and therefore mediated by the internal-external and intentional-unintentional dimensions of attributions, whereas the risk aspects were related to expectations or predictions and therefore mediated by the stable-unstable dimension.

Thus, consider the following four explanations for why a businessman might be engaged in illegal business (or political) activities and their judgmental consequences. First, he lacks moral knowledge of right and wrong. This is an internal-unintentional and stable cause which should lead to high blame (hence, high punishment) and high risk predictions (hence, high incapacitation). Further, to the extent that an internal cause is perceived as intentional, that is, under the control of the person, blame would be even higher. Second, he was following supposedly typical business practice in the corporate community. This is an external and stable cause which should lead to low blame but high risk predictions. Third, he made an unusually bad decision during a period of depressed mood. This is an internal, unintentional, and unstable cause which should lead to moderately high blame (not as high as an internal-intentional cause) but low risk predictions. Fourth, he was under unusual pressure from business associates to go along. This is an external and unstable attribution which should lead to low blame and low risk predictions. The precise response, as a prison term or treatment plan, would depend upon the relative importance of the punishment and incapacitation aspects of the decision.

In order to test these hypotheses, we followed the logic of experimental social psychology: manipulate the independent variable, eliminate or control extraneous variables, and measure dependent variables. The independent variable was the causal attribution—would people react to the same crime but different attributions in appropriately different ways? Extraneous variables were everything else about the parole applicant, such as crime, record, and social history. Dependent variables included time in prison, risk predictions, desire to punish, desire to incapacitate, attributions of responsibility and criminality, and manipulation checks.

Causal attributions were manipulated by writing background information items designed to suggest plausible causes of crime that were either internal or external, stable or unstable, and intentional or unintentional. These were pretested by having college students rate the causes on the above three dimensions. A final set of eight were chosen to fit into the $2 \times 2 \times 2$ design. The extraneous variable of crime was controlled by writing eight crime descriptions that represented eight major crime categories with four personal crimes (murder, rape, assault, robbery) and four property crimes (burglary, theft, forgery, drugs). All other variables were controlled by making the descriptions brief, making all offenders male between 22 and 30, and giving all offenders no prior history of arrests. We felt that record would be an important source of attributional inferences and that it would be inferred from the crime unless given. By providing gender, age, record, crime, and cause, we hoped we were providing a few important items of case information consistent with studies showing that experts use only a little information about a case (Wilkins et al., 1973).

Sixty-four college students were presented with a questionnaire packet consisting of eight crime reports. Each crime report included one of the eight crime descriptions and one of the eight pieces of background information. Crime descriptions were paired with different background information for different subjects, such that each subject saw each crime and each background only once, in combinations and orders determined by a Latin square design. An example of one crime report from this study was the following, which includes the murder crime description followed by the external, stable, unintentional cause:

Mr. Green is a 25-year-old male convicted of second-degree murder. He was in a bar having a drink and talking to the victim when they began to argue, push and punch each other. He pulled out a gun and shot the victim several times; the victim was pronounced dead on arrival at the hospital. Mr. Green surrendered himself to police called by the bartender. He has no previous record of convictions. Interviews indicated that he could not find a good job because his skill had been replaced by mechanization. The circumstances around the crime had been acting on him for some time.

After each crime report, subjects responded to a two-page battery of questions regarding crime seriousness, suggested prison term, predictions about recidivism, and so forth. These questions related to all aspects of a parole case and therefore supported the cover story of making simulated parole decisions. Only some of these questions were actually analyzed.

The results provided several important insights. Most important, there was clear evidence that the background information suggesting causal attributions was used to evaluate crimes and offenders in ways predicted by attribution theory. Attributions to causes internal to the offender led to generally more negative affect—less liking, higher ratings of crime severity, responsibility, purpose of prison is punishment, and longer prison term. Attributions to stable, long-term causes led to higher expectations for recidivism, higher ratings of criminality, responsibility, purpose of prison is incapacitation, and longer prison term. Prison term was assigned on the basis of both punishment and incapacitation factors, and thus was an additive sum of internal-external judgments and stable-unstable judgments. For example, crimes with internal-stable causes were given an average prison term of 9.1 years, crimes with internal-unstable causes were given 6.6 years, external-stable causes received 5.2 years, and external-unstable causes were given an average of 3.7 years.

The results regarding the role of intentionality as the third attributional dimension were only suggestive. The manipulation checks showed that the manipulation of intentionality was not at all strong and intentionality also was inferred from the crime descriptions. There was also some contamination from the other dimensional manipulations (e.g., stable causes were more intentional than unstable causes). However, the pattern of results was still consistent with the hypotheses: Intentionality had significant effects on responsibility judgments and the appropriate manipulation checks.

A very similar questionnaire was prepared for use with expert parole decision makers. We first took the questionnaire to one local parole decision maker in order to get a reading on validity. He gave it a clean bill of health but questioned whether the brief material about each case was really supposed to be a summary of the case. We decided to change our cover letter to indicate that these statements were selected by us out of interview material rather than an official-sounding summary.

In the spring of 1976, the questionnaires were distributed by mail to 44 experts throughout Pennsylvania with self-addressed return envelopes. This was the entire group of people working for the board who had discretionary power to evaluate parole cases and make recommendations. Over the next two weeks, we quickly found out something was wrong. We received a few letters, a few notes on our questionnaire forms, some relayed conversations, and a lot of missing respondents. The response rate was barely over 50%, and we had to add a couple of local Pittsburgh parole staff in order to complete three repetitions of our eight-cell Latin square. What the experts objected to was the task of evaluating someone about whom so little information was provided. In contrast to college students who found the task interesting and rich, the experts found the task sparse and inadequate for their goal of making individualized recommendations.

The results obtained from the experts showed both substantial agreement and substantial disagreement with those from students. The experts showed a clear tendency on nearly all judgments to consider internal-stable causes as different from any other types of causes. These causes led to higher judgments of both crime seriousness and recidivism risk than any others. Moreover, recommended prison term was 5.9 years for internal-stable causes, as compared to 3 to 4 years for other causes. Thus, while attributional information was important to both students and experts, only the students clearly showed the predicted separability of the internal-external and stable-unstable dimensions and the resultant punishment and incapacitation judgments. Further, the impact of the attributional information was clearly much greater for the students than for the experts.

It is interesting to note that students and experts were in high agreement over crime seriousness, but less on prison term, and still less for risk of recidivism. For example, experts rated a murderer as least likely to commit another crime while students saw him as third most likely. This is probably an instance of experts knowing that murderers are statistically good risks. The background which described the offender as aggressive in personality was reacted to much more unfavorably by experts, as was a background of recent divorce, which students treated leniently as an excuse but experts perhaps as a pattern of social instability. Further, the same attributional cue had different implications for the experts on different crimes: A cue of long-term, technological unemployment paired with a murder case received mild judgments compared to other cues, but paired with a heroin arrest it was the cue with the highest ratings of seriousness and offender's responsibility.

In order to explicate the role of intentionality, multiple-regression reanalyses were conducted using the manipulation checks to predict other judgments. The results suggested the following conclusions: For students, internal-intentionality does influence the same judgments as does internality, and it is of particular importance in judging responsibility for the crime; for experts, the results are more confusing, in that effects for internality appear only as internal-intentionality and are more important for judgments of responsibility, criminality, and risk of recidivism.

In conclusion, the results of this study suggested that attributions indeed play a role in parole decisions, but that our hypotheses were most consistent with what college students did on simulated parole tasks. Our results were seriously deficient for experts in that the task lacked validity. Even on our sparse task, the experts demonstrated specific detailed knowledge about crime and criminals that the students and we researchers lacked. We should also note that we asked subjects to suggest a time in prison. However, in

Pennsylvania, parole decisions are generally release/not release after serving a certain number of months decreed by the judge (the minimum sentence). As it turns out, this in/out decision differs substantially from a time-setting (sentencinglike) decision. For all these reasons, it became obvious that more valid, naturalistic tasks were necessary which would allow the experts to reveal their specialized knowledge.

Our difficulties highlight the difference between real tasks with experienced subjects and packaged tasks with college students. Social psychologists typically run experiments under conditions in which subjects utilize knowledge provided by the experimenters; the subjects are considered more objective the more they are experimentally naive. Subjects need only apply reasonably logical analyses of cues that are made salient to them. In contrast, real tasks demand that subjects apply or demonstrate what they *know* about the situation. In this sense, field research requires the psychologist to know a lot about the setting as well as the theory employed, challenging our ability to abstract critical features without destroying the essence or validity of the judgment.

We lost some credibility with the Parole Board by doing the previously described study. We got some useful information, but we aroused some bad feelings in the process. In order to recoup and retain the cooperation of the board, we moved into studies that had more meaning to the board and potential application to the problems the board was confronting.

ARCHIVAL DATA FROM CASE FILES

During the summer of 1976 we turned to a different type of data about parole decisions by coding the case files of parole applicants interviewed between January and March 1975.[3] By relating data taken from case files to parole decisions, we hoped to accomplish several goals. First, identify the major variables such as crime seriousness, prior record, and institutional conduct that influence parole decisions. Second, code the recommendations made by the various people who evaluate parole cases—psychologists and counselors, the institutions, Case Analysts, Hearing Examiners—to see how they influence each other and the final board decision. Third, use the resultant descriptions of what influences parole decisions to select valid samples of cases for experimental and process-tracing studies. Fourth, use the descriptions to validate that experimental and process-tracing studies could reproduce the major predictors of the decision, addressing critiques of "simulation" research by Ebbesen and Konecni (1975). Fifth, provide the board with data useful for preparing guidelines, such as the description of board policy, the relationship of crime seriousness and parole decisions, and an empirical risk prediction scale derived by relating case variables to subsequent measures of parole success (i.e., whether the parolee had committed a crime in the 12 months following release).

Over 60 variables were coded from the case files of over 250 offenders who were initially interviewed for parole from January to March 1975. Roughly 80% of cases were granted parole. We found that board decisions were identical in almost every case to Hearing Examiner recommendations. Essentially, decision making is decentralized so that the Hearing Examiner makes the crucial determination. Hearing Examiners base their judgments mainly on the Case Analyst's recommendation (which primarily reflects past record), the Institutional Staff recommendation (which primarily reflects conduct in the institution), and the presence of assault in the offense.

In an initial attempt to examine the predictors of parole success, parole outcomes (current status of parolees) were obtained for 210 parolees who had been released either in early 1975 or at later hearings, and who were under supervision in the community: 34% of these parolees were in some type of trouble, either returned as technical or convicted parole violators, detained pending disposition of charges, or whereabouts unknown (absconders). The two most important factors separating those in trouble from the rest were more prior adult arrests and poorer job skills.

This pilot study became the model for a very extensive series of studies of parole release and revocation decisions (see Carroll and Ruback, 1980). It also carried our research in the applied direction of aiding the board to design decision guidelines.

ONE THOUSAND PAROLE CASES

During the summer of 1977 the first author wrote another grant proposal, again with John Payne assisting by discussing ideas, contributing ideas, and reading and critiquing drafts. The second proposal was much more mature and a better proposal. We knew where we were going in terms of theory, research, and funding agencies. We had a track record of publications from the NSF grant and assured cooperation of the Pennsylvania Parole Board. The emphasis of the second proposal was attribution theory, reflecting the fact that John Carroll was the Principle Investigator and John Payne was a consultant. Six studies were proposed to be carried out over a two-year period.

A central part of our research project was to collect archival data on actual parole release decisions enabling us to produce a description of the case factors predictive of decisions. A set of 1000 cases were to be coded in a similar manner to the 250 case pilot study previously described. These cases would also provide a population from which cases could be sampled later to create experimental stimuli or cases for process-tracing studies. Moreover, similarities in the predictors of parole decisions in archival and controlled studies would provide evidence of validity. Finally, this study would assist the Parole Board in its desire to expand the guidelines approach to the parole release decisions. In one massive data collection, we hoped to satisfy our own needs for data and those of the board.

We prepared a posthearing questionnaire[4] which contained over 70 items and included two open-ended assessments of causal attributions enabling the questionnaire to serve as a research instrument regarding attributions. These items were: "Opinions on underlying cause for offense committed" and "Opinion on reason for criminal record/history."

The board used this questionnaire for 272 parole release hearings during September and October of 1977. At this time, the board notified us that they had revised the questionnaire and were now using the revised form. This new questionnaire dropped all open-ended items including the attribution questions and a few alterations were made in other items. These changes came out of the blue, apparently as a response to two months of using a very time-consuming instrument. We were upset but knew that we could do nothing positive about it except hope that we had enough attribution data for our purposes. The revised questionnaire was used through May 1978, bringing the total number of cases to over 1000.

In the summer of 1978, two undergraduates (Veronica Kelly and Jacqueline Wooley) worked full time in Parole Board offices in Harrisburg retrieving these 1000 case files and coding them on over 140 variables. By the end of the summer over 800 cases were coded, with a few cases missing in each month and the month of May never reached. The missing cases have not as yet been coded and may never be coded.

The responses from the first set of postdecision questionnaires containing attributions were initially analyzed in early 1978. Two coders, Tim Elig and Howard Snyder, who were familiar with coding attribution statements, coded each case on five-point scales for internality, stability, and intentionality each for cause of crime and cause of criminal history. In responses containing multiple statements, statements were combined to concentrate on underlying causes whenever apparent or else coded individually and averaged (noninteger values were used when appropriate).

A multiple-regression analysis showed that stability of the cause of the offense affected parole recommendations with board member, crime type, sentence, and number of convictions controlled. Stability had its effect upon parole by affecting the perceived risk of subsequent crime, such that more stable causes produced more perceived risk which made board members reluctant to parole the offender.

Thus, half the original model of parole decisions had been confirmed, and internal or internal-intentional attributions had no effect because the parole decision in Pennsylvania lacked a punishment component. Differences between these results and the earlier experiment manipulating attributions seem adequately explained by the fact that the experts made recommendations about *prison sentence* in that earlier study but about *parole release* in this study. Sentencing brings in the punishment component.

PAROLE DECISION GUIDELINES

The data we collected on these 1000 cases were also used to help the board develop parole decision guidelines. The parole decision has three possible outcomes: grant parole, refuse parole, or continue pending some specific information. The purpose of the guidelines was to identify factors which were most strongly related to these different outcomes in past parole decisions. In this way, the past implicit policy of the board could be made more explicit and could be used to structure and standardize future parole decisions. Our specific aim, then, was to develop a system of rules which accurately reflected past decisions and could be easily applied to future ones.

We began with a sample of 801 cases for which parole decisions had been made: 77% of these cases had been granted parole, 14% were refused, and 9% were continued. We then conducted discriminant analyses to see which variables could best account for the separation of these cases into these three groups. We found that factors such as severity and dangerousness of the crime or the length and seriousness of the criminal record were not significantly related to parole decision outcome. Clearly, the board did not see the punishment of past criminal offenses as the purpose of the parole decision.

What did turn out to be strongly related to parole decisions, however, were ratings of institutional discipline. The better the inmate's behavior and conduct while in the prison, the more likely he or she was to be paroled. By using only the ratings of institutional discipline in a discriminant analyses, we could correctly classify 84% of the past decisions into the parole, refuse, and continue categories (as compared to a 77% accuracy by predicting all paroles). Since this factor could explain more of the variability in past decisions than any other, we decided to use it as a first step in constructing a sequential model of the parole decision. We divided the total sample into three groups: those with good, fair, and poor institutional discipline. We then conducted discriminant analyses on each of these subgroups to see whether the addition of other variables could produce a more precise categorization of previous parole cases. The results of these analyses were used to develop a sequential decision tree which fairly accurately predicted past parole decision outcomes. The first consideration or branch in the tree was the applicant's institutional discipline.

When discipline was good, parole was the likely outcome. When discipline was only fair or poor, the decision outcome was determined by one or more of seven other variables, such as prognosis for parole supervision or progress in counseling programs. By applying these rules to the 801 past cases, we were able to correctly classify 87% into the paroled, refused, and continued categories. Other analyses, including discriminant analyses with as many as 18 variables, could not reach this level of accuracy.

Since the decision tree which we developed offered a simple system which could fairly accurately account for past parole decisions, we offered it to the board as guidelines for structuring future decisions. We also informed the board of a number of reservations concerning these guidelines. First of all, for all the sophisticated analyses and considerations of additional variables, the precision with which we could predict past decisions was not greatly enhanced over what it would have been using institutional discipline ratings alone. Further, the sequential model we developed may have capitalized on chance, since we sifted and selected for those particular variables which worked best in our sample. Applying the same decision guidelines to an entirely new sample could well result in less accurate classification.

The board did not adopt the guidelines for use exactly as we presented them. However, after discussion and consideration, they are currently piloting a set of guidelines which are similar to the ones we developed. They agreed that institutional discipline was of primary importance in their deliberations, and this is the first factor considered in their current guidelines. Once discipline has been taken into account, the board's second concern is with parole prognosis. Obviously, the lower the chances of parole violations, the more likely the applicant is to be released. Assessment of parole prognosis is based on factors such as the applicants' age, previous record, parole plan, and past or current drug involvement. The board was able to use our work as a starting point, from which they could revise and amend to meet the particular goals and concerns which they felt were most important.

WRAPPING UP

The parole decision research we have described represents a growth process. We began the research trained in laboratory experiments and now are consulted by parole boards about very real-world problems. In the process, we have come to appreciate many different kinds of research, goals that research is directed toward, and how to get to do research. Our work exemplifies issues that researchers must face when they let go of the modality of laboratory experiment. In the final part of this article, we turn to a discussion of these issues.

LEAVING THE LAB

The roots of social psychology in the 1930s and 1940s were in real-world social problems. Later, driven by a desire for scientific rigor and theory development, social psychologists of the 1950s and 1960s moved into the laboratory. Only in the 1970s has major recognition grown that the extreme emphasis on laboratory research may have been a false maturity. Many now believe that the degree of control made possible in laboratory studies and the restrictions necessary to maintain that control have constricted the progress of social psychology (McGuire, 1967, 1973; Helmreich, 1975; Weissberg, 1976).

The importance of research in naturalistic settings (e.g., parole decisions) is not simply that we address and attempt to solve "social problems." Social psychologists certainly can be good social technicians. However, we feel that in order to be good social psychologists, good theorists, we must take our ideas out to confront phenomena we cannot control. In our labs we have power, we stage manage, we select stimuli and situations, and we have a captive cooperative group of subjects. The process of theory development and testing becomes solipsistic: We pilot test, we select, we refine until we get the supposedly right answer. The world out there will not hold still for this—it has an existence beyond what we give to it. As a result, it is more of a test of our theories, more valuable for developing theories, and uniquely capable of testing the connections between our theories and everyday events.

Had we remained in the laboratory using college students, our study of parole decisions would have reached the conclusion that attribution theory had been confirmed. Instead, our work with experts revealed that parole decisions were far more than crime plus attribution and that the attribution process was likely to be different than that traditionally proposed (Carroll, 1978). In short, the growth of our theoretical concepts, although slow, was directly dependent upon confrontation with real parole decisions that we could neither control nor intuit as we do with students in artificial laboratory tasks. This has been an enduring and important lesson.

GETTING SOMEWHERE

If one wants to do research in the criminal justice system, or any applied setting for that matter, one has to make a lot of adjustments from the academic laboratory. First of all, drop preconceptions. When the parole project started, we had the mentality of liberal 1960s students and academics. We expected parole boards to be conservative, dogmatic, racist, with a Nixon-like distrust for others. The Pennsylvania Parole Board disabused us of those stereotypes. They were open, intelligent, conscientious, sincerely concerned about making the best decision, innovative, and diverse individuals. They are also stuck with a difficult job with little resources, no right answers, and tremendous responsibilities.

The next thing to recognize is that our aspirations are completely out of synchrony with this setting. Academic researchers typically expect to get in and get out with the data in a few weeks and verify an experimental hypothesis which is one small piece of a very large puzzle. The goal is to solve the puzzle and the solution involves years of effort by generations of researchers. We have found that research with the parole board always takes more time than one imagines. It is not our lab, our subject pool, our turf, our ethics committee. Each study must be defended and approved, the resources assembled, the subjects located, the travel across the state, and so forth. When we are done with a study, the board would like to have a usable product. They rarely work on the whole puzzle (let us solve crime) but are very pleased with a small contribution that actually works (let us make parole decisions a bit more uniform). If academics focus on the big picture, they by definition cannot contribute. But if they address problems in the terms of a practitioner, we find we can make a serious contribution.

Related to the above point, when asked to assist the board, we have continually made the error of collecting too much data, and often the wrong kind of data. Because academics want to get the big picture, we throw in every variable we can think up, straining both our subjects and ourselves. We get the wrong kind of data if we fail to use the categories generated by the practitioners and rely only on our own ideas instead. Interviews and discussions, as messy and soft and lengthy as they are, are still the best way to do this and simultaneously to impress the practitioners with one's interest in their ideas. We have had absolutely no progress generated from questionnaires asking the board to tell us how they do things. And, whatever one does, *listen*. When one is told what they want, make that the basis of the research, and simplify everything as much as possible.

Access to an agency requires that somebody thinks a contribution can be made in some way. One must demonstrate credibility through a track record, credentials, and the ability to make a cogent presentation. One must present one's skills or products in such a way that someone will recognize that one can provide a service and will advocate the project.

Besides having something to offer, one has to minimize the risks one poses. Make few demands. If a parole board thinks that its time will be taken up unduly, or one requires space and other resources, then their ability to function will be threatened. If one *brings* resources (Xeroxing, money, computer time, one's own staff), it is a plus. A big risk for parole boards is the possibility of lawsuits. Can a parole applicant who is denied parole drag the board into court because one's questionnaire led to an unfair hearing? Can a disappointed parole applicant demand that the researcher testify about what he or she heard at the hearing or testify that parole decisions are arbitrary and capricious? Law suits hang over the heads of parole boards and they are justifiably wary. What one has to be is sensitive to their needs—be flexible and understanding.

The best thing for research is good ideas. If one has them, a parole board will probably appreciate them. Better yet, parole boards have their own ideas and are often unable to implement them. One may find that the board has some excellent thoughts and needs the researcher to help achieve them.

Finally, watch out for politics. Do not assume that everyone is one big happy family. Sometimes researchers are brought in as part of a power play. An administrator is fighting to save his job and uses the research as a demonstration of his innovative approach. Or an administrator wants to make a change and uses the researcher's analysis as an impetus to fire people or whatever. In these cases the content of the research will not get taken seriously. More common still is that one gets agreement from some people (e.g., parole board chairman) but not from others crucial to one's work (e.g., the rest of the board). The risk here is that some people will feel pressured to participate in the research and give low quality responses. Every effort should be made to make everyone feel as if they are contributing, that they have chosen to participate, that their collaboration is valued, and that they will benefit from the results.

Right now the parole system is going through a political upheaval. The largest criminal justice debate in 50 years is being waged over how to reduce and reallocate discretion among judges, parole boards, and legislatures. Arguments have been raised that individualized rehabilitation does not work (e.g., Martinson, 1974) and that individualized judgments about offenders are inaccurate, inconsistent, and therefore unjust (e.g., Kasteinmeier and Eglit, 1973; Von Hirsch and Hanrahan, 1978). The movement to reduce discretion generally seeks to restrict the range of indeterminacy and to have time served in prison more closely reflect criminal behavior by one or more of three means: (1) legislative specifications of the relationship between crimes and time in prison in determinate sentencing laws, (2) sentencing commissions to watch over and regularize equitable judicial sentencing, and

(3) guideline development to produce equitable parole decisions. Major changes are underway accompanied by hot debates over justice, treatment, safety, prison population size, prison discipline, and the practicalities of how the system will actually work under various attempted reforms. (For a concise discussion of these issues, see *Corrections Magazine,* September 1977, and Von Hirsch and Hanrahan, 1978). In the course of this debate, research has been a tool used to aid policy development and clarify issues but also to justify and defend oneself and attack others. Clearly, the researcher must be cognizant of the political context in order to be effective, to talk the language and concerns of the practitioners, and to be credible.

KINDS OF RESEARCH

The criminal justice system has most often been studied by descriptive or correlational techniques. For example, our study of Pennsylvania case files revealed that the strongest determinant of parole decisions was institutional discipline. In order to predict parole decision, then, a knowledge of discipline is important. This tells what is *common* in parole decisions, but tends to confuse strength of effect with breadth of effect. That is, discipline could be important because it is a crucial factor in some cases or because it is taken into account in all cases (whereas other factors operate sporadically). We cannot tell why discipline is important since it is correlated with other variables. Discipline is important in its own right, but also reflects risk, rehabilitation, and so forth. Because predictors are highly correlated in the real-world parole data, most successfully predicted decisions could be predicted by several models employing different combinations of these predictive variables.

Social psychologists typically use experiments to tell whether a particular effect exists. To test this, we usually restrict the task to one in which the effect is highlighted and easy to measure. Thus, Carroll and Payne (1977a, 1977b) manipulated contrived attribution statements and Carroll (1979a, 1979b) manipulated risk statements so that responses to a few cases would test whether the manipulation makes a difference. However, the number of things that make a difference is potentially infinite, especially if we reconstruct and select stimuli each time. Experiments rarely test how one effect relates to everything else or checks the naturalistic occurrence of the manipulated variable. In a sense, experiments miss the forest for the trees. Experiments check whether a tree exists, and how the tree looks, whereas descriptive studies view the forest at the expense of knowing less about specific trees.

We have brought in yet a third type of research from information-processing psychology. Process-tracing techniques such as information acquisition monitoring (Carroll and Payne, 1976, 1977a) and verbal protocols (Carroll and Payne, 1977a) have the potential to give a detailed portrayal of how parole decisions are made. In regard to the analogy of forest and trees, process tracing is like finding paths through the forest that meander from tree to tree. However, without the services of a good guide, the researcher can find himself in a very deep and dark wood, buried under transcripts. The better able the researcher is to identify the structure of the decision task, the better able he or she is to benefit from the level of detail offered in process tracing. We again confront the fact that the psychologist must know about parole in order to study it in detail. To ask a good question and get a useful answer, one must already know a good part of the answer.

WHAT HAVE WE LEARNED ABOUT PAROLE?

Our study of parole in Pennsylvania has revealed that the parole decision is based upon institutional conduct, incapacitation, and rehabilitation goals, although different decision makers appear to value and conceptualize these goals in somewhat different ways. Attributions are made in this process, and attributions regarding the cause of crime are important in judgments of recidivism risk. The precursors of these attributions in case information and individual attitudes are not well understood, although it appears that specific case information generates specific causal hypotheses which are then tested against case information.

Parole decision makers are also flexible in how they use information, depending on their conceptualization of the decision task. In Pennsylvania, the parole release decision is nonpunitive in regard to past criminal behavior although possibly punitive (in the sense of deterrence) toward institutional misconducts. However, the parole revocation decision is basically punitive, using back time as a punishment for the seriousness of the violation offense (Carroll and Ruback, 1980).

This flexibility is also evident in the willingness of the board to create a policy that will change its decision making in a desired direction. Parole systems in the various states are in a process of innovation—some by choice, some as a defense against pressure, and some by force of law. It is unquestionably an interesting time to be involved in the criminal justice system.

NOTES

1. The senior author wrote the historical description.
2. Carol Shapiro assisted with this project.
3. Coders were Tim Devinney, Barry Ruback, John Herstein, and Sally Goldin. Steve Schact carried out the data analyses at the University of Chicago.
4. Barry Ruback assisted in the development of this questionnaire. Shirley Tucker assisted on the study.

REFERENCES

CARROLL, J.S. (1979a) "Judgments of recidivism risk: the use of base-rate information in parole decisions" in P.D. Lipsett and B.D. Sales (eds.), New Directions in Psycholegal Research. New York: Litton.

———(1979b) "Judgments by parole boards" in I.H. Frieze et al. (eds.), New Approaches to Social Problems: Applications of Attribution Theory. San Francisco: Jossey-Bass.

———(1978) "Causal attributions in expert parole decisions." Journal of Personality and Social Psychology 36: 1501-1511.

——— and J.W. PAYNE (1977a) "Judgments about crime and the criminal: a model and a method for investigating parole decisions" in B.D. Sales (ed.), Perspectives in Law and Psychology (vol. 1): Criminal Justice System. New York: Plenum.

———(1977b) "Crime seriousness, recidivism risk, and causal attributions in judgments of prison term by students and experts." Journal of Applied Psychology 62: 595-602.

——— (1976) "The psychology of the parole decision process: a joint application of attribution theory and information processing psychology" in J.S. Carroll and J.W. Payne (eds.), Cognition and Social Behavior. Hillsdale, NJ: Lawrence Erlbaum Associates.

——— and R.B. RUBACK (1980) "Sentencing by parole board: the parole revocation decision" in B.D. Sales (ed.), Perspectives in Law and Psychology (vol. 2): The Jury, Trial and Judicial Processes. New York: Plenum.

Corrections Magazine (1977) Special Issue on "Determinate Sentencing" 3(3).

EBBESEN, E.B. and V.J. KONECNI (1975) "Decision making and information integration in the courts: the setting of bail." Journal of Personality and Social Psychology 32: 805-821.

GENEGO, W.J., P.D. GOLDBERGER, and V.C. JACKSON (1975) "Parole release decision-making and the sentencing process." Yale Law Journal 84: 810-902.

GOTTFREDSON, D.M., P.B. HOFFMAN, M.H. SIGLER, and L.T. WILKINS (1975) "Making paroling policy explicit." Crime and Delinquency 21: 34-44.

——— L.T. WILKINS, P.B. HOFFMAN, and S. SINGER (1973) The Utilization of Experience in Parole Decision-Making: A Progress Report. Davis, CA. National Council of Crime and Delinquency Research Center.

HELMREICH, R. (1975) "Applied social psychology: the unfulfilled promise." Personality and Social Psychology Bulletin 1: 548-560.

HOFFMAN, P.B. (1973) Paroling Policy Feedback. (Supplemental report 8). Davis, CA: National Council on Crime and Delinquency Research Center.

JONES, E. and K. DAVIS (1965) "From acts to dispositions" pp. 219-267 in L. Berkowitz (ed.), Advances in Experimental Social Psychology (vol. 2). New York: Academic Press.

KASTENMEIER, R. and H. EGLIT (1973) "Parole release decision-making: rehabilitation, expertise, and the demise of methodology." American University Law Review 22: 477-525.

KELLEY, H.H. (1972) Causal Schemata and the Attribution Process. Morristown, NJ: General Learning Press.

_____(1971) Attribution in Social Interaction. Morristown, NJ: General Learning Press.

_____ (1967) "Attribution theory in social psychology" in D. Levine (ed.), Nebraska Symposium on Motivation. Lincoln: University of Nebraska Press.

MARTINSON, R. (1974) "What works? Questions and answers about prison reform." Public Interest 35 (Spring): 22-54.

McGUIRE, W.J. (1973) "The yin and yang of progress in social psychology: seven koan." Journal of Personality and Social Psychology 26: 446-456.

_____ (1967) "Some impending reorientations in social psychology: some thoughts provoked by Kenneth Ring." Journal of Experimental Social Psychology 3: 113-123.

PAYNE, J.W., M.L. BRAUNSTEIN, and J.S. CARROLL (1978), "Exploring pre-decisional behavior: an alternative approach to decision research." Organizational Behavior and Human Performance 22: 17-44.

STANLEY, D.T. (1976) Prisoners Among Us: The Problem of Parole. Washington, DC: Brookings Institution.

TVERSKY, A. and D. KAHNEMAN (1974) "Judgment under uncertainty: heuristics and biases." Science 185: 1124-1131.

VON HIRSCH, A. and K.J. HANRAHAN (1978) Abolish Parole? Washington, DC: Government Printing Office.

WEINER, B. (1974) "Achievement motivation as conceptualized by an attribution theorist" in B. Weiner (ed.), Achievement Motivation and Attribution Theory. Morristown, NJ: General Learning Press.

WEISSBERG, N.C. (1976) "Methodology or substance? A response to Helmreich." Personality and Social Psychology Bulletin 2: 119-121.

WILKINS, L.T. (1973) "Information overload: peace or war with the computer?" Journal of Criminal Law and Criminology 64: 190-197.

_____D.M. GOTTFREDSON, J.O. ROBISON, and A. SADOWSKY (1973) Information Selection and Use in Parole Decision-Making (Supplemental report 5). Davis, CA: National Council on Crime and Delinquency Research Center.

ELLIOT ARONSON
NEAL OSHEROW

7

COOPERATION, PROSOCIAL BEHAVIOR, AND ACADEMIC PERFORMANCE:
Experiments in the Desegregated Classroom

Over the past several years, we have observed scores of classrooms anywhere from 30 days to three years after their schools were desegregated. From these observations, we learned that desegregating a school system does not necessarily mean integrating its students. Indeed, if we were to take an aerial photograph of the playground or cafeteria at a recently desegregated school, it most frequently would reveal a striking pattern, depicting several discrete clusters of children gathered in their own ethnic groups. Students in the classroom might be arbitrarily mixed—teachers often assign seats alphabetically. But when the children get up to talk with their friends, go outside to play, or sit down to eat, they tend to separate along ethnic lines.

This configuration presents quite a different picture than expectations when the Supreme Court outlawed school segregation in 1954. At that time, and for several years afterward, there was a great deal of hope that desegregation would produce true integration, reducing racial prejudice and increasing the self-esteem and academic performance of minority children. But there is little evidence that desegregation efforts have fulfilled any of these goals. In this chapter, we will examine hypotheses to account for the apparent failure and we will consider changes in the classroom structure and learning process that we consider necessary to achieve those benefits. We will go on to describe the "jigsaw" technique, an interdependent learning environment that we developed and implemented in order to instill the values and skills of cooperation in its participants. We also will report the findings and analyze

AUTHORS' NOTE: The term *We* will be used primarily in reference to a research team under the direction of Elliot Aronson and whose personnel shifts from year to year and project to project. Occasionally, it will be used to designate the authors of this essay. Research reported herein was supported by National Institute of Mental Health grant MH27736-03 and National Science Foundation Grant GS28847.

the methodology of the research we conducted to evaluate the method's success.

RATIONALE AND EXPECTATIONS FOR DESEGREGATION

In its landmark decision in *Brown v. Board of Education,* the Supreme Court held that segregation deprived minority group children of their rights to equal educational opportunities. The unanimous opinion argued that psychological barriers precluded schools from being "separate but equal"; the mere fact of segregation implied to the minority group that its members were inferior to those of the majority. This reasoning was based, in part, on the testimony of social psychologists. As Stephan (1978) has pointed out, their research helped establish the inferiority of segregated schools and their analyses outlined how this resulted in harms to minority students.

Stephan's description makes it clear that social psychologists perceived interethnic prejudice, minority self-esteem, and minority academic performance to be interrelated in a vicious circle. White prejudice against Blacks was seen as causing segregation. Being separated and deemed inferior lowered Blacks' self-esteem. Black students' expectations were reduced, hurting their academic achievement. This increased Blacks' prejudice as they turned out their frustrations onto Whites. This also reinforced Whites' prejudice as they attributed Blacks' poor performance to their abilities and as they felt and feared Blacks' hostility.

Several social scientists explained this sequence in an *amicus curiae* brief they filed in the *Brown* case. Furthermore, some of its coauthors and cosigners had been responsible for the findings underlying the model. Clark and Clark (1947) had given projective tests to children and concluded that discrimination, prejudice, and segregation harmed Black children's self-esteem. They found that Black children as young as three years old were already convinced that being Black was not a good thing, rejecting Black dolls in favor of White ones which they saw to be prettier and generally superior. The Clarks also stated that these feelings of inferiority led to resentment and hostility directed both inward against themselves and outward in heightened prejudice against Whites. A survey of social scientists conducted by Deutscher and Chein (1948) indicated that the Clarks' conclusions were widely shared, 90% of the respondents agreeing that segregation had "detrimental psychological effects" on the group being excluded, even when facilities were equal. And several psychologists suggested that segregation set into motion a vicious cycle of negative self-fulfilling prophecies. Black children felt inferior and learned to expect failure and rejection. They lost motivation and tended to perform according to those lowered expectations. Segregation was thought to hurt members of the majority group, too. As they treated the minority with hostility, superiority, and aggression, their attempts to bring their actions into line with their concepts of justice caused Whites to intensify their hatreds and fears.

Desegregation was expected to break this cycle. Minority children, no longer separated and branded as second-rate, should show improvements in their self-esteem, expectations, motivation, and achievement. Feeling less frustrated and having more contact with Whites, their prejudice should decrease. Whites should reduce their prejudice as well, as they experience more interethnic contact and are denied the institutionalized sanction for their discrimination and hostility.

It would be oversimplistic to assume that these benefits would result automatically from desegregation. Certain preconditions must be satisfied to break the cycle and produce the advantageous effects on self-esteem, performance, and prejudice. Allport stated these prerequisites most articulately in his classic, *The Nature of Prejudice,* published in the same year as the Supreme Court decision:

Prejudice . . . may be reduced by equal status contact between majority and minority groups in the pursuit of common goals. The effect is greatly enhanced if this contact is sanctioned by institutional supports (i.e., by law, custom, or local atmosphere), and provided it is of a sort that leads to the perception of common interests and common humanity between members of the two groups [1954: 281].

Today, a quarter of a century after desegregation was begun, an assessment of its effectiveness is not encouraging. We have had to confront evidence that its effects are not inevitably better either for minority children or for White children, and it does not always bring racial peace. A good example of this evidence stems from an impressive longitudinal study, the Riverside project, conducted by Gerard and Miller (1975). They found, as we did, that long after the schools were desegregated, White, Black, and Mexican-American children tended not to integrate but to stay in their own ethnic groups. Moreover, anxiety increased and remained high long after desegregation occurred.

These trends are echoed in the majority of studies. The most careful, scholarly reviews of the research show few, if any, benefits (see St. John, 1975; Stephan, 1978). Even more distressing, there is some evidence of harms. According to Stephan's review, of 20 studies that measured the self-esteem of minority children following desegregation, none found a significant increase; on the contrary, in 25% of them desegregation was followed by a significant *decrease* in the self-esteem of young minority children. Similarly, Stephan reported that the expected reductions in prejudice and gains in performance have not been demonstrated. Desegregation reduced the prejudice of Whites toward Blacks in only 2 of the 15 school systems studied, and the prejudice of Blacks toward Whites *increased* in almost as many cases as it decreased. Studies of the effects of desegregation on the academic performance of minority children also present a mixed and highly variable picture. Thus we reluctantly face the admission that the hopes that knowledgeable social psychologists pinned on desegregation may have been terribly naive.

OBSERVING THE DESEGREGATED CLASSROOM

What went wrong? And how can it be corrected? In the early 1970s, our research team at the University of Texas at Austin had been doing laboratory research on the antecedents of interpersonal attraction. One of our interests was the problem of decreases in interpersonal attraction across ethnic groups that occurred as a result of desegregation. The outbreak of racial tensions and hostility that followed the desegregation of the Austin schools made the question a timely one to investigate. The fact that the schools were in a state of crisis encouraged a high-ranking administrator, who had earned his Ph.D. from Texas and had worked with the first author on research and as an associate in encounter groups, to call in our research team. We promised an investigation of the problem and began systematic observation and research in the classrooms. Though some administrators were a bit leery at first, the positive results of our initial pilot study reinforced the respect and trust that already existed to swing the doors open wide for us.

The most typical situation we observed in the elementary schools worked something like this: The teacher stands in front of the class and asks a question. Six to 10 eager students strain in their seats and frantically wave their hands, anxious to be called on to show the teacher how smart they are. Several others hide in their seats, eyes averted, trying to make themselves invisible. When the teacher calls on one student, usually one of those with their hands raised, looks of disappointment and dismay appear on the faces of the other eager students. The cringing students look relieved that the spotlight has passed them by, at least for the moment. If the fortunate student comes up with the right answer, the teacher nods and smiles approvingly, a great reward for the child. And an audible groan can be heard from his or her rivals, who apparently have been rooting for the child to fail so that they themselves might have the opportunity to demonstrate how smart (or how much smarter) they are.

On a few occasions the teacher bypasses the volunteers and calls on one of the students who is trying to avoid being called on. The child may not know the answer, might be very nervous speaking in front of the class, or, in the case of Mexican-Americans, could have trouble with English. It is an uncomfortable moment. The student feels put on the spot. His classmates get impatient waiting for his response and want to show off their own superiority. They might snicker or even verbally insult the intelligence or the accent of the respondent. The teacher is also in an uncomfortable position. He or she wants to give attention to the child, but does not want to subject him to ridicule or embarrassment. Therefore, these occasions *are* few and far between. The teacher and student forge an unwritten agreement. The child becomes anonymous and avoids getting caught stumbling over an answer, and the teacher, in turn, does not call on him. By ignoring him, however, the teacher has, in effect, written him off. The message that the other students get, and that the child in question almost certainly comes to believe, is that he must be stupid and not worth bothering with.

Our observations made it clear that this classroom game is fiercely competitive and that the stakes are high. The kids are competing for the attention and approval of an important person in their world, as well as for status and grades. The process does not encourage friendliness and understanding among any of the children, who are led to view one another as foes to be heckled and vanquished. This state of affairs exists in most classrooms—even segregated ones. Desegregation adds racial tensions and exacerbates prejudices in this already volatile atmosphere of one-upmanship and resentment.

How might this situation be rectified? One does not need to look far. Let us return to Allport's prediction: When sanctioned by authority, equal-status contact in the pursuit of common goals will produce beneficial effects. Social psychological research has demonstrated the importance of each of these preconditions.

SANCTION BY AUTHORITY

Local authorities have differed in their willingness to accept and their efforts to enact desegregation rulings. Some localities were quick to implement the *Brown* decision, but in many areas there has been resistance and a policy of gradualism has been adopted.

The firm support of local authorities is important for desegregation to positively affect people's values, as the theory of cognitive dissonance predicts. Research has demonstrated that children who believe that they must eat a vegetable they dislike will convince themselves it is not so bad (Brehm, 1959), and that women who expect that they must work intimately with a particular person will emphasize her positive qualities (Darley and Berscheid, 1967). This "psychology of inevitability" explains that if I do not like you but I know that you and I will inevitably be in close contact, I will reduce the tension arising from these conflicting cognitions by convincing myself that you are not as bad as I had previously thought.

Studies of the process and effects of desegregation have supported this reasoning. Pettigrew (1961) has shown that desegregation proceeded more smoothly and with less violence in those districts where integration had the support of a forceful leadership. Clark (1953) discovered that immediate desegregation was much more effective than gradual desegregation. But, as we have seen, accomplishing desegregation smoothly does not, in and of itself, produce all of the beneficial effects that were hoped for. Even where authorities clearly sanction desegregation, in most cases variables such as self-esteem and prejudice do not necessarily change for the better. While sanction by authority may be a necessary prerequisite, it is not sufficient for desegregation to produce those benefits.

IN PURSUIT OF COMMON GOALS

Deutsch (1949) performed seminal research exploring competitive and cooperative relationships. He specified the critical difference between competition and cooperation to lie in the consequences of the interaction between two or more people: With competition, they have different outcomes; with cooperation, individuals share the same outcome. In competitive interactions, if you win, I lose. If we cooperate, when you win, I win, too. Deutsch suggested that this would influence the feelings between the participants, with people in competition inclined to be suspicious and hostile while people who cooperate would tend to be more concerned with each other's welfare. He tested these ideas in his college classrooms by inducing some students to compete for individual grades and having others work together for group grades. As he predicted, the latter groups showed more coordinated efforts and displayed greater friendliness and attentiveness than the competitive ones.

While Deutsch's work helped define the conditions that encouraged competition and cooperation, a series of experiments on group conflict by Sherif and his colleagues discovered a means to transform a competitive environment into a cooperative one. Sherif explained that their working hypotheses were that when two groups have conflicting aims—i.e., when one can achieve its ends only at the expense of the other—their members will become hostile to each other even though the groups are composed of normal well-adjusted individuals. There is a corollary to this assumption . . . Just as competition generates friction, working in a common endeavor should promote harmony. It seemed to us, considering group relations in the everyday world, that where harmony between groups is established, the most decisive factor is the existence of "superordinate" goals which have a compelling appeal for both but which neither could achieve without the other [1956: 56].

They tested these hypotheses experimentally by setting up a series of boys' summer camps. In the 1954 camp at Robber's Cave, they separated the boys into two groups, the Eagles and the Rattlers. They engaged the groups in competitive interactions, such as tournament games. This led to aggressive and hostile actions between them. After being defeated in a game, the Eagles discovered and burned a banner left behind by the Rattlers. Retaliation was swift, as the Rattlers seized the Eagles' flag the next morning.

The antipathy between the groups was pervasive. Even benign interactions between them became opportunities for insults and confrontations. Social events such as movies or meals increased the conflict, indicating that repeated social contacts between opposing groups do not necessarily reduce the friction between them.

Then Sherif and his associates created a number of urgent situations to test their corollary, that working in a common endeavor should promote harmony between the groups. For instance, they staged a breakdown in the camp's water supply. Members of both groups volunteered to help search for the problem in the water line. They worked together to successfully discover the difficulty and correct it. The superordinate goal replaced their competitive aims and compelled the groups to cooperate. Sherif reported that while the old attitudes were not dispelled immediately, after a series of cooperative efforts the groups displayed less friction between them and more liking and friendships among their members.

EQUAL-STATUS CONTACT

A demonstration by Elliott (1970) with her third graders exemplified the impact on children of being assigned to an inferior status. She told her class one day that brown-eyed people were more intelligent and better people than those with blue eyes. The brown-eyed students, though in the minority, would be the "ruling class" over the inferior blue-eyed children. They were given extra privileges as the blue-eyed kids were "kept in their place" by such restrictions as being last in line, seated in the back of the class, and given less recess time.

Elliott noticed that within a very short time, the blue-eyed children began to do more poorly in their schoolwork and became depressed and angry. They described themselves with more negative words. And the brown-eyed children grew mean, oppressing the blue-eyed children and making derogatory statements about them.

To show the irrationality of prejudice, the next day in class the teacher announced that she had lied, that it was really blue-eyed children who were better. The patterns of discrimination, derogation, and prejudice quickly reversed themselves. Finally, Elliott debriefed the children by talking with them about being the targets of prejudice and about the need to empathize with others. Several similar studies have replicated this scenario and process with other populations of subjects.

While this illustrates the effects resulting from a lack of equal-status contact, an analysis by Cohen suggests a method to cultivate its presence. She reasoned that even in environments which apparently allow equal-status contact, biased expectations for the groups could sustain the superior position that one of them enjoys. She explained that both groups might believe that one group's dominance is caused and justified by its competence. And she suggested that a temporary exchange of majority and minority roles is required as a prelude to reaching equal status, in order to reverse these often unconscious expectations.

One of her studies (Cohen and Roper, 1972) corroborated her analysis. Black children were taught how to build radios and how to teach others to do so. Then a group of White children and the newly trained Black children viewed a film of themselves building the radios. This was followed by some of the Black children teaching the Whites how to construct radios while others taught a Black administrator. When all of the children were joined into small groups, equal-status interactions were found only in the groups where Black children had been teaching the Whites. The other groups showed the usual white dominance.

While these experiments and other social psychological investigations have underlined the significance of fulfilling these prerequisites in order to achieve the advantages expected from desegregation, our observations of the elementary school classrooms indicated that few of them were being met consistently. Institutional sanctions sometimes were lacking. In some communities, desegregation proceeded forcefully and smoothly, but in other localities there is still great resistance. Many citizens have protested angrily against busing, and some local authorities have acquiesced to court rulings only reluctantly.

Though Allport speaks about sanction by authority on a governmental level, it is relevant to the classroom process as well. In the classes we visited, the types of cooperative interactions necessary to promote prosocial behaviors among the children usually were not condoned by the teacher. They prohibited conversations between students during class, viewing them as distractions for the students involved and as interruptions to the class. They preferred to deal with the children individually, turning their attention to and rewarding one respondent at a time.

The children clearly do not pursue common goals. One student's success is another's missed opportunity. As we described, if Mary knows the answer but the teacher calls on John, Mary probably hopes for John to make a mistake so she can show her knowledge. She is disappointed if he answers correctly. The students who often answer incorrectly or who do not even raise their hands to compete probably envy and resent their more successful classmates. They might put them down as teachers' pets or seek some kind of revenge through physical aggression against them on the playground. The successful students, for their part, often hold the less successful children in contempt, calling them "dumb" or "stupid."

This competitive process interacts with the lack of equal-status contact to wreak a special hardship on ethnic children. Many of the minority students originally attended schools where the atmosphere and facilities were not conducive to high academic achievement. Some have difficulties with English. Following desegregation, they are forced to compete with Anglo children who are usually better prepared and more accustomed to the competition. Their disadvantages are made more salient, the situation virtually guaranteeing a decrease in relative, if not absolute, performance. An additional burden is furnished by some teachers who are overtly prejudiced, their classrooms displaying clear differences in the students' status that are correlated with their ethnicity (see Gerard and Miller, 1975). These factors are almost certain to exert a negative effect on self-esteem as well as on feelings of friendship across ethnic lines.

After just a few days of observation, it became increasingly clear to members of our research team that students learn more than the content of the material explicitly taught in the classroom. The medium is the message; they learn implicit lessons from the process as well. We came to realize that it would be greatly advantageous if, in addition to acquiring specific skills and information, children could use the classroom to experience productive ways of relating to others and to develop a reasonable and positive view of themselves as people. But it appeared that the traditional classroom structure imparted a very different message. The children learned to obey the rules. They viewed their classmates as competitors for a limited resource, the approval of the teacher. They perceived the teacher as the sole source of information and reward in the classroom and recognized that the payoff came from pleasing her by giving the correct answer—the one which the teacher had in her head.

INTERDEPENDENT LEARNING: THE JIGSAW METHOD

Our observations and our reasoning led us to the conclusion that the basic classroom structure would have to be changed so that children could learn to like and trust each other. While desegregation might be a necessary first step toward getting students of different races together, it clearly was not enough. We felt that it was crucial for teachers to encourage cooperative interactions among the children. In order to concretize such interactions, it would be helpful to transform the classroom's competitive goal structure into a cooperative one. Such a structure should be accompanied by an emphasis on the need for participants to work together and to treat each other as resources. We wanted to replace individual aims with superordinate goals for the group and to utilize reciprocal peer teaching between students in order to foster equal-status contact.

This reasoning led us to hypothesize that interdependent learning environments would establish the conditions necessary to achieve the benefits previously expected to occur as a function of desegregation. Toward this end, we developed a technique for classroom instruction that attempted to incorporate the beneficial features of cooperation and peer teaching into the highly structured atmosphere of the traditional classroom (see Aronson et al., 1975; Aronson et al., 1978). We dubbed the process the "jigsaw" method, for reasons which will soon become obvious.

In this technique, the students are placed in small learning groups consisting of five or six participants. They might meet in these jigsaw groups for about an hour a day, to learn one subject, while following their usual routine the rest of the time. Each student in the jigsaw group is assigned one portion of the day's lesson and is responsible for teaching that segment to the other members of the group. Since the other members have no other access to this information, without which they cannot put together the entire picture, interdependence is established for them to learn the complete lesson.

For example, suppose the students are to learn the biography of Eleanor Roosevelt as part of a unit in social studies. The teacher would arrange the biography so that it consisted of six paragraphs of approximately the same length. Each child would be given one paragraph. The first paragraph would be about Eleanor Roosevelt's early childhood; the second, her young adulthood; the third, her years as a wife and young mother; the fourth would be about her husband's paralysis and her role in his quest for the presidency; the fifth, her years in the White House; the sixth, after World War II, about her coming into her own as a world political figure, her work for the United Nations, and so on. Thus, each learning group would have within it the entire biography of Eleanor Roosevelt, but each individual child would have no more than one-sixth of the story. In order to learn "Eleanor Roosevelt," the students would have to master their paragraph, teach it to the others in their group, and listen closely to each of the participants.

Each student first would take his or her paragraph, read it over a few times, and then join his or her counterparts from the other groups. For instance, if Julie is given Eleanor Roosevelt's White House years, she would consult in a counterpart group with Ted, Pam, and Juan, each of whom is a member of a different jigsaw group and who have also been given that portion of the biography. They could use each other as sounding boards and as consultants, to be sure that they had understood the important aspects of that phase of Eleanor Roosevelt's life and to rehearse their presentations to their jigsaw group. This procedure enables the poorer readers to get assistance in learning their section of the material, and it encourages the more advanced children to assume a teaching role.

A short time later the children would return to their six-person jigsaw groups to teach their parts of the biography to one another. The teacher would inform them that they would have a certain amount of time to communicate that knowledge to each other and that they would be tested on the whole life of Eleanor Roosevelt. Though each student will be evaluated individually, clearly they would have to depend on one another to learn all of the material. The process is highly reminiscent of a jigsaw puzzle, with each student possessing a single vital piece of the larger picture.

The children must work together and teach each other. It is a situation in which students are reinforced for helping one another. In addition, the jigsaw structure demands that the students utilize one another as resources rather than depending on the teacher as the sole provider of information, a state of affairs that is the hallmark of traditional education. In this situation, the only way a child can be a good learner is to begin to be a good listener and interviewer. The students also reward each other instead of allowing the teacher to be the major source of reinforcement in the classroom.

When left to their own resources in such a situation, the children eventually learn to teach and to listen to each other. They come to two important realizations: First, none of them could do well without the aid of every other person in the group and, second, each member has a unique and essential contribution to make.

The jigsaw technique is not a loose, "anything goes" situation. On the contrary, it is highly structured and very demanding. The structure induces children not only to imitate and model skills of group dynamics and social interaction, such as listening carefully and asking good questions, but also requires them to integrate these skills cognitively in their interactions with fellow group members. Indeed, group process receives explicit consideration as the members spend the last few minutes of their meeting reviewing how their group proceeded and suggesting improvements.

What is the role of the teacher in this cooperative process? Instead of being primarily a lecturer and provider of substantive information, the teacher now assumes the role of facilitator of group process. He or she keeps close watch on the functioning of the jigsaw groups and intervenes on occasion in order to enhance constructive group interactions. The teacher still maintains the task of planning the particular curriculum and adapting the material to the jigsaw format. (For specific details and examples to implement this method in the classroom, see Aronson et al., 1978.)

It should be noted that problems may arise when the jigsaw technique is introduced. Cooperation does not occur smoothly or all at once; old, competitive habits die hard. Moreover, not all students easily adapt to a cooperative classroom. For example, some students, because they are extremely poor readers, have great difficulty in holding their own. Others, because they are extraordinarily shy or antisocial, prefer to work alone. With the aid of a little ingenuity, though, the teacher often finds ways to turn some of these difficulties into strengths.

The experience of a Mexican-American child in one of our groups serves as a useful illustration. We will call him Carlos. Carlos was not very articulate in English, his second language. Because he was often ridiculed when he had spoken up in the past, over the years he learned to keep quiet in class. He was one of those students we discussed earlier who had entered into an implicit contract of silence with his teacher, he opting for anonymity and she calling on him only rarely.

While Carlos hated school and was learning very little in the traditional classroom, at least he was left alone. Accordingly, he was quite uncomfortable with the jigsaw system, which required him to talk to his groupmates. He had a great deal of trouble communicating his paragraph, stammering and hesitating. The other children reacted out of old habits, resorting to insults and teasing. "Aw, you don't know it," Susan accused. "You're dumb, you're stupid. You don't know what you are doing."

One of the researchers, assigned to observe the group process, intervened with a bit of advice when she overheard such comments: "OK, you can tease him if you want to. It might be fun for you, but it's *not* going to help you learn about Eleanor Roosevelt's young adulthood. And let me remind you, the exam will take place in less than an hour." Note how this statement brings home the fact that the reinforcement contingencies have shifted considerably. Now Susan does not gain much from putting Carlos down. And she stands to lose a great deal, not just from the teacher singling her out for criticism but because she needs to know Carlos's information.

Gradually, but inexorably, it began to dawn on the students that the *only* chance they had to learn about Carlos's segment was by paying attention to what he had to say. If they ignored Carlos or continued to ridicule him, his segment would be unavailable to them and the most they could hope for would be an 80% score on the exam—an unattractive prospect to most of the children. And with that realization, the kids began to develop into pretty good interviewers, learning to pay attention to Carlos, to draw him out, and to ask probing questions. Carlos, in turn, began to relax more and found it easier to explain out loud what was in his head. What the children came to learn about Carlos is even more important than the information about the lesson that they got from him. After a couple of days, they began to appreciate that Carlos was not nearly as dumb as they had thought he was. After a few weeks they noticed talents in him they had not seen before. They began to like Carlos, and he began to enjoy school more and to think of his Anglo classmates as helpful friends and interested colleagues rather than as tormentors.

Do you believe this?

EVALUATING THE JIGSAW TECHNIQUE

Over the course of several experiments, we have evaluated the effects of participating in jigsaw learning groups on students like Carlos and Susan. We began on a small scale, carrying out pilot studies in individual classrooms. Finding that the jigsaw method seemed to be successful, we conducted more systematic and comprehensive experiments implementing the technique in many classes in several schools. Then we brought the research back into the social psychological laboratory to investigate some of the mechanisms we hypothesized to underlie the beneficial changes we measured in jigsaw participants.

Taken together, the results of our project show a strong positive pattern of feelings, behaviors, and abilities which can be attributed to the jigsaw groups. It appears that relative to traditional classrooms, this interdependent learning method increases the students' liking for their classmates and for school, enhances their self-esteem, improves their academic performance, decreases their competitiveness, and helps them view their classmates as learning resources. Children exposed to the jigsaw method also demonstrate a greater ability to place themselves in the role of another person and tend to make ego-enhancing attributions for themselves *and* for their peers.

Long before the data from our evaluations was accumulated and analyzed, however, it was clear to most of the teachers in our studies that the jigsaw technique was working. Experienced teachers are sensitive to subtle changes in the attitudes and performance of individual students; they do not need complex statistics, graphs, or tables in order to assess the viability of an instructional innovation. Indeed, one of the most gratifying aspects of our research was listening to the excitement of many of the teachers as they shared anecdotes and success stories with us—long before the final results were tabulated.

Though the teachers' testimony was dramatic and important, it cannot be accepted at face value as proof of the method's effectiveness. Experimenter bias is a well-known phenomenon to be avoided in social psychological experimentation and a particular hazard of evaluation research: There is a tendency for those involved with a project to unconsciously edit their observations and reports. It is possible that because of their commitment to the effort or their agreement with its goals, observers may selectively emphasize positive incidents and relegate negative ones to the back of their minds. It is also conceivable that in the absence of adequate controls, the progress that occurs in some classes could be due to special circumstances unrelated to the jigsaw technique itself.

These problems have hampered many educational innovations. In many instances, the initial responses of students and teachers seems promising, so the innovation is widely publicized and adopted. Only later might there be any systematic evaluation. Furthermore, the researchers who create the new technique often enter a few classrooms, institute their changes, gather their data, and then leave. It is rare that they explain their reasoning and results fully enough or train teachers sufficiently for whatever positive changes they effect to be sustained beyond the time of their departure. Thus many supposedly fantastic innovations turn out to be ineffective, either because the techniques are flawed or as a result of their being implemented incorrectly. And many teachers and school administrators grow skeptical and reluctant to adopt them.

For these reasons, we felt that it was essential to conduct unbiased, carefully controlled research to evaluate the effects of the jigsaw method and to help develop it fully. One of our goals was to determine whether it was a valuable way to educate individual students, eliciting the benefits of increased liking, self-esteem, and performance that were originally predicted to follow desegregation. So we designed a meticulous assessment, rigorous enough to pass the scrutiny of our scientific colleagues. At the same time, we endeavored to refine a set of techniques that teachers could readily apply to their classrooms. Thus emerged a strategy of "action research" to improve the effectiveness of our method and to plant the seeds for jigsaw groups to spread from classroom to classroom.

THE JIGSAW PILOT STUDIES

To test the feasibility of the jigsaw method, our first step was to run a two-week exploratory study on two fifth-grade classes. All of the students were divided into small groups of five or six children. Half of the groups were taught in the traditional manner, by their teacher or one of our graduate students. The other half were the experimental groups, with the students using the jigsaw method to teach each other. The small groups met for one hour each day.

At several intervals in the study, we measured the students' liking for one another in order to determine whether it changed due to their participation in a competitive or an interdependent group. While there were no differences in the ratings prior to the beginning of the study, after a week the members of the jigsaw groups grew to like each other more than the members of the teacher-taught groups did. At that halfway point, the traditional groups were also changed to the jigsaw format. By the end of the study a week later, their liking ratings also increased to the levels found among the original jigsaw groups. We also tested the children on the material they studied. While the students in the original jigsaw groups performed slightly better than the controls, the difference did not reach statistical significance.

By altering the classroom routine for members of both of the groups, our design attempted to equalize Hawthorne effects, the tendency for people to perform better and appear happier when they think their superiors are trying to improve their working conditions. All of the children seemed to enjoy meeting in the smaller groups, even the control students in the competitive ones. But it was only when they joined the jigsaw groups that they exhibited the increase in liking for their groupmates. Simply working in small groups was not sufficient—interdependence makes the difference in liking.

Soon after this initial study, we replicated the experiment in a sixth-grade classroom in a poorer neighborhood. The results were similar. The jigsaw groups fostered more friendship and at least as much learning as the traditional teaching method.

OUR FIRST FULL-SCALE EXPERIMENT: BLANEY ET AL. (1977)

Encouraged by the results of these pilot studies, we believed that the jigsaw technique was a workable and effective teaching method; accordingly, we began planning a more systematic and comprehensive experiment (Blaney et al., 1977). We wanted to test a greater number of students, in several different schools, across more measures. Before discussing its procedure and results, we will focus on two methodological issues raised by the larger scale investigation: the problems of gaining the support of teachers and of acquiring equivalent experimental and control groups.

Whereas a decision to expand a laboratory experiment might entail recruiting more subjects and perhaps hiring another research assistant, increasing the scope of our intervention in the schools necessitated enlisting the cooperation and participation of many teachers. Some of them would have to volunteer to implement the jigsaw technique in their classrooms, and others were needed to teach their classes in the traditional manner so that we could use them as control groups.

Our preliminary studies had demanded very little from the teachers. They merely taught one of the small groups in their usual manner; we helped the children learn the jigsaw system, adapted the curriculum to it, and observed the groups. Now we would have to motivate and train teachers to use our method and take over those responsibilities. We also needed to ensure that the technique would be used similarly in all of the jigsaw classes.

To accomplish this, we conducted a five-day workshop for 14 fifth- and sixth-grade teachers a few weeks before the school term started. (See Aronson et al., 1978, Appendix D for details.) Its goal was to change the teacher's role from that of being a dispenser of information to that of being a facilitator of the group process. The teachers learned how to use the jigsaw method by experiencing it themselves. They were trained to handle problems that might arise and given instructions and exercises to help them introduce the technique. Most important, the great majority came to realize that temporarily relinquishing the awesome power they held in the classroom allowed them to be more creative, to face new challenges, and that it would be valuable and fun for them and their students.

Ten of the teachers who participated in the workshop volunteered to implement the jigsaw technique, and their classes became the experimental condition in our experiment (Blaney et al., 1977). We wanted the control teachers and classes to be as similar to these as possible, so we rejected the idea of using teachers who had originally offered to try the jigsaw method. Since they had volunteered to learn a new teaching technique, we reasoned that those teachers might not be deeply committed to their old styles. We wanted good teachers who believed in the traditional manner of teaching.

To obtain our control groups, we asked our experimental teachers to recommend other teachers from their schools whom they considered to be at least as competent as themselves and who would be willing to donate time in their classes for testing. In this way we tried to ensure that they would be capable, and as committed to their mode of teaching as the jigsaw teachers were to theirs. Thus, our control group (of students) differs from a traditional control group in that the classroom teachers were not sampled from precisely the same population. Technically speaking, this turns our experiment into a quasi experiment. At the same time, because of the high motivation of the teachers in the control condition, we believe this to be a conservative strategy—reducing the possibility of committing a type I error. In addition, by selecting teachers from the same schools, we could match the racial composition and socioeconomic status between the conditions. To make certain that the traditional classrooms acted as legitimate control groups, we asked their teachers to refrain from employing any small-group or cooperative teaching methods during the course of our study.

PROCEDURE

Since the Blaney et al. (1977) study served as a precursor for many of the follow-up investigations, we will describe its procedure, measures, hypotheses, and results in some detail. About a month after the school year began, the jigsaw technique was introduced in the 10 fifth-grade classrooms, which were from seven elementary schools in Austin, Texas. Three classes were utilized as controls. Over 300 students participated. The experimental classes met in jigsaw groups for about 45 minutes a day, three days per week. Students were assigned to groups with an eye toward evenly distributing children according to ethnicity, academic ability, and sex. We also tried to avoid having close friends or bitter enemies as members of the same jigsaw group. The curriculum was basically the same for the experimental and the control classes.

At the beginning and at the conclusion of the six-week experiment, we administered a sociometric instrument to measure the students' liking for their classmates and had them complete questionnaires to assess several of their attitudes relating to school. We trained undergraduates to give the tests, reducing experimenter effects by having them read from standardized scripts when questioning the children. Though they observed the classes, we prohibited these students from intervening in the process in any way—the teachers facilitated the groups. We tried to minimize demand characteristics on the participants' responses by keeping the jigsaw students unaware that this questioning was related to their learning groups. We informed them that the information they were providing was part of a study of the entire school system and assured them that their teachers would not see their answers.

MEASURES

We developed a sociometric instrument to measure the students' liking for their fellow group members (in the jigsaw condition) and for the remaining children in the class. We considered simply asking them to designate whom they liked or disliked, but advice from the teachers changed our minds. They feared that such explicit statements might lead to hurt feelings among the students. Our highest priority in carrying out this research was to avoid causing either physical or emotional disruptions, so we tried to devise a measure that would be pleasant for the students while also yielding valuable information. The instrument emerged as our alternative.

Our data collectors asked the students to imagine taking a trip to an exciting island. They could bring their classmates, but since they had to travel in a small boat they could carry only a few of them at a time. But they could make several trips. We gave class rosters to the students and had them assign numbers to each of their classmates according to which boatload they would have them ride. They would assign a seven to those classmates who would join them on the first trip, a six to those who would come over in the second boatload, and so on down to those who would get a one and would join them on the last trip. We assumed that these preferences would reflect the students' liking for those classmates.

We also designed a questionnaire to assess the students' attitudes toward school, their feelings about themselves, and their opinions concerning cooperation and peer teaching. Each of its 22 questions was read aloud twice, and students were asked to respond by marking one of the seven boxes beneath each item (see Figure 1). Each of the boxes was accompanied by a verbal description, and they were of increasing size to present a picture of the degree of feeling represented by the labels. We found that this way of presenting the questions was helpful, especially for students with reading difficulties.

"How much do you like school this year?"

□	□	□	□	□	□	□
like not at all	like very, very little	like very little	like some	like a lot	like very much	like very, very much

FIGURE 1   Student Questionnaire

HYPOTHESES AND RESULTS

On the basis of the psychological research and our own reasoning, observations, and preliminary studies, we were able to make several predictions about what we would find. We expected that students in jigsaw groups would show increased liking for their groupmates. We also thought that, compared to children taught in traditional classrooms, students in jigsaw classes would like school more, increase more in self-esteem, decrease in feelings of competitiveness, and have a stronger belief that they could learn from other children.

Peer liking. The previous research comparing the effects of competitive and cooperative relationships, including the classic experiments by Deutsch and by Sherif, supported our prediction that the children in our interdependent groups would come to like their groupmates more than the children taught in the traditional manner would like their classmates. As we have mentioned, the results of our pilot studies confirmed this hypothesis. We were concerned, however, that the jigsaw students' increased liking for their groupmates not come at the expense of isolating themselves from or growing to dislike the other students. So we totalled two liking scores: one representing the average ratings the jigsaw children gave their groupmates and the other (the only one for the control classes) representing the average of the ratings assigned to the other classmates. Notice that our instrument is flexible enough to reflect changes in students' liking for individuals as well as for overall levels of liking for their classmates. Since the instructions do not specify the number of children that can be accommodated on each boatload, the liking score assigned to one classmate need not be compensated by a reduced ranking for another. Thus, individual rankings and average liking scores could vary.

We found that students in the jigsaw classes grew to like the others in their groups more than they liked their other classmates, even though they liked their groupmates slightly less than the others at the beginning of the study. Moreover, this increase did not come at the expense of their liking for the other classmates, as this score also increased, though not nearly so dramatically. This is important, not only for its direct consequences of more friendship in the classroom but also because increased liking for a student is a first step for the child being accepted and given support by his or her classmates. According to Coopersmith and Feldman (1974), this acceptance is a major prerequisite for the development of positive self-esteem.

Liking for school. Our observations and our memories of attending school suggested that in traditional classes, boredom and dissatisfaction grow as the school year progresses. We thought that the jigsaw method would help prevent this decline in interest, and we hypothesized that stu-

very probably!
Bravo!
Hawthorne effect?!

dents in the jigsaw classes would come to like school better than students in the control classes. We tested this hypothesis by summing the students' responses to three questions: "How much do you like school this year?"; "When you are in the classroom, how happy do you feel?"; and "When you are in the classroom, how bored do you feel?"

Significant differences over time and between groups were obtained for this measure. By the end of six weeks, students in the control classes liked school less than they had at the beginning. Students in the jigsaw classes, however, liked school about as well. This confirmed our hypothesis: Jigsaw groups help students sustain the interest in school which most children have at the beginning of a new school year. These results indicate that participating in jigsaw groups tends to forestall the decline that we found in teacher-oriented classrooms.

When we examined the responses by members of different ethnic groups, we found differences between Anglo, Black, and Mexican-American students. Anglos in the jigsaw groups grew to like school more during the six weeks, while Anglos in the control classes liked school less. Black students in the experimental classes came to like school slightly less than they had at the beginning, but in the traditional classes their liking decreased substantially. Unexpectedly, the trend was reversed for Mexican-American children. Mexican-Americans in the control classes showed a marked increase in liking for school that was greater than the minor increase they exhibited in the jigsaw classes. We speculated that the most likely explanation for this unexpected difference was traceable to the language problems faced by Mexican-Americans, which were highlighted by the students being forced out of their usual silence in the classroom to participate in the peer teaching required by the jigsaw format. A replication of our study by Geffner (1978), which we will describe shortly, helped verify this speculation.

Besides our data demonstrating the increased liking for school due to the jigsaw technique, we also learned of its positive effects in more casual ways. Both students and teachers commented on the fun they had and the freedom they felt in the groups. The students also expressed satisfaction with their involvement in their own learning, and after a while they were heard to exclaim, "How come it's only such a short time that we get to meet in small groups?"

Self-esteem. We considered the self-esteem of the students to have crucial importance on their attitudes and performance in school. Our observations in the classrooms meshed with various psychological conceptualizations to lead us to hypothesize that our interdependent groups would have beneficial effects on their participants' feelings of self-esteem.

A short theoretical discussion will help to illuminate our reasoning. A person's self-concept is thought to consist of all the attitudes, abilities, and assumptions that the individual holds about himself or herself that act as a guide to behavior (Coopersmith and Feldman, 1974). Self-esteem is the evaluative component of the self-concept, and can be defined as the amount of worthiness or power that the person perceives himself or herself to possess. Evidence about one's worthiness or power is provided by two main sources: from the individual's interpersonal interactions and as a function of the person's experiences, accomplishments, and abilities. Thus, self-esteem can be viewed as having an "outer" component, resulting from social comparison processes and the appraisals of relevant others, and an "inner" component, developing from objective data pertaining to successes or failures in one's interactions with the environment (Franks and Marolla, 1976). These two dimensions of self-esteem are not mutually exclusive; they may overlap as well as interact with each other. Both factors can be vitally important in the classroom.

In education, these two dimensions of self-esteem develop from children's interpretations of the feedback from teachers and classmates as well as from their own learning experiences. Recalling our observations of the traditional classrooms will help to illustrate how these interpretations and experiences can operate to enhance or to cripple children's self-esteem. As we have seen, the emphasis on competition creates a situation in which there are winners and losers in the classroom. A few fortunate students win their teacher's praise, attribute their success to their abilities (e.g., "I did well on the exam because I am smart."), and expect to do well in the future. The research suggests that this leads to a cycle of positive self-fulfilling prophecies, in which the students' high self-esteem leads to better achievement and, conversely, their high performance elevates their self-esteem (Covington and Beery, 1976; Purkey, 1970).

Unfortunately, successes are all too rare and rewards all too scarce in the traditional classroom. Its system of education exacts high performance partly by instilling students with a fear of failure. The lack of successful experiences and scarcity of rewards can lead some students to give up and to stop trying to succeed. Low self-esteem and low achievement are maintained through a cycle of negative self-fulfilling prophecies.

We thought that changing from a competitive to a cooperative environment in the classroom would promote situations in which all students could have successful experiences that would build their self-confidence and self-esteem. The emphasis for all participants to work together to accomplish mutual goals virtually eliminates the production of "losers." Under these circumstances, it is likely that the students will experience positive outcomes, as well as receiving more support from their classmates. As these phenomena occur, they will almost certainly produce increases in self-esteem from the positive feedback that the children receive and from the skills they gain when they help their classmates.

As we hypothesized, over the six-week period, the students in the experimental classrooms increased in self-esteem to a greater extent than those in the competitive classes. To measure self-esteem, we combined the results of four questions: "How much do you like being yourself?"; "When you are in the classroom, how important do you feel?"; "When you are in the classroom, how smart do you feel?"; and "When you are in class, how often do you feel you can learn whatever you try to learn?" In general, the results indicated that the students in the jigsaw classes significantly increased in self-esteem while the control students decreased.

Competitiveness. Does the jigsaw experience change students' attitudes toward competing and winning at all costs? We hypothesized that compared to students in the control classes, students who participated in the jigsaw groups would show less of a preference for competitive behaviors. This hypothesis was tested by the questionnaire item, "I would rather beat a classmate than help him." The responses indicate that students in the jigsaw classes grew less competitive over the six weeks while students in the control condition became more competitive. This lowered competitiveness appeared to extend beyond the jigsaw groups themselves. Jigsaw teachers reported that even the music or physical education teachers remarked about the improved attitudes and behavior of the jigsaw students.

Learning from others. We also hypothesized that students in jigsaw classes would come to believe that they could learn from other students. The question "Can you learn anything from the other kids in your class?" was the test for this prediction. We found that students in the jigsaw groups increasingly believed that they could learn from other students, while students in the control classes decreased in this belief. The experiences of teaching and being taught by classmates helped them learn to use their peers as resources.

AN ATTEMPTED REPLICATION

Thus the results from the Blaney et al. experiment confirmed our hypotheses. The data, our observations, and the reports from teachers and students corroborated that participating in the jigsaw groups increased the students' liking for their groupmates, maintained their interest in school, improved their self-esteem, reduced their competitiveness, and increased their belief that they could learn from their classmates. Our evaluation of the jigsaw technique indicated that it had been successful on these measures and that it was a valuable way to educate students.

Accordingly, we turned to the second goal of our action research: to refine the method and to encourage its adoption in the schools. We wanted to demonstrate that the program could be grafted onto the existing classroom process with little stress or strain. So we redesigned and shortened our teachers' workshop, trained 14 teachers to implement the jigsaw groups in their classrooms and recruited 4 more to be the teachers in the control classes, and began the experiment again.

The results astonished us. Predictably, we obtained the characteristic advantages to the jigsaw students' friendship with their peers, their satisfaction with school, and so forth. But the children in the control classrooms also showed shifts in these directions, and the differences that we expected between the experimental and the traditional classes failed to materialize.

Our researchers who observed the classrooms helped to explain why they failed to occur. The traditional classes were not traditionally competitive—most of their teachers were employing some form of small-group learning. Therefore the control classes did not act as controls, instead becoming an intermediate condition in which cooperation was used but was not as extensive or systematic as in the interdependent groups, and which had an impact on the children, though it was not as significant as in the jigsaw classes.

In scientific circles it might be charged that our experiment had been contaminated, invalidating our results. But our experience exemplified that we had been successful in perhaps a more important role, that of change agents. It appeared that some of the teachers who were enthusiastic about our method had spread word-of-mouth accolades across the school system. Six months after we had introduced the jigsaw technique in our first classrooms, it was hard to find a purely traditional fifth-grade class in the Austin public schools. We had contributed to a minirevolution in education, which frustrated our replication effort but which gratified us as more classes adopted our method.

A REPLICATION AND EXTENSION: GEFFNER (1978)

In his Ph.D. dissertation, Geffner (1978) followed a similar methodology to investigate the implementation of the jigsaw method in the Watsonville, California, elementary schools. He conducted the research over an eight-week period in 10 fifth-grade classes in Santa Cruz County, where the composition of the schools is approximately 50% Anglo and 50% Mexican-American. To control for Hawthorne effects and to formally operationalize the three conditions that arose from the replication, he compared classes that instituted the jigsaw method to traditional classes and to classes taught with innovative cooperative techniques other than interdependence. He explored self-esteem in more depth by using a modified version of "A Pictorial

Self-Concept Scale for Children" (Bolea et al., 1971), and he also studied the students' interethnic and intraethnic perceptions.

Geffner's results replicated those of Blaney et al. in most respects. Students in both the interdependent groups and the other cooperative classes improved or maintained positive attitudes about their peers, about school, and about themselves, with the jigsaw students improving more. Students in the traditional classes suffered declines. The inconsistently smaller gain in liking for school by Mexican-American students taught by the jigsaw technique, found in the Blaney et al. research, was not obtained in Geffner's. The Mexican-American students in the Texas schools were strongly in the minority and were in a new situation; this, combined with some language barriers, probably accounted for those inconsistent results. The Mexican-American children in the Watsonville schools were much more familiar and comfortable with their school environment since they comprised nearly half of the population and had been in the situation for a few years, and showed the greater liking for school characteristic of participating in the jigsaw groups.

The modified self-esteem scale he adapted consisted of cartoonlike pictures of stick figures in various types of situations and included five dimensions of self-esteem deemed important by the students themselves: scholastic abilities, athletic abilities, physical appearance, social interactions, and family interactions. Relative to the traditional classrooms, the cooperative conditions enhanced the students' self-images regarding their social interactions and their scholastic abilities and even generalized to increase their confidence in athletic abilities and family interactions. Having more successful experiences and getting more feedback and support probably led to the generalized improvement in self-esteem and feelings of competence.

An important goal for desegregation was the reduction of interethnic prejudice; and Geffner's research also found that, to a far greater extent than students in control classrooms, the Anglo and Mexican-American children in jigsaw classes improved their general attitudes toward their own ethnic group as well as toward members of other ethnic groups.

TESTING ACADEMIC PERFORMANCE: LUCKER ET AL. (1977)

These studies made it clear that the jigsaw method can produce benefits in peer liking, attitudes toward school, and self-esteem, but its effect on academic performance still needed to be assessed. A recent analysis of various innovative classroom procedures suggesting that these methods do not necessarily improve or even maintain academic achievement (Chalupsky and Coles, 1977) and current publicity that national test means are falling and that some students are graduating from high school without being able to read, write, or compute adequately have created a "back-to-basics" sentiment that threatens educational innovation. We expected that the advantages to students' attitudes resulting from the jigsaw technique would increase their achievement by changing the cycle of self-fulfilling prophecies that we discussed earlier. In the aforementioned experiments we also examined the students' grades, which improved in the jigsaw condition while decreasing in the traditional classes. Though these results and the teachers' impressions about academic performance were encouraging, the teachers' assignment of grades as well as their observations may be subject to bias or expectancy. Thus a well-controlled study was required.

Our research team designed and carried out such an experiment (Lucker et al., 1977). The subjects were 303 fifth- and sixth-grade students from five Austin schools. Six classes met in jigsaw groups for about 45 minutes each day, while five classes were taught in the traditional manner by highly competent teachers and represented the control condition. The social studies curriculum for both groups was standardized during the two-week study and consisted of a unit on colonial America taken from a fifth-grade textbook along with supplemental materials. A standardized test about the lessons was given to the children both before and after they studied the unit.

Though the pretest showed no discernible differences between the students in the two conditions, the posttest demonstrated that those in the jigsaw classes showed significantly more improvement than those in the control classes, $F(1, 280) = 6.73$, $p < .02$. An analysis of the data reveals that this was mainly due to the increased performance of minority students in the

TABLE 1   Performance of Anglo and Minority Students in Interdependent and Traditional Classrooms (Lucker et al., 1977)

Group	N	DV-Performance	
		Pretest Score	Adjusted Posttest Score*
INTERDEPENDENT			
Anglo	122	29.00	64.47
Minority	36	25.40	64.66
TRADITIONAL			
Anglo	120	29.40	62.65
Minority	25	26.20	57.02

*Raw posttest scores (which followed the same pattern) adjusted for reading level and pretest score by covariance analysis.

jigsaw groups. Anglo students performed as well in the jigsaw classes as they did in the traditional classes (F < 1.0). But minority students performed significantly better in the interdependent groups than in the control class-rooms, $F(1, 280) = 8.77$, $p < .01$. Only two weeks of jigsaw activity narrowed the performance gap between the unadjusted scores of Anglos and minorities by over a third. Interestingly, the jigsaw method does *not* work a hard-ship on high-ability children: Students in the top quartile in reading ability benefited just as much as students in the lowest quartile. Two integral features of the jigsaw method safeguard their interest and achievement: the new role for them of teaching and the exam's being a function of individual performance so that they are not penalized by others' lower grades.

INVESTIGATING UNDERLYING MECHANISMS

Having established that several advantages accrue from the jigsaw method, we sought to illuminate some of the mechanisms assumed to under-lie its positive effects. We investigated jigsaw participants' role-taking abili-ties and their attributional processes to focus more directly on why coopera-tive interactions enhance prosocial behavior.

MEASURING ROLE-TAKING ABILITIES: BRIDGEMAN (1977)

We believed that one of the crucial mechanisms underlying the effects of cooperative behavior on liking, positive attributions, self-esteem, and perfor-mance is *empathy.* According to Piaget's (1932) theory, children construct their ways of viewing the world by actively interacting with their environ-ment to resolve social and cognitive conflicts. He suggested that egocen-trism and role taking are negatively correlated in children's development. Therefore, if they engage in cooperative interactions, the process of modify-ing their intended behavior in anticipation of the others' needs and responses would diminish their egocentrism and provide a framework for increasing their abilities to take another's perspective.

Bridgeman (1977) tested this hypothesis about the relationship between cooperative learning and role-taking abilities in her Ph.D. dissertation. She tested 120 fifth-grade students from three Santa Cruz County schools. Roughly half of the students spent eight weeks participating in jigsaw groups while the others were taught either by traditional methods or in innovative small-group classrooms. She revised Chandler's (1973) role-taking cartoon series to assess the students' perspective-taking abilities.

Each of Chandler's cartoon sequences depicts a central character caught up in a chain of psychological cause and effect, such that the character's subsequent behavior is shaped by and fully comprehensible only in terms of the events preceding it. In one of the series, for example, a boy who had been saddened by seeing his father off at the airport began to cry when he later received a gift in the mail of a toy airplane similar to the one which had carried his father away. Midway into each sequence, a late-arriving bystander is introduced, such as the mailman, who witnessed the resultant behavior of the principal character but who was not privy to the antecedent events. Thus it is possible to place the subject in a privileged position relative to the story character whose role the subject is later asked to assume and to specify the degree to which the subject is able to set aside facts known only to him or herself and adopt a different perspective. For instance, when asked to explain the child's behavior, both adults and children usually can explain the association which caused him to cry. It is when they are asked to assume the role of the latecoming mailman that differences in egocentrism emerge. When they take the role of the mailman, young children tend to give the egocentric explanation that he knew that the boy's father had recently left town and that the boy would cry. Adults would answer that the mailman probably would be confused by the boy's crying.

The results of Bridgeman's experiment indicated that the jigsaw students manifest less egocentrism than was found among the controls. Both role taking of rational thought (considering the logical perspective of another) and role taking of affective thought (considering the emotional perspective of another) showed significant increases after students experienced eight weeks in the cooperative groups. There was no change for students taught in more traditional ways. Bridgeman's results are consistent with both Piaget's theories and the assumptions underlying the cooperative process. And they point out that the effects of the curriculum-incorporated role-taking experience from the cooperative interactions generalized to the noncurriculum tasks of the Chandler stories. Further, these data support the notion that empathic role taking may be a key ability which mediates other prosocial behaviors.

ATTRIBUTIONAL PATTERNS: TWO LAB EXPERIMENTS

Another important influence on the way students perform and relate to each other comes from the attributions that they employ to explain their own and their classmates' behavior (see Heider, 1958; Jones and Davis, 1965). Earlier we described how students who experience successes or failures in the classroom will make attributions that are consistent with their experiences and self-esteem. Students who perform well generally will make dispositional attributions to explain their successes (e.g., "I did well because of my ability.") and will protect their self-esteem by making situational attributions to account for their failures (e.g., "I did poorly because the room was noisy."). This tends to be reversed for low-achieving students. They come to believe, along with their classmates and even some teachers, that their occasional successes are due to situational factors (to luck) and that their failures are traceable to dispositional factors (to poor ability and low self-worth). These patterns initiate cycles of positive or negative self-fulfilling prophecies which perpetuate the students' success or discouragement.

As the jigsaw groups improve the self-esteem and achievement of students who might be considered "losers" in many traditional classrooms, we hypothesized that the change from a competitive to a cooperative or an interdependent environment would transform their own and others' attributions about their performance from negative ones to more ego-enhancing ones. To investigate this, we designed and conducted two laboratory experiments, in which students were removed from the hustle and bustle of the classroom and tested under more controlled conditions. By taking our research into the laboratory, we were able to test refinements without disrupting the classroom procedure. This enabled us to perform a quick study on children who had not been exposed to the jigsaw technique and then return them to their usual classroom routine.

In one such study, Stephan et al. (1977a) demonstrated that these attributional patterns are more complex. Their results suggested strongly that once friendship and empathy have been established, competition appears not to produce the kind of one-upmanship that can be demoralizing to the loser and harmful to the relationship between the competitors. The researchers set up a situation in which sixth-grade students succeeded or failed at a motor task (throwing bean bags at a target) that was performed competitively, independently, or cooperatively. They found that when the children *beat a friend* in a competitive situation, the usual ego-enhancing attribution process was reversed such that winners were more likely than losers to attribute their performance on the task to luck. It looks as though children are reluctant to gloat and boast at the expense of a friend's ego, at least temporarily.

A similar experiment was designed to look more closely at the type of attributions made by college students in competitive, cooperative, and interdependent interactions with other students (Stephan et al., 1977b). The subjects' results were manipulated to indicate that they succeeded or failed on a task involving artistic judgments. Generally, ego-enhancing attributions were made by the students to explain their success or failure. In the cooperative and interdependent conditions, similar attributions were made for their partner's success or failure (i.e., attributing success to ability and failure to luck). In the competition condition, however, the process was reversed such that their partner's failure was attributed to personal abilities and success to situational variables. In short, cooperation leads individuals to treat their partners in the same kind of ego-enhancing manner in which they treat themselves. Competition creates a harsh difference.

This line of research lends credence to the model of self-fulfilling prophecies developed earlier, yielding evidence that an interdependent, cooperative environment can change the self-defeating attributions and negative self-fulfilling prophecies made by the students who are considered by themselves and others as failures. The experiments demonstrate that these cycles can be reversed, not only by enhancing the performance of the individual but also by changing the attributions that tend to be made as a function of a cooperative (rather than a competitive) interaction.

EVALUATING THE RESEARCH

The direction of the results of our studies assessing the jigsaw technique's effectiveness is clear: It appears to be a valuable way to educate students. Our research consistently finds that on a variety of measures, participants in the interdependent groups give more positive responses over time and relative to students in traditional classrooms. Still, it is possible to question some of our reasoning, methodology, or results and to point out issues still requiring consideration.

One might assert that the advantages claimed for the jigsaw method result from aspects of the learning technique other than interdependence or that they arise from artifacts of the research. The increased liking for peers could be due merely to the effects of increased exposure in the small groups. Greater liking for school might be encouraged by instituting any change that would make the classroom less boring. Gains in performance may not be caused by the interdependent groups themselves but by the increased participation and practice that the students experience. The data could be affected by Hawthorne effects or demand characteristics coming from innovating and testing in the classroom.

No experimentation is perfect or completely rules out alternative interpretations. But while methodological flaws can be discovered in individual studies and alternative explanations might be advanced to account for single findings, we feel that the weight of the evidence points to the legitimacy of our reasoning and research. One should assess our series of experiments as steps in a more comprehensive research strategy, each study attempting to correct flaws or to answer questions raised in the preceding one. For example, the increased liking for groupmates found in the Blaney et al. experiment could be due to mere exposure. But this would not explain the increase in liking for other classmates, and the other small group conditions that were added in the Geffner experiment (and indeed, in the pilot studies) demonstrate that interdependence yields additional benefits compared to the other small-group learning methods. (This finding of increased liking for groupmates relative to other classmates, however, causes us to recommend that when the groups are used over the course of a complete term, their membership should be rotated every few weeks.)

The characteristic increases in self-esteem found to result from jigsaw participation appear to comprise a crucial advantage. It is difficult to trace these gains to sources other than the interdependent groups and the cooperative interactions that they generate in the classroom. Furthermore, our analysis and research on the mechanisms responsible for the jigsaw method's effectiveness indicate that the students' self-esteem might be an important mediating variable, acting as a catalyst to pass along the gains in self-worth to facilitate improved interpersonal liking, attitudes about school, and academic performance.

The research on the jigsaw technique continues. For his Ph.D. dissertation, Gonzalez (1979) tested the method in several high school classes in Watsonville, California. Besides extending the interdependent groups to investigate their effectiveness with an older population of students, Gonzalez also considered three additional factors. He varied the ethnic composition of the jigsaw groups, predicting that they would be more effective as the ratio of majority and minority group members became more balanced. He studied the students' locus of control, as measured by achievement, hypothesizing that participating in the jigsaw groups would promote their perception of control being located internally. He also revised the measure of interethnic and intraethnic perceptions, seeking to explicate Geffner's findings that negative stereotyping is reduced by interdependent learning. Gonzalez's results confirm these hypotheses, with the jigsaw's positive effects most pronounced in those groups where the ethnic composition was most balanced.

Several aspects of the jigsaw method still merit exploration. Among them are its influence on the motivation or cognitive development of the participants and the effect of sex differences. The dynamics of the groups, such as the distribution of power among the members, deserve consideration. An important issue still to be addressed concerns the long-term effects of the jigsaw technique. Systematic longitudinal studies are needed to determine if the advantages found in jigsaw classrooms are maintained over time and whether they generalize to other situations and environments.

The results of our research thus far seem promising. They illustrate how, by utilizing social psychological theory and research, the solution for a social problem might be suggested and advanced. A problem arises, and the psychological literature is consulted and analyzed to design a method to solve it. A program is implemented and its effectivenss is evaluated in the field. Mechanisms assumed to be influencing the process are isolated and brought back into the laboratory to be investigated. Thus the theories continue to be tested and the program becomes increasingly refined.

The first goal of our research strategy was to evaluate the effectiveness of the jigsaw method. We have shown that beneficial effects occur as a result of structuring the social psychological aspects of classroom learning so that children spend at least a portion of their time in pursuit of common goals. These effects are in accordance with predictions made by social scientists 25 years ago in their testimony favoring desegregation, and they confirmed our hypotheses for the jigsaw technique as well.

It is necessary to go beyond the results of measures and the confirmation of hypotheses when evaluating the implementation of a social program. Thus emerged the second goal for our strategy of action research: to perfect the jigsaw technique and encourage its widespread adoption in the schools. Evaluating a social intervention demands the explicit consideration of the impact and side-effects of the program. Its goals must be specified. And whether the program meets its goals in a workable and efficient manner must be determined.

We have described two instances in which the impact of our research and intervention received our scrutiny. On the first occasion, we tried to avoid having an impact, attempting to minimize the disruption caused by our research and adjusting the measures that we employed accordingly. On the second, our replication of the Blaney et al. study was contaminated by our program having too much impact, spreading cooperative learning methods to some of our control classrooms. Our observations and the comments from teachers and students indicated that any side-effects arising from the jigsaw method were positive ones.

The goal of the jigsaw technique is not to train young people to be so cooperative that they will be out of place in a highly competitive society. Rather, the aim is to teach cooperation *as a skill* so that the individual can call on that skill under suitable conditions, when cooperation is the most appropriate way to perform a task. And it is quite clear that some success has been achieved: Children in the experimental classes can and do cooperate under appropriate conditions. Moreover, a year later, when the students have moved on to a classroom in which competition predominates, informal reports from teachers indicate that they perform as well as they ever did.

Apparently they have not lost anything important, only their tendency to compete and try to outdo the other person in situations in which cooperation would be a more reasonable strategy.

Finally, it appears that the jigsaw method is a workable and efficient way to meet that goal and to achieve those advantages previously cited. Its use entails no extra costs. Most teachers like it, and they are easily trained to introduce and facilitate the groups in their classrooms. The jigsaw groups improve the performance of less successful students without hampering high achievers. The technique is flexible and may be used with students of a wide range of ages and to teach material from many subject areas. And the program does not need to replace the existing classroom structure—the benefits we have described result from using the jigsaw groups for only an hour or less each day.

Thus, an aerial photograph of a jigsaw classroom usually would show a familiar configuration, with students seated in rows and being taught in a traditional manner. During one subject, for about an hour, that pattern would change to depict several small circles of students working together and teaching each other. Most important, we have observed that the clusters that appear in the cafeteria or on the playground would also change, to include more students from different ethnic groups.

REFERENCES

ALLPORT, G. (1954) The Nature of Prejudice. Reading, MA: Addison-Wesley.

ARONSON, E., N. BLANEY, J. SIKES, C. STEPHAN, and M. SNAPP (1975) "Busing and racial tension: the jigsaw route to learning and liking." Psychology Today 8: 43-59.

ARONSON, E. and D. BRIDGEMAN (forthcoming) "Jigsaw groups and the desegregated classroom: in pursuit of common goals." Personality and Social Psychology Bulletin.

—————— and R. GEFFNER (1978a) "The effects of a cooperative classroom structure on students' behavior and attitudes." in D. Bar-Tal and L. Saxe (eds.), Social Psychology of Education: Theory and Research. Washington, DC: Hemisphere.

—————— (1978b) "Interdependent interactions and prosocial behavior." Journal of Research and Development in Education 12: 16-27.

—————— C. STEPHAN, J. SIKES, N. BLANEY, AND M. SNAPP (1978) The Jigsaw Class-room. Beverly Hills, CA: Sage Publications.

BLANEY, N.T., C. STEPHAN, D. ROSENFIELD, E. ARONSON, and J. SIKES (1977) "Interdependence in the classroom: a field study." Journal of Educational Psychology 69: 139-146.

BOLEA, A., D. FELKER, and M. BARNES (1971) "A pictorial self-concept scale for children in K-4." Journal of Educational Measurement 8: 223-224.

BREHM, J. (1959) "Increasing cognitive dissonance by a fait-accompli." Journal of Abnormal and Social Psychology 58: 379-382.

BRIDGEMAN, D. (1977) "The influence of cooperative, interdependent learning on role taking and moral reasoning: a theoretical and empirical field study with fifth grade students." Ph.D. dissertation, University of California, Santa Cruz.

CHALUPSKY, A. and G. COLES (1977) "The unfulfilled promise of educational innovation." Presented at the meeting of the American Educational Research Association, New York City.

CHANDLER, M. (1973) "Egocentrism and antisocial behavior: the assessment and training of social perspective-taking skills." Developmental Psychology 9: 326-332.

CLARK, K. (1953) "Desegregation: an appraisal of the evidence." Journal of Social Issues 9(4).

_____ and M. CLARK (1947) "Racial identification and preference in Negro children" in T.M. Newcomb and E.L. Hartley (eds.), Readings in Social Psychology. New York: Holt, Rinehart & Winston.

COHEN, E. and S. ROPER (1972) "Modification of interracial interaction disability: an application of status characteristics theory." American Sociological Review 6: 643-657.

COOPERSMITH, S. and R. FELDMAN (1974) "Fostering a positive self concept and high self-esteem in the classroom" in R.H. Coop and K. White (eds.), Psychological Concepts in the Classroom. New York: Harper & Row.

COVINGTON, M. and R.G. BEERY (1976) Self-Worth and School Learning. New York: Holt, Rinehart & Winston.

DARLEY, J. and E. BERSCHEID (1967) "Increased liking as a result of the anticipation of personal contact." Human Relations 20: 29-40.

DEUTSCH, M. (1949) "An experimental study of the effects of cooperation and competition upon group process." Human Relations 2: 199-231.

DEUTSCHER, M. and I. CHEIN (1948) "The psychological effects of enforced segregation: a survey of social science opinion." Journal of Psychology 26: 259-287.

ELLIOTT, J. (1977) "Personal communication to authors" pp. 598-599 in P.B. Zimbardo and F. Ruch, Psychology and Life. Glenview, IL: Scott, Foresman.

FRANKS, D. and J. MAROLLA (1976) "Efficacious action and social approval as interacting dimensions of self-esteem: a tentative formulation through construct validation." Sociometry 39: 324-341.

GEFFNER, R. (1978) "The effects of interdependent learning on self-esteem, inter-ethnic relations, and intra-ethnic attitudes of elementary school children: a field experiment." Ph.D. dissertation, University of California, Santa Cruz.

GERARD, H. and N. MILLER (1975) School Desegregation: A Long-Term Study. New York: Plenum Press.

GONZALEZ, A. (1979) "Classroom cooperation and ethnic balance." Ph.D. dissertation, University of California, Santa Cruz.

HEIDER, F. (1958) The Psychology of Interpersonal Relations. New York: John Wiley.

JONES, E.E. and K.E. DAVIS (1965) "From acts to dispositions" in L. Berkowitz (ed.), Advances in Experimental Social Psychology (vol. 2). New York: Academic Press.

LUCKER, G., D. ROSENFIELD, J. SIKES, and E. ARONSON (1977) "Performance in the interdependent classroom: a field study." American Educational Research Journal 13: 115-123.

PETTIGREW, T. (1961) "Social psychology and desegregation research." American Psychologist 16: 105-112.

PIAGET, J. (1932) Judgment and Reasoning in the Child. New York: Harcourt Brace Jovanovich.

PURKEY, W. (1970) Self-Concept and School Achievement. Englewood Cliffs, NJ: Prentice-Hall.

ROSENTHAL, R. and L. JACOBSON (1968) Pygmalian in the Classroom. New York: Holt, Rinehart & Winston.

SHERIF, M. (1956) "Experiments in group conflict." Scientific American 195: 53-58.

ST. JOHN, N. (1975) School Desegregation: Outcomes for Children. New York: John Wiley.

STEPHAN, C., J. KENNEDY, and E. ARONSON (1977b) "The effects of friendship and outcome on task attribution." Sociometry 40: 107-111.

————N. PRESSER, J. KENNEDY, and E. ARONSON (1977) "Attributions to success and failure on cooperative, competitive and interdependent interactions." European Journal of Social Psychology 8:269-274.

STEPHAN, W. (1978) "School desegregation: an evaluation of predictions made in Brown vs. the Board of Education. Psychological Bulletin 85: 217-238.

CAMILLE B. WORTMAN
ANTONIA ABBEY
A. ELIZABETH HOLLAND
ROXANE L. SILVER
RONNIE JANOFF-BULMAN

8

TRANSITIONS FROM THE
LABORATORY TO THE FIELD:
Problems and Progress

How do people respond when they are told that they or a loved one has cancer? How does the victim of a serious automobile accident cope with permanent paralysis? The authors of this chapter share a long-standing interest in control and in how people react when they are confronted with outcomes they are unable to alter or influence. In addition to our fascination with the question of how people come to terms with major life crises, we have also been curious about how individuals deal with the more minor annoyances that confront them daily. How do people respond, for example, when they move into a supposedly quiet apartment building and subsequently learn that their neighbor's child is an aspiring drummer for a rock and roll band, or when they rush to get to the airport on time only to learn that their flight has been delayed or cancelled?

In this chapter, we will describe a research program conducted by the first author and her students on reactions to uncontrollable negative outcomes. We will try to illustrate how our thoughts on this topic have changed and developed over the past several years, necessitating a departure from the safe and predictable confines of the laboratory into richer but more chaotic and frustrating real-world settings. This transition has been accompanied by a host of problems and issues for which we were unprepared. Below, we discuss some of these problems and describe our attempted solutions.

AUTHOR'S NOTE: The research reported in this article was supported by National Science Foundation grants SOC 75-14669 and BNS 78-04743 to the first author. We would like to thank Anita Siegel, and the other cancer patients and family members from the Chicago Make Today Count groups, for the special role they have played in shaping this program of research.

INITIAL THINKING ABOUT CONTROL

The first author first began to pursue her interest in reactions to loss of control while a graduate student in psychology at Duke University. This graduate program was traditional in its focus on theory and on laboratory research. However, students were encouraged to pursue their own interests and received support from the faculty in doing so. The first author sought out theoretical frameworks that might help her understand how individuals react to uncontrollable outcomes. At that time, most psychologists were focusing their attention on people's responses to outcomes that they had voluntarily chosen. The most popular theories of the day, such as Festinger's (1957) theory of cognitive dissonance, reflected this concern. However, one of Duke's faculty members had recently developed a theory that seemed relevant to the issue of control. This was Brehm's theory of psychological reactance, which concerns how people respond to restrictions in their personal freedom. According to this model (see Brehm, 1966; Brehm and Sensenig, 1966; Wicklund, 1974), individuals become aroused when their freedom is threatened. This arousal, called reactance, motivates people to try to restore their freedom. According to Brehm an individual is motivated to believe "that he can do what he wants, that he does not have to do what he doesn't want, and that . . . he is the sole director of his own behavior" (1966: 9). The theory predicts that if a person expects to control or influence an outcome and the freedom to do so is threatened, he or she will experience psychological reactance. The stronger the threat and the more important the outcome, the greater the amount of reactance. The theory predicts that individuals will respond to loss of freedom or control with hostile and angry feelings and with enhanced motivation to engage in the threatened behaviors.

In many of the early attempts to test this model, subjects were exposed to others' verbal statements that threatened their freedom (see e.g., Brehm and Sensenig, 1966; Hammock and Brehm, 1966). These studies demonstrated, for example, that if a subject expected a choice between two options and an experimental confederate pressured the subject to select option A, the subject became much more interested in option B. Although such studies provided support for the theory, they did not seem very relevant to the first author's interest in uncontrollable life events. But outcomes such as serious illness, disability, or even air traffic delays can certainly threaten people's freedom to do as they please. Therefore, the first author thought that reactance theory might be pertinent to her interests. When applied to these situations, the theory suggests that people may react to such outcomes with frustration and with enhanced motivation to alter or influence the outcome in question.

Although the first author felt that reactance theory provided an accurate description of some people's reactions to uncontrollable events (including her own), she did not think it told the whole story. While interviewing for a job at the University of Pennsylvania during her third year of graduate school, she encountered another theory quite by accident that seemed relevant to her concerns. In the course of this interview, she met with Seligman and learned for the first time about his theoretical work on learned helplessness.

Seligman and his associates had developed their ideas about learned helplessness while conducting research with animals on Pavlovian fear conditioning. These investigators (e.g., Overmier and Seligman, 1967; Seligman et al., 1968) had found that exposure to uncontrollable aversive stimulation subsequently interferes with the acquisition of escape-avoidance learning. If naive dogs are placed in a two-compartment shuttle-box, they quickly learn to jump from one compartment to the other and thus avoid electric shocks. However, this is not the case for dogs who have previously received uncontrollable electric shocks. These dogs are very slow to learn to avoid or escape the shocks. They seem to give up and passively accept as much shock as the experimenter chooses to give.

On the basis of these studies, Seligman and his associates proposed that exposure to uncontrollable outcomes results in learned helplessness. The organism is said to have learned that its outcomes are not contingent on its responses. According to Seligman, this state is characterized by a motivational deficit and passivity, thereby interfering with subsequent learning that one's behavior can influence one's outcomes (Seligman et al., 1971). Seligman has also suggested that the data from helplessness studies may provide a model of reactive depression. He has maintained that, like learned helplessness, depression may have its roots in feelings of lack of control (Seligman, 1974; Seligman et al., 1976). When the first author visited Penn, Seligman and his associates were just beginning to test some of their ideas on human subjects. Wortman and Seligman were both intrigued by the obvious relevance of theories in social psychology, such as reactance and attribution, to the problems on which Seligman was working.

The first thing that struck the first author about the learned helplessness model is that it seemed to make predictions about reactions to loss of control that were quite different from those of reactance theory. She sought out Jack Brehm as soon as she returned from Pennsylvania, and together they read Seligman's articles and studied his theory more closely. The more they read, the more they became intrigued by the apparent inconsistencies between the two models. According to reactance theory, exposure to loss of control will result in feelings of hostility and anger; the learned helplessness model predicts that organisms who are exposed to uncontrollable outcomes will become passive and depressed. Reactance theory predicts that people will react to threatened loss of control with enhanced motivation to influence or attain the outcome; the learned helplessness model predicts that exposure to loss of control will result in a motivational deficit and in impairments in active problem solving.

Some equally puzzling inconsistencies began to emerge in the experimental literature as investigators began testing Seligman's notions with human subjects (see Miller and Norman, 1979; Roth, forthcoming; Wortman and Brehm, 1975, for reviews). While some of the experiments have suggested that exposure to uncontrollable outcomes results in performance decrements, others have found precisely the opposite: That subjects pretreated with uncontrollable stressors actually perform better in a subsequent testing session. Clearly, there is no way that either the reactance model or the learned helplessness model alone could account for this diverse pattern of findings.

AN INTEGRATIVE MODEL

Although the first author left Duke to take a job at Northwestern University that year, she and Brehm continued to explore these issues. They felt that in order to understand these varied reactions to uncontrollable outcomes, they could not continue to focus on loss of control per se. Instead, they believed that it was imperative to consider the meaning that this loss was likely to have for the subject involved. They attempted to identify a number of factors that might influence or determine the meaning of the uncontrollable outcome. Drawing from reactance theory, they hypothesized that such factors as whether people expected to control or influence the outcome in question, whether the outcome was important to them, and how long they had unsuccessfully attempted to gain control over the outcome might determine their reaction to that outcome. Perhaps because they were working primarily with animals, early helplessness researchers had not given much attention to these and other more cognitive variables.

Using these theoretical constructs, the first author and Brehm attempted to integrate the reactance and helplessness models into a single theoretical statement (Wortman and Brehm, 1975). They suggested that if a person expects to be able to control an outcome and if this outcome is important, then psychological reactance should be aroused when one discovers that he or she cannot influence the outcome. Initially, individuals should experience hostility, anger, and increased motivation to exert control over the outcome in question. But individuals may learn through repeated exposure to the situation that control is not possible, and their expectations of control may diminish over time. The stronger the expectation of control over the outcome, the longer it should take people to become convinced that they cannot control the outcome, and the more controlling behavior or persistence they should show before giving up. Once they realize the outcome is uncontrollable, repeated exposure to it will result in lowered motivation, passivity, and depression. The more important the outcome, the more intense the reactance or helplessness effects will be.

This model predicts that for individuals who initially expect control, a period of heightened activity will precede helplessness effects. However, individuals who do not expect to control the outcome in question should not go through this invigoration phase, and should become helpless relatively quickly when exposed to an uncontrollable outcome. Studies that have manipulated the relevant theoretical variables (e.g., Baum et al., 1978; Roth and Kubal 1975) have provided reasonably good support for this model (see Wortman and Brehm, 1975, and Wortman and Silver forthcoming, for reviews).

BROADENING THE MODEL

In addition to the factors spelled out in the formal model, Wortman and Brehm discussed some additional variables that they thought might influence reactions to uncontrollable outcomes. They felt that people's responses might be affected by such considerations as whether the outcome was common to a lot of people (e.g., inflation, gasoline shortages) or unique to the individual in question, whether it was regarded as deserved or undeserved (cf. Lerner, forthcoming), and whether the inability to influence the outcome was attributed to one's personal inadequacies or to situational factors. While they were not confident enough about how these variables affected reactions to uncontrollable outcomes to incorporate them into their formal model, they argued that more research attention should be devoted to these issues (see Wortman and Brehm, 1975).

Combining an interest in attributions (cf. Wortman et al., 1973) with her thoughts about control, the first author and her students designed a study to examine the role of attributions in predicting reactions to uncontrollable outcomes (Wortman et al., 1976). When people are confronted with an uncontrollable outcome, there are several different attributions of causality that they might make for their inability to influence, avoid, or cope with the outcome to their satisfaction. People can blame the environment, themselves, others, circumstances, or fate (see, e.g., Jones et al., 1972; Weiner et al., 1972) for their failure to exert control. How do the attributions they make influence their affective state and future performance?

As a first step toward answering this question, they conducted a laboratory experiment designed to assess the relationship between subjects' attributions of causality for their inability to influence an outcome and the amount of stress and helplessness they experience. The experiment employed the traditional paradigm for human helplessness experiments. Subjects were randomly assigned to one of four groups. In three of these groups, the subjects were led to believe that they had no control over the outcome (aversive noise bursts) and were led to attribute this lack of control to (1) their own lack of ability, (2) the situation, or (3) were given no information about causality. In the fourth group, subjects were led to believe that they had controlled the outcome and were given no information about the locus of causality. Dependent variables included measures of self-reported stress, performance on a problem-solving task administered in the same situation, and performance on a task administered in a different setting and presented as a completely different experiment.

The results of this experiment revealed that subjects' attributions of causality for their inability to influence the noise bursts had a strong effect on their subjective feelings of distress and on their subsequent problem-solving ability. Subjects who attributed their failure to their own incompetence reported considerably more stress than subjects who made situational attributions. In fact, the latter subjects experienced no more stress than subjects who believed they were successful in controlling the aversive stimulation. Surprisingly, subjects whose attributions for performance led them to feel personally incompetent performed significantly better than the remaining subjects on both the problems administered in the same situation and on problems administered in a new and different situation.

The authors were intrigued by the finding that subjects who blamed themselves for their inability to exert control performed better in subsequent situations than those who blamed the situation. This study provided tentative evidence that attributions can mediate responses to uncontrollable outcomes and that they are deserving of further attention. However, the study raised more questions than it answered. For example, how would self-attributions for loss of control affect subjective distress and subsequent performance if the uncontrollable outcomes were of longer duration or greater importance?

Other studies have also explored the role of attributions in learned helplessness (e.g., Diener and Dweck, 1978; Hanusa and Schulz, 1977). Interestingly, Seligman and his associates have come to believe that attributions of causality may be important mediators of the helplessness effect. In a major reformulation of the original model, Abramson et al. (1978) argued that the type of attributions made for an uncontrollable outcome will influence the nature of the person's deficit, as well as how far it will generalize and how long it will last. For example, a person who attributes failure on the Graduate Record Examination to a factor that occurs across many situations (e.g. "I'm stupid") should show subsequent deficits in more settings than a person who attributes failure to a more specific factor (e.g. "I was ill on the day of the test"). This analysis addresses many of the shortcomings of the original model, which provided no means of predicting the generalizability or the duration of the deficits. But because the authors fail to specify the conditions under which particular types of attributions will be made, it can be argued that their model is circular and lacks predictive power (Wortman and Dintzer, 1978). Nonetheless, we support this focus on cognitive factors and are hopeful that it will have a positive impact on subsequent helplessness research (Dweck and Wortman, forthcoming).

LIMITATIONS OF THE LABORATORY PARADIGM

Although we were excited by the implications of our own and others' studies on helplessness, the shortcomings of the laboratory approach were becoming increasingly apparent. These problems fall into two major categories: (1) limited external validity or generalizability and (2) ethical concerns.

EXTERNAL VALIDITY

A major problem with studying reactions to uncontrollable outcomes in the laboratory is that investigators are constrained to examine reactions to relatively minor outcomes that occur for relatively short durations. Most researchers studying reactions to loss of control have utilized outcomes such as electric shocks or noise bursts (e.g., Glass and Singer, 1972; Roth and Bootzin, 1974), losing an experimental credit (Apsler and Friedman, 1975), eating an insect (e.g., Comer and Laird, 1975; Foxman and Radtke, 1970), or failing on a problem-solving task (e.g., Roth and Kubal, 1975). While the data from such studies may be useful in determining how subjects react to mild stressors, it is not clear whether these results would generalize to more serious outcomes. Moreover, most investigators have exposed subjects to these outcomes for a relatively short period of time, in large part because of the ethical implications of longer exposure. Even when the outcome is as mild as failure on a problem-solving task, exposure over a period of days without debriefing would raise serious ethical questions. The inability to examine subjects' reactions to an outcome over time makes it difficult to test predictions from Wortman and Brehm (1975) and other models that specifically predict a time course (e.g., Klinger, 1977). Furthermore, some of the most interesting methods of coping with uncontrollable stress, such as changes in one's self-concept or the development of psychosomatic illness, may develop over a long period of time (cf. Lazarus and Launier, 1978).

External validity is also threatened because there are unique features of a laboratory setting that differentiate it from the situation encountered outside of the laboratory. Some of these features stem from human subjects' guidelines, which require that subjects be forewarned of the stressor and freely consent to participate. In the Comer and Laird experiment, for example, subjects were led to believe that they would be required to eat a worm, but were informed that they were "free to refuse or to terminate participating at any time in the study if, for any reason, you find it difficult to participate" (1975: 95). In noise or shock experiments, subjects are typically exposed to a sample burst of the noise or shock and asked whether they would be willing to continue with the study. Research within the dissonance and self-perception literatures (see, e.g., Abelson et al., 1968; Brehm and Cohen, 1962) has clearly demonstrated the effect of choice on subsequent attitudes and behavior. Certainly an awesome feature of most uncontrollable life events is that they often occur without forewarning and are not freely chosen. The psychological processes that affect an individual's reaction to an implicitly chosen outcome may be completely different from those which occur when the outcome has been purely involuntary.

As Bulman and Wortman (1977) have noted, another unique feature of most laboratory experiments is that subjects are generally provided with a rational explanation for any discomfort that they are asked to endure. For example, subjects may be told that the investigator is interested in learning more about how people react to urban stress, and that he or she is attempting to simulate such stress in the laboratory. In fact, there are data to suggest that the availability of a rational explanation for an outcome may influence the coping process (Wortman and Silver, forthcoming). Such a rational explanation is rarely present in many of the uncontrollable outcomes (e.g., rape, life-threatening illness) that occur outside the laboratory.

Finally, the unique relationship between the experimenter and the subject, as well as the experimenter's position of authority, may artificially constrain the subject's behavioral responses to any stressors encountered in the laboratory. Despite their rights as subjects, individuals may be reluctant to engage in such coping mechanisms as challenging the experimenter or leaving the experiment. In most settings outside the laboratory, people are free to choose among a larger variety of reactions to distress.

ETHICAL CONCERNS

There are certainly good theoretical and methodological reasons for subjecting participants to uncontrollable outcomes of some importance. Increasing the importance of the stressor would help to address the issues of external validity raised above. Manipulating importance would enable us to test predictions derived from the Wortman and Brehm (1975) model. For ethical reasons, however, enhancing the importance of the outcomes studied is obviously not a solution to the problem. In fact, researchers struggling with this problem are left with an unappealing choice. If they utilize outcomes that are relatively unimportant, they are likely to produce findings that are ultimately trivial; if they expose subjects to aversive outcomes of real significance, the research may well be unethical.

The ethical problems encountered with this type of research were highlighted for us by the Wortman et al. (1976) study described earlier. In this experiment, the stressors were relatively mild—subjects were induced to fail on a few trials of a problem-solving task that had no special significance and were consequently exposed to some moderately loud noise bursts. One of the authors (Lisa Shusterman) who had been trained in clinical psychology handled the debriefing and devoted considerable skill and effort to making subjects feel positively about their participation in the study. Despite our precautions, the situation created more distress for our participants, and hence for our experimenters, than we would have preferred. This was especially true in the condition in which subjects were induced to attribute their performance to their own personal incompetence. In this study, personal attributions for failure were associated with considerable distress, but resulted in improved performance on a subsequent task. For theoretical reasons it would have been interesting to follow up this research. Would subjects continue to show facilitated performance if they were induced to attribute a larger number of failures, or failure on more significant tasks, to their own incompetence? Because of all the problems that we have outlined above, however, we felt that it would not be appropriate to conduct such a study.

A MOVE TO NATURAL SETTINGS

We still have a great deal of respect for laboratory methodology and feel that the laboratory is a highly appropriate setting to answer a wide variety of questions. For example, Glass and his associates (e.g., Glass, 1977; Glass et al., 1974) are currently involved in an exciting program of laboratory research on Type A, or coronary-prone behavior. Building on the pioneering studies by Glass and Singer (1972), these investigators are attempting to identify the characteristics of performance settings (e.g., time pressure) that can exacerbate the Type A's difficulties. Specifying the conditions under which Type A individuals are especially likely to hide their fatigue and continue with a strenuous task, or to show physiological responses that can be damaging, has obvious theoretical as well as practical significance. Similarly, laboratory experiments by Dweck and her associates (e.g., Diener and Dweck, 1978) have helped to identify the pattern of cognitions that differentiate children who become helpless in the face of failure from those who respond more adaptively. Such research not only sheds light on the antecedents of helpless behavior but also provides a sound basis for designing interventions that may alleviate maladaptive responses (see Dweck and Wortman, forthcoming).

The question of how others react to victims of uncontrollable life events (Coates, et al., 1979; Kleck, 1968) is also amenable to laboratory investigation, and we are currently carrying out a program of research in this area. But for all of the reasons outlined above, we do not believe that the laboratory is an appropriate setting to examine individuals' reactions to the significant negative life events that may befall them. Therefore, we felt that it was necessary to broaden our research program by moving into more natural settings. This shift from the laboratory to the real world was facilitated by the general climate at Northwestern, where the first author's colleagues Donald Campbell and Thomas Cook had been working in field and evaluation research long before these areas were popular.

Wortman had her first exposure to Northwestern's unique atmosphere during her first quarter on campus. She was asked to discuss one of her research projects at a weekly "sack lunch" at which faculty and students informally present and exchange ideas. She decided to describe a laboratory study she had planned at Duke to determine how responsibility is assigned for an accident. In order to discriminate among several theoretical frameworks (e.g., Lerner, 1965, 1970; Shaver, 1970; Walster, 1966), she was planning to stage an accident in the laboratory, vary the nature and severity of the consequences, and examine the victim's and the perpetrator's attributions of responsibility. The students listened politely to the description of this study, but seemed puzzled that anyone would want to do such an experiment. Finally, one of them said, "If you are interested in how people react to accidents, why don't you just go interview some people who have been involved in accidents?" At the time, the first author was quite annoyed with this response, since she felt that the advantages of the experimental method should be obvious to anyone. A few years later, however, she found herself doing exactly what the student had recommended.

The graduate students at Northwestern again exerted a positive influence to move these ideas outside the laboratory while they were enrolled in the first author's graduate seminar on stress. Although the seminar critically examined a large number of laboratory studies on stress, the students did not find these studies to be very helpful in understanding how people cope with more serious life problems. They felt it would be more illuminating to speak with people who were dealing with stress in their own lives and they encouraged the first author to invite some guests for a class discussion. Since the first author had always felt that coping with a life-threatening illness would be particularly difficult, she called the director of the local chapter of the American Cancer Society to ask whether there were any cancer patients available who might be willing to share their experiences with some psychologists. The director was quite enthusiastic and mentioned that she knew some patients who would love to say a thing or two to psychologists. She graciously arranged for four patients to attend the class the following week. In making the arrangements for this seminar, we got our first exposure to some of the barriers and problems that cancer patients typically encounter. We made plans to hold the class in a special seminar room so that the participants would be as comfortable as possible. Some faculty members from another department strongly objected to our plans, stating that since cancer is contagious, they did not want any cancer patients using the seminar room or the other facilities (cf. Wortman and Dunkel-Schetter, 1979).

The class was exciting and stimulating for all of us. The guests were willing to share their experiences from the time of diagnosis to the present and to describe the difficulties and problems they had encountered. Afterward, we began to explore how some of the variables that Wortman and Brehm had proposed would influence reactions to life-threatening illness. We were intrigued, for example, about whether these individuals typically go through an invigoration/anger—depression/passivity sequence, as Wortman and Brehm (1975) had suggested. We were also interested in such questions as whether people who feel responsible for their illness cope better or worse than those who attribute responsibility to other factors such as their environment, chance, or fate. On addressing these theoretical issues, we were struck by the richness and complexity of these patients' reactions. Our laboratory experiments, and the theories that were based on them, did not begin to capture, predict, or explain their concerns or their varied and multifaceted reactions to what was happening to them.

Our experience with these cancer patients, in combination with our growing disillusionment with laboratory studies on helplessness, encouraged us to broaden our research focus by studying people who had been victimized by uncontrollable life events. Since that time, we have attempted to familiarize ourselves with the literature on reactions to uncontrollable life events, have sought practical and clinical experience in dealing with individuals who have been exposed to serious problems, and have conducted a pilot study to assess the reactions of severe spinal-cord-injured patients to permanent paralysis.

REVIEW OF LITERATURE

During the past several years, we have examined the literature on reactions to a number of uncontrollable aversive outcomes including life-threatening illness, accidents, separation, death of a loved one, and rape (Wortman and Silver, forthcoming). Although social psychologists have devoted little attention to these problems (for notable exceptions, however, see Langer and Rodin, 1976; Schulz, 1976; Taylor and Levin, 1977), they have frequently been addressed by physicians, nurses, psychiatrists, clinical psychologists, social workers, and by patients and victims themselves. The majority of published reports in these areas consist of personal accounts, case studies, or general impressions from clinical practice, although more methodologically sophisticated studies are beginning to appear with increasing frequency. Moreover, it has been rare for investigators to apply theoretical notions to these problems and test them in a programmatic fashion.

In reviewing this literature, we were especially interested in locating studies that assessed variables we had identified as theoretically important, such as expectations of control and attributions of causality. These factors have received almost no consideration from investigators studying uncontrollable life events. There are also few methodologically rigorous studies that have assessed changes in people's reactions to uncontrollable events over time (see Wortman and Silver, forthcoming, for a more detailed discussion of this literature). Nonetheless, the articles, case studies, and personal accounts we examined were invaluable in suggesting hypotheses, variables, or processes that may be important. One article that influenced us was written by Harker (1972), a nurse who had cancer. Her eloquent portrayal of the communication problems that cancer patients encounter encouraged us to examine these problems more carefully. Similarly, we found Gullo et al.'s (1974) presentation of case history material for cancer patients, and portrayal of the "stages" they went through to be very useful. A number of the patients in this study attempted to influence their disease by "bargaining" with God. They promised to change their lifestyle and to make various improvements if they were granted more time. Since we are especially interested in patients' attempts to influence their outcomes, this article suggested some new avenues for exploration.

PRACTICAL AND CLINICAL EXPERIENCE IN DEALING WITH VICTIMIZED POPULATIONS

Over the past few years, each of the members of our research team has made an effort to learn more about the coping process by working directly with people who have encountered aversive life events. The first author has been working primarily with cancer patients. This occurred as a result of her experience in the graduate seminar described earlier. During the class, guests were asked what had been most helpful to them in dealing effectively with their illness. Interestingly, these patients viewed professionals as "irrelevant at best" in meeting their support needs. Without exception, each guest indicated that their interactions with other cancer patients had been their most important source of emotional support. The first author found this intriguing and approached one of the guests after class to inquire further about the value of peer support. She was invited to attend a local peer support group for cancer patients and their family members affiliated with a national organization called Make Today Count. The major purpose of these groups is to provide an opportunity for cancer patients and their family members to communicate openly and honestly about the problems encountered in living with cancer. The group discussion is facilitated by a professional person who volunteers his or her time.

The first author was highly skeptical of the value of these groups when she arrived the first night. About 15 cancer patients and their family members were present. One woman of about 35 years of age was attending the group for the first time and was obviously very distraught. She had recently been diagnosed with uterine cancer and was waiting for surgery to be scheduled. During the course of the evening, the group attempted to support her by sharing their experiences and feelings (e.g., "Waiting for surgery is the worst time of all, because you don't know what to expect."). The first author was struck by the group's effectiveness in alleviating this woman's distress and began attending the group on a regular basis. After working with cancer patients under the supervision of personnel from a local hospital for some time, she was asked by a group of patients to begin a second group. She has been serving as a facilitator since that time.

The first author's students have also taken the opportunity to work more closely with various victim populations. For example, Elizabeth Holland has received training for Parental Stress Services' hotline, and has served as a volunteer counselor for abusive parents and their children. Holland, Antonia Abbey, and Ronnie Janoff-Bulman have also become involved with rape crisis programs in Chicago and Boston and have received training to counsel rape victims. Roxane Silver has been working for the past several years with social workers, counselors, and other professionals from the Rehabilitation Institute of Chicago, a nationally renowned center for the treatment of spinal cord injuries. She has also been meeting regularly with parents who have lost a child to the Sudden Infant Death Syndrome.

These experiences have had a major impact on us and on our work. One benefit of this experience is that it has enriched our perspective on the issues that concern us. Our clinical work has forced us to think more precisely about the theoretical constructs of interest to us. For example, when one attempts to apply a term such as "loss of control" to rape victims or spinal-cord-injured patients, some questions arise. What kind of control is important? Control in the sense of causing the outcome, in the sense of altering the consequences that have accrued, or in the sense of preventing future occurrences?

Our clinical work has also helped us to identify additional theoretical variables that may be important in understanding reactions to uncontrollable negative life events. One such variable, for example, is the social support available to the individual. In the cancer patients groups described earlier, we have been struck by the frequency with which patients appear to be troubled by interpersonal problems. Patients have repeatedly recounted incidents about spouses who withhold affection, children who become hostile and demanding, friends who avoid them, and doctors and nurses who are completely lacking in compassion. These comments have been so compelling and have occurred so often that we simply could not ignore them. As a result of this experience, we have made perceived support an important focus of our subsequent research. We have also been working to formulate new theories that center around the dissolution of the support network (see, e.g., Coates and Wortman, 1980; Wortman and Dunkel-Schetter, 1979).

A third consequence of this clinical experience is that it has stimulated our professional interest in the stresses and rewards of the helping role. Coping with the frustrations inherent in helping people with overwhelming and difficult problems may be comparable, in some ways, to coping with other types of uncontrollable life events. Holland is currently planning a theory-based, longitudinal study among hotline volunteers to examine this possibility.

In short, we have found this clinical work to be invaluable in shaping our subsequent theoretical thinking and research. One thing that we were relatively unprepared for, however, was the impact of this work on the rest of our lives. Speaking to a distraught rape victim who is afraid to walk to the local grocery store in shorts because she might provoke another attack or listening to a young quadraplegic in a Stryker frame recount his plans to play professional football may provide a great deal of insight into the psychological processes involved. However, such experiences have forced us to realize that outcomes such as permanent paralysis or life-threatening illness can happen to anyone at any time, and this realization has been accompanied by a great deal of anxiety and distress. Especially at the initial stages of our work, each of us was in a perpetual state of concern that disaster might strike us at any moment. The most minor ache was regarded as evidence of bone cancer, if not multiple sclerosis. If one of us spotted an oncoming car or truck, we expected the worst and prepared for impact; if a man approached us at any time, for any reason, we saw him as a potential rapist. Interestingly, we have since learned that patients and victims themselves share many of these same fears.

Another problem that some of us have encountered, especially at the initial stages of our clinical work, concerns the impact of these experiences on our interpersonal relationships. As a result of working with people who have extremely serious problems, it is sometimes difficult to muster much sympathy when friends or spouses confront us with their relatively insignificant problems. After spending several hours with cancer patients or permanently paralyzed individuals, for example, it is not easy to be sympathetic when a colleague complains that her office is too small or a friend is upset because her coworkers have been annoying her.

Of course, our experience with these victim populations has had many positive effects on our lives as well. Over time, our training and experience have provided insights about the helping role that have been beneficial. When we first began this work, we shared a common misconception (see Coates, et al., 1979): When someone discussed a personal problem with us, we felt responsible to find a solution. Needless to say, this created a great deal of distress. When a cancer patient tells you that the prognosis is poor, she is in constant pain, her finances are in chaos, her husband is having anxiety attacks, and her children are "acting out" at school, what can you possibly say? We are slowly beginning to realize that others are often most in need of an attentive listener, not answers or advice for their problem. This recognition has helped us to feel more comfortable with the helper role in our personal lives as well as our clinical work.

Another positive consequence of this kind of work is that it inevitably causes one to think about priorities and the use of time. The heightened awareness that tragedy could befall us or our loved ones at any time, for example, seems to enhance the value of one's interpersonal relationships. It also forces one to realize that it is not the end of the world if a manuscript is rejected, and it is only a minor disaster if a grant is not funded.

In short, the psychological impact of this kind of work can be substantial.

We strongly believe that social psychologists who become involved with clinical populations should be prepared for this impact. Perhaps more important, they should attempt to structure opportunities to discuss their feelings about these experiences and to share their coping strategies with others (cf. Maslach, 1976).

PILOT WORK

Examination of the literature revealed a clear need for methodologically sophisticated studies of reactions to uncontrollable outcomes which examine the relationship between subjects' attributions of causality for these outcomes and their ability to cope effectively with them. Bulman and Wortman (1977) conducted a pilot study that was designed to focus on this concern. Respondents were young men and women who had been involved in sudden, traumatic accidents (e.g., shooting, fall, automobile accident, or injury during work or while engaging in sports such as diving, hang-gliding, or football) that resulted in paraplegia or quadriplegia. Subjects were asked how much blame they assigned for their accident to themselves, others, the environment, or chance and whether they perceived the accident to be avoidable. A measure of how well each participant was coping with his or her disability was obtained by eliciting a rating from his or her social worker and nurse. Respondents were identified as coping well if they had accepted the reality of their injury and were attempting to deal positively with their paralysis (e.g., working toward improvement of their physical abilities, attending physical therapy, and so on). Patients were considered to be coping poorly if they denied the extent of their injuries despite clear medical evidence to the contrary, if they expected to get better miraculously, or if they showed little or no interest in attending physical therapy sessions and improving their physical condition.

Three factors emerged as the best predictors of coping: the attribution of blame to others, the perceived avoidability of the accident, and the degree of self-blame. The more victims blamed another or the more they believed they could have avoided the accident, the worse they coped. The more they blamed themselves, however, the better they coped with their paralysis. In trying to decide whether they could have avoided the accident, many patients appeared to consider whether the activity they were engaging in was common or unusual for them. If the activity was a common one, that they participated in frequently (e.g., swimming, diving, or outdoor activity), they tended to view the accident as unavoidable. If the activity was unusual—something they normally did not do—they were more likely to see the accident as avoidable. In deciding whether they were to blame for the accident, many respondents seemed to be influenced by whether or not they were alone at the time of the accident and whether they voluntarily chose the activity that they were participating in because it was something they enjoyed. Thus, the findings suggested that individuals victimized while voluntarily engaging in leisure activities may cope most successfully.

OUR CURRENT RESEARCH FOCUS

On the basis of the review of the literature on reactions to life crises, our clinical work with victimized populations, and the pilot study by Bulman and Wortman (1977), it became clear that in the future, our research program should involve further testing of the theoretical model in applied settings; as well as an extension of the theoretical model by considering the role of variables not included in the original analysis.

FURTHER TESTING OF THE CURRENT THEORETICAL MODEL

Since a review of the literature revealed few methodologically sophisticated studies that permitted an examination of victims' responses to serious life events over time, it became clear to us that only through a longitudinal approach would it be possible to ascertain whether victims go through an invigoration/anger-depression/passivity cycle, as Wortman and Brehm (1975) have suggested. Of course, a longitudinal approach does not permit the clean manipulation of variables such as expectation and importance that is possible in a laboratory study (cf. Roth and Kubal, 1975). However, we felt that a careful measurement of subjects' expectations of control, assessments of importance of the outcome, and emotional reactions to the outcome would make it possible to explore the relationships among these variables. Also a longitudinal approach would enable us to investigate how expectations of control and perceived importance change over time and to examine whether people who initially expect control show a different sequence of emotional reactions than those who do not.

EXTENDING THE THEORETICAL MODEL

The original model Wortman and Brehm (1975) developed identified only three variables that might be important in understanding reactions to uncontrollable outcomes: expectations of control, affective responses (invigoration/anger and/or passivity/depression), and judged importance of the outcome. Our review of the literature, clinical experience, and the pilot study have suggested several new variables that may influence reactions to uncontrollable life events. The additional factors that have emerged are discussed below.

ATTRIBUTIONS OF CAUSALITY

Wortman and Brehm (1975) and Wortman (1976) speculated that people's attributions of causality for uncontrollable outcomes might affect their ability to cope and adjust to such outcomes, and this speculation was borne out in the pilot study which revealed a significant relationship between self-blame and coping. However, the questions measuring subjects' attributions in the pilot study were rather limited in scope. It became apparent that any future research should assess these concepts more carefully, perhaps distinguishing among attributions of causality, judgments of foreseeability, and assignment of fault or blame. In fact, different types of self-blaming responses may have different implications for adjustment. Janoff-Bulman (1979) has recently suggested that there are two types of self-blame. One involves attributions to one's behaviors (e.g., "If I had not been walking late at night, I would not have been raped.); another concerns attributions to one's character or personality (e.g., "If I weren't such a gullible, stupid person with such poor judgment, I would not have been raped."). Janoff-Bulman (1979) has found that behavioral self-blame is more common among rape victims than characterological self-blame and has speculated that it may also be more adaptive, since it provides the woman with feelings of control over her future outcomes (cf. Wortman, 1976).

ABILITY TO FIND MEANING IN THE EXPERIENCE

Many times in our clinical work, we have noted that victims of uncontrollable life events seem to have a powerful motivation to find meaning or make sense of what has happened to them. The pilot study also suggested that the participants were concerned with meaning. (See Bulman and Wortman, 1977, for a further discussion of this issue.) Although the need for meaning has sometimes been mentioned by individuals studying reactions to life stresses (see, e.g., Frankl, 1963), this concept has received relatively little attention from social psychologists. We plan to examine whether individuals who are able to find some meaning in the outcome cope better than individuals who are not. We also hope to determine whether different types of explanations for uncontrollable life events are more adaptive or functional than others. Will a person who views permanent paralysis as a punishment for past misdeeds, for example, cope differently than a person who views his paralysis as a challenge that will help him to grow and develop as a person? (See Lipowski, 1970, and Wortman and Silver, forthcoming, for a more detailed discussion of the issue.)

EXPECTATIONS ABOUT THE OUTCOME

Although Wortman and Brehm (1975) argued that the expectation of control over an outcome is an important determinant of one's response, they did not consider the possible role played by the expectations about the outcome itself. Our clinical experience with various victimized populations has suggested, however, that this variable may be quite important. For example, if a cancer patient expects to live no more than six months, how will the patient or his or her family cope if he or she is bedridden but lives much longer? In contrast, how do spinal-cord-injured patients who maintain that they will walk again despite clear medical evidence to the contrary cope with permanent paralysis compared to those patients who accept their doctors' prognoses? Some studies have suggested that individuals who have accurate expectations about a stressor cope better with that stressor than individuals with unrealistic expectations (e.g. Janis, 1958). Few investigators, however, have systematically questioned respondents about their expectations regarding an undesirable life event and related these to indices of effective coping (see Wortman and Silver, forthcoming, for a review).

COPING STRATEGIES

In our clinical work, we have been struck by the diversity of coping strategies used by people in attempts to minimize their distress. Some individuals seek as much information about their problem as possible; others actively avoid it and distort any information they are given. Some are eager to discuss their problems and feelings; others are not. Some people make a conscious effort to keep themselves busy and try not to dwell on their problems; others turn to alcohol or drugs or spend a great deal of time daydreaming, fantasizing, or pretending that they are well.

This topic has generated a great deal of interest over the past several years (Lazarus and Launier, 1978; Lazarus et al., forthcoming; Lipowski, 1970). In fact, recent research with cancer patients (Penman, 1979; Weisman and Worden, 1976) suggests that certain coping strategies may be more effective than others in minimizing emotional upset as long as four months after diagnosis. We therefore feel that a systematic examination of the relationship among such strategies and long-term psychosocial adjustment is crucial to a complete understanding of the coping process following a negative life event.

INTERPERSONAL RELATIONSHIPS

As noted earlier, perhaps the strongest impression we have obtained from our clinical experience with victims concerns the serious problems they face because of the derogation, blame, and avoidance they receive from others.

As we have detailed elsewhere (cf. Coates et al., 1979; Coates and Wortman, forthcoming; Wortman and Dunkel-Schetter, 1979), we believe this topic to be one of extreme importance and have chosen to investigate it carefully in our current research program.

OVERVIEW OF THE RESEARCH PROGRAM

Over the last few years we have designed a number of longitudinal studies to investigate how individuals react to uncontrollable negative life events and how these reactions change over time. The largest project currently underway is an extension of the Bulman and Wortman pilot study.[1] Its major purpose is to identify the predictors of successful coping among severely spinal-cord-injured patients. This longitudinal study involves a large sample of spinal-cord-injured persons and their family members at several points in time. Systematic interviews are being conducted from the first week after the accident through acute care hospitalization, rehabilitation, and their return home. Hopefully, our data will shed light on the relationships among the variables discussed in the preceding section and will clarify the ways in which these variables affect the patient's adjustment to permanent paralysis. In assessing coping, we are obtaining medical status data, physical therapy and occupational therapy attendance and progress over time, as well as ratings of each patient from social workers, nurses, physical and occupational therapists, and interviewers. In addition, we are collecting information about the resumption of social and vocational activities after the return home. These data will enable us to explore the relationship between patients' psychological reactions to sudden, traumatic injury at several points in time and their ability to deal effectively with the disability.

Of course, uncontrollable life events differ in the problems in adjustment they pose for the victim. Victims of violent crimes may suffer no permanent physical harm from the incident; spinal-cord-injured patients must learn to deal with permanent limitations. Similarly, victimizations that are obvious to others (e.g., spinal cord injury, amputations) pose different problems in adjustment than those that may be hidden (cancer, rape). Theoretical variables that predict successful coping in one setting may not be effective in predicting adjustment to a second kind of victimization. For example, feelings of self-blame may be adaptive for the spinal cord injured, since successful rehabilitation involves active and vigorous efforts and cooperation from the patient. By actively participating in the rehabilitation program, patients can improve their skills and greatly increase the number of activities accessible to them. In contrast, such feelings might be quite maladaptive for parents who have lost a child to the Sudden Infant Death Syndrome, since there is no action that they can take to alter or improve their situation vis-à-vis the child.

For these reasons, our current research program also includes two additional investigations of more limited scope. These projects focus on different kinds of victimized populations, each of which is theoretically interesting in its own right. Unlike spinal cord injury, for example, future avoidability is an important issue in coping with rape. Therefore, we are conducting a yearlong study of rape victims. The key variables in this study are the attributions of responsibility that the victim makes for the attack, her perceptions concerning whether she can avoid recurrence, and her ability to obtain social support. We plan to examine how these variables affect subsequent adjustment and recovery.

Because the medical cause of Sudden Infant Death Syndrome has not yet been identified, self-blame and guilt are reported to be quite common among parents following the death of their baby (Stitt, 1971). Moreover, there is reason to believe that the attributions of blame, combined with the distress from the death itself, can have deleterious effects on the marital relationship (e.g., Cornwell et al., 1977). For this reason, we are planning a longitudinal investigation of 50 couples who have lost an infant to this syndrome.

METHODOLOGICAL ISSUES AND PROBLEMS

In moving from the laboratory to the field, we soon realized that while we had an adequate theoretical and conceptual understanding of the issues, we were ill-equipped to handle the plethora of methodological and practical issues confronting us. We had little training or experience with such issues as gaining access to victimized populations, motivating them to participate in research, or conducting interviews with them. Accustomed to the control which investigators have in the laboratory, we were ill-prepared for the relative chaos that exists in the field. Moreover, there were few books or articles available to guide us in dealing with these issues. In order to obtain information about these problems, we have contacted other researchers who are conducting field studies and who have encountered similar problems. For the most part, however, we have learned about these issues by plunging in and attempting to do the research. We have made our share of mistakes in this process, but these have been instructive.

It quickly became apparent that the success of our projects hinged on developing satisfactory relationships with three categories of people: (1) the host agency or organization from which we plan to access respondents, (2) the individuals who actually collect the data for the project, and (3) the respondents who provide the data for the study. Below, we will share some of the highlights of our experience in each of these areas. This information is not meant to be all-inclusive or comprehensive, but simply to provide some preliminary ideas about problems that might be encountered and how they might be resolved.

ESTABLISHING A RELATIONSHIP WITH THE COOPERATING AGENCY

While in some field research respondents can be approached directly, it is usually necessary to work through an agency or organization which has access to potential respondents. In our work, for example, we have had to establish contact with the Rehabilitation Institute of Chicago, the Rape Victim Advocate program, the National Sudden Infant Death Syndrome Foundation, and some local medical centers. Establishing a good relationship with the host agency not only provides access to appropriate respondents but also helps insure that the project will be carried out smoothly and efficiently. If a sound relationship is to be established, researchers must first identify and approach the appropriate contact person within the organization and then lay careful groundwork so that the project is endorsed and supported for its duration. Each of these issues is discussed below.

APPROACHING AGENCY PERSONNEL

Before approaching key personnel to describe the project, it is important to become as fully informed as possible about the agency. In many organizations there are several levels of authority and it may be difficult to identify the actual "gatekeeper" to the desired subject population (Crano and Brewer, 1973; Richardson et al., 1965). In complex agencies, particularly those with multiple leadership, many individuals must be approached for permission. In fact, the chief gatekeeper may not have direct access to his or her own subjurisdictions (Schatzman and Strauss, 1973). Based on his experience with welfare agencies, Beck (1970) suggests that one approach "someone high enough in the hierarchy to empower you (formally or informally) to enter the places you want to observe, to interview the people you want answers from and to read documents you want to analyze" yet "low enough in the hierarchy to have working knowledge of routine operations and material impact on those operations" (1970: 13).

In learning about the agency, the researcher should pay particular attention to the relationship among the key personnel, especially the power alignments among these people. One of our colleagues learned this the hard way with a project on coping with cancer. She contacted a well-known physician at a local medical center and proposed that they submit a research proposal on their mutual interests. The physician was quite interested. After several months of work, the proposal was completed and sent to the medical school for some signatures prior to its submission to the federal agency. To her shock, the Director of the Cancer Center at this medical school vetoed her proposal and indicated that he would not allow the physician to work with her or permit access to patients from the hospital. She later learned that this veto was the result of an ongoing political power struggle between the Director and the physician with whom she had been working. If she had been aware of the situation earlier, she could have met with the Director herself to ensure that he would support her project before she began writing the grant.

GAINING COOPERATION

Once the investigator has identified key agency personnel and provided an adequate description of the project, he or she must bargain with the agency for approval of the research (see Geer, 1970). We have found several techniques to be helpful both in soliciting cooperation and in developing a good working relationship with agency personnel. Naturally, the researcher will stress the potential knowledge to be derived from the research and its applicability to the target population and the agency itself. Agency personnel are often suspicious of researchers, viewing them as unconcerned outsiders more interested in data and publication than in the welfare of the respondents. Several writers have discussed the value differences between service- and research-oriented individuals (Fairweather and Tornatzky, 1977; Riecken et al., 1974). To bridge this gap, researchers must demonstrate to the agency that they are truly concerned about the respondents.

This can be done in several ways. If the researcher is fortunate enough to have prior experience, special expertise, or a history of past work with this population, it should certainly be mentioned. When we have approached local hospitals to discuss access to cancer patient populations, for example, our five years of clinical experience is usually regarded as evidence of our good intentions. Willingness to invest time in learning more about the agency or the respondents is also helpful. For example, once we decided that the Rape Victim Advocate program (a Chicago-based service organization for rape victims) would be the best organization with which to work on our rape project, Abbey and Holland were trained as qualified advocates. Not only did this familiarize us with their procedures but it also established our credibility with the agency personnel (Cook and Campbell, 1976).

Also, we have learned that it is important to respect the staff's practical experience and to make an effort to involve them in the project. In addition to seeking their advice about what we can expect to be of concern to the victims we are interviewing, we also routinely ask for their critique of our data-collection instruments. Not only does their involvement make agency personnel feel committed to the project but it is also highly useful in its own right. Since these individuals have far more experience with the populations under study than we do, their insights and suggestions about the project have been invaluable.

Researchers must be sensitive to any burdens which may be created for the agency due to their participation in the project. Administrators are often anxious about the extent to which the research project will disrupt their daily routine; the experimenters must attempt to alleviate these fears (Riecken et al., 1974). Promising to make periodic reports about the progress of the research and to discuss any and all problems that develop with the staff will often help mitigate the administrator's concerns (Fairweather and Tornatzky, 1977). Researchers can also attempt to compensate the agency more directly for its cooperation. For example, it might be possible to add a few items to the interview schedule which are of special interest to the agency staff yet consistent with the researcher's objectives. Alternatively, the researcher could volunteer to teach some type of in-service course for the staff or respondents. Some agencies ask the researcher to help them evaluate their service.

Agency personnel are often apprehensive that any research conducted through their agency may reflect negatively on them and their organization (Weiss, 1972). We have found that it is important to confront this issue directly. When appropriate, allowing agency personnel to examine preprints of any articles prior to publication will usually alleviate this fear.

Once the bargaining process has led to host approval (a process which is apt to take from several weeks to several months), it is a good idea to spell out the responsibilities of both the research and agency staff in a written legal agreement signed by both the principal investigator and the director of the agency. This agreement not only openly delineates the researcher's goals and expectations for administrative personnel (and vice versa) but also helps insure cooperation from the organization throughout the investigation. Fairweather and Tornatzky (1977) warn that a verbal agreement may not be viewed as binding by a cooperating agency. We know of one researcher who was forced to terminate a longitudinal project before its completion because the staff member with whom he had been working decided to leave the agency. Since the staff replacement had no interest in the project, he refused to allow it to continue. A written legal agreement serves as explicit evidence of an agreement made with the agency and is likely to convince the new staff member as to the seriousness of the research endeavor and the agency's prior commitment. Fairweather and Tornatzky (1977) suggest that any agreement include a discussion of the manner in which the research budget and procedures should be administered, potential respondents selected, and personnel shared. This agreement should clarify the rights and responsibilities of both parties.

ESTABLISHING A RELATIONSHIP WITH THE DATA COLLECTORS

The success of any project is largely determined by the skill, talent, and commitment of the people who do the actual data collecting. Principal investigators may find it useful to collect the data themselves in small-scale interview studies, for this affords them the invaluable knowledge and insights derived from face-to-face contact. In pilot studies which entail unstructured interviews, competence at the level of the principal investigator may be required (see Richardson et al., 1965). However, in large-scale studies which involve structured interviews, principal investigators generally rely upon data collectors whom they must select, train, and supervise.

While on the surface it may appear easier to utilize agency staff as interviewers if the cooperating agency director approves it, our experience has suggested that hiring and training one's own interviewers is more cost efficient and will ensure greater quality control. As we learned in a pilot study of psychosocial adjustment to chronic lung disease, an agency director is often unable to secure an adequate level of cooperation and commitment from his or her staff. The director of this medical project ordered his employees to administer our instruments. Because these individuals resented having an additional task added to their daily routine, they were uncooperative and the data they collected were often incomplete. Even when staff members are willing to cooperate, however, problems may emerge. Particularly in social service agencies in which they are accustomed to assuming the helping role, staff may have difficulty collecting data in the objective, standardized manner required in research.

SELECTION

The quality of the interviewer-respondent interaction is critical to the maintenance of high subject commitment and low attrition rates. In selecting interviewers, researchers should seek out individuals with the interpersonal skills to build rapport with respondents (Cannel and Kahn, 1968; Richardson et al., 1965; Yancy and Rainwater, 1970).

The schedule interviewer must maintain an appearance of spontaneity and interest with each new respondent; even after having used the schedule in scores of earlier interviews. In every interview, he must maintain painstaking attention to accuracy and detail in asking the questions and recording and coding the responses; ... he must tolerate the difficulties of locating respondents and sometimes encountering refusals and rebuffs; finally, he must have sufficient self-confidence to initiate contacts with one stranger after another and not display anxiety and hesitancy [Richardson et al., 1965: 274].

This is hardly an easy bill to fill and the researcher should make it apparent to the interviewers that he or she recognizes the difficulty of the task.

In addition to recruiting individuals with social skills, the principal investigators should also attempt to match interviewers with respondents (see Crano and Brewer, 1973). For instance, women would presumably be more appropriate than men as interviewers of rape victims. In the Bulman and Wortman (1977) study, it became apparent early in the interviews that similarity of age was an important factor contributing to the ease of rapport between interviewer and respondents (Erlich and Riesman, 1961).

TRAINING

Once hired, the interviewers should undergo a detailed training program, covering the general content area under investigation, interviewing techniques, and the necessity for methodological rigor. In our current research projects, interviewers learn specific information about the victimized population with which they will be working, and they are taught to recognize and deal with potential distress in respondents.

In learning the interview schedule, we also ask interviewers to carefully review each question and discuss their reaction to it with us. If an interviewer is uncomfortable with a question or sees no reason why it should be asked, he or she might skip the question or change the wording, thereby jeopardizing the scientific integrity of the findings.

In addition to learning about interviewing techniques (how to approach the respondent, how to respond to particular answers, when to pause, and so on); interviewers need to be sensitized to the effects that their expectations may have on the subject's responses (Cannel and Kahn 1968; Converse and Schuman, 1974; Hyman et al., 1975). As one of Converse and Schuman's interviewers confessed, it is not easy to "listen to what someone *says*, not what you think they are going to say" (1974: 18). Converse and Schuman suggest that researchers teach interviewers to broaden their perspective on what is a supposedly acceptable answer (see their suggested techniques, 1974: 18).

The greatest emphasis and the most training time should be spent on interviewing practice. While books and articles (e.g., Cannel and Kahn, 1968; Hyman et al., 1975; Richardson et al., 1965; Whyte, 1976) on interviewing are helpful in developing familiarity with the technique, actively engaging in interviews is requisite for good training. Role playing is a particularly effective means of practicing interview techniques (Cannell and Kahn, 1968), and one which we have relied upon in our work. Like Farber (1970) our data collectors tape record interviews with one another and then give each other feedback on their performance. Then, the principal investigator works with each interviewer, purposely taking the role of a reluctant, rude respondent. In the final stage of training, our interviewers conduct pilot interviews with volunteer victimized individuals; this provides them with their most valuable training experience.

SUPERVISION

During the data-collection phase, the principal investigator should attempt to foster quality control in the interviews and continued interviewer commitment to the project. To check on quality, researchers should listen to selected tapes of the interviews and/or review interviewers' notes (Farber, 1970). Sudman (1966) presents a quantitative coding scheme for determining the quality of an interviewer's data which the researcher could utilize.[2] We have also found that it is important to maintain close contact with the interviewers, so we conduct weekly meetings to determine how the study is progressing. Because interviewers are involved in the day-to-day details of the study, they have access to valuable information that is otherwise unavailable to the researcher. They may alert the researcher to potential problems with the questionnaire or procedures before they become serious.

In addition, these meetings provide an opportunity for the interviewers to receive emotional support, which we have found vital (see Maslach, 1976). Talking with rape victims and paralyzed individuals can be anxiety provoking, threatening, and depressing, and the group meetings are often therapeutic in reducing these feelings. Further, within the groups we are able to stress our interest in the interviewer's feedback, our appreciation of their work, and our recognition of their importance to the success of the project.

ESTABLISHING A RELATIONSHIP WITH RESPONDENTS

The success of a longitudinal field study depends not only on locating a representative sample of respondents and obtaining their consent to participate but also on maintaining their participation throughout the study and encouraging them to provide data that are reliable and valid. While a full discussion of these difficult and complicated matters would clearly be beyond the scope of this chapter, some of the more salient issues are presented below.

MAXIMIZING PARTICIPATION

In our judgment, the researcher should not underestimate the importance of a clear and informative introduction to the project. In some investigations, the information provided to respondents is limited to that required by human subjects guidelines on a consent form. In introducing our studies to the respondents, our interviewers try to build rapport with the subject, attempt to get him or her as excited about the project as we are, and go into some detail about why the respondent's participation is important to us.

As Cannel and Kahn (1968) have noted, the interviewer should describe the project and its purpose to respondents in enough detail so that they can truly understand it, but not in so much detail that they become overwhelmed. The selection procedures should also be explained; respondents should understand why they were singled out. Particularly in studies on coping and adjustment, respondents may assume that they have been chosen because the staff thinks they are having problems; the researcher should alleviate this anxiety. Respondents should also be informed as to what agency is sponsoring the research so that they can be assured of its legitimacy.

In order to introduce the project so as to maximize participation, it may be helpful to consider what motivates people to become involved in research. According to Richardson et al., (1965), there are three major factors that affect participation: altruism, emotional satisfaction, and intellectual satisfaction. If altruism is a motivating factor, the respondent will see himself or herself as being in a position to help the interviewer or others in society. In such cases, the interviewer will want to stress the social utility of the study. For example, Farber (1970) reports that many parents of mentally retarded children were willing to participate in his research because it gave them an opportunity to help other parents avoid the difficulties they had encountered and because they wanted to advance scientific understanding of the mentally retarded.

For other people, the interview provides an opportunity to express their opinions and to talk in the presence of a sympathetic listener. Such considerations may be especially important to victims of aversive life events, who are ordinarily surrounded by people who do not appear willing to listen to their problems (Coates and Wortman, 1980). Finally, interviews offer some respondents intellectual satisfaction. There are some people who enjoy discussions and the exchange of ideas, but who lack such stimulation on an everyday basis. These individuals may find an interview a novel and highly rewarding experience.

This notion that different respondents may be motivated to participate by different factors received confirmation from Burgess, who has recently completed a four- to six-year longitudinal study of rape victims (Burgess and

Holmstrom, 1978). Burgess suggested that the interviewer try to build some rapport with the respondent before discussing the possible reasons for participation, and then try to emphasize those reasons that may be especially appealing to each respondent.

In order to enhance participation, researchers must also consider the needs and problems of the target population. In our own work we avoid discussing the project with respondents at a time when they are under acute emotional stress. For example, we describe our investigation to rape victims a few days after the assault, rather than doing so when they are brought into the hospital emergency room. Similarly, we postpone the initial contact with our spinal cord patients until intense physical pain has been brought under control. It would clearly raise serious ethical questions to burden respondents when they are in acute distress. Moreover, it would be impossible for them to focus on our introductory material and make a reasoned choice about participation at that time.

No matter how skillfully the introduction to the project is delivered, of course, some individuals will decline to participate. Researchers face a difficult dilemma here: If a large number of respondents decline, the results will obviously have limited generalizability. This is especially problematic if those who refuse to participate are the very individuals who are having the most serious difficulties in coping with their situation. If potential respondents do not wish to discuss the project or reject participation out of hand, one final effort may be attempted. In our study, we try to ascertain why the respondent does not want to participate. Some respondents are not in the mood to discuss the project when the interviewer initially approaches them, but are perfectly willing to be contacted at another time.

A second suggestion for enhancing the likelihood of participation has been suggested by Aaron Rosen and Arthur Shulman, who are conducting a large-scale study of bereavement in the St. Louis, Missouri, area. They have established a Council of Widows who serve as informed, volunteer consultants to the project. If individuals decline to participate, they are contacted by a member of this council, who attempts to stress the benefits of the project for other widows. If this option is available to the researcher, it promises to be highly effective. A danger of this and similar techniques, however, is that they can become rather coercive. Researchers can easily become so overzealous in their efforts to procure participants that they fail to treat respondents as intelligent, responsible persons capable of making their own decision about participation.

MAXIMIZING ACCURACY OF REPORTS

Once the potential participants agree to be interviewed, researchers should be concerned with the validity and reliability of information provided by respondents. According to Cannell and Kahn (1968; see also Richardson, 1960), there are several factors which operate to maximize the respondent's motivation to provide complete and accurate information. These factors include liking for the interviewer, prestige of the research agency, self-image as a dutiful citizen, and loneliness. The factors which they identify as operating against complete and accurate reporting are the press of competing activities, embarrassment at ignorance, dislike of the interview content, and fear of consequences.

In some of our research with victimized populations, the issue of accuracy of reporting is particularly salient due to the nature of the victimization (i.e., rape) and the resulting potential for embarrassment and anxiety in responding to interview questions. If respondents are feeling anxious or depressed, will they share their feeling with the interviewer or will they attempt to create the impression that they can handle what has happened to them? A comfortable relationship between interviewer and respondent is perhaps the best protection against inaccuracy. The interviewer should explain that there are no right or wrong answers; that negative reactions are common when people are under stress; and that while it may be difficult to admit these negative responses, it is important to do so; otherwise inaccurate results will be passed on to the scientific community as well as health care professionals.

Although it is vital that the respondent and interviewer develop a trusting relationship, it is also possible that they become so close that it may be difficult for the subject to freely disclose embarrassing information. If the interviewer's attitudes become too important to the respondent, he or she may be more likely to engage in impression management. Although the likelihood of achieving a too-great affinity between respondent and interviewer seems small, it is increased by the use of young and idealistic interviewers who are drawn to the project by their personal concern for the victim population. In order to minimize this problem, it should be confronted directly in interviewer training.

Cannell and Fowler (1975) review literature suggesting that reporting is significantly more accurate if respondents are given clear instructions at the beginning of the study which stress the importance of giving accurate responses to all questions, of mentioning all relevant incidents even if the subject considers them unimportant, and of thinking carefully about each response. They also discuss the results of a pilot study designed to increase respondents' commitment to a research project. Before the initial interview, respondents were asked to sign a document which stated that the respondent agreed to provide complete and accurate information to the interviewer.

Respondents were told that they should not participate in the study unless they were willing to make this commitment. The interviewer also signed the form as an indication of his or her commitment to keeping the data confidential. They report that the large majority of the subjects agreed to sign this document and the accuracy and quality of the data was improved significantly.

Another technique for increasing the accuracy of one's data, also reported by Cannell and Fowler, concerns the interviewer's use of positive and negative feedback. Respondents are rewarded for giving adequate answers and given negative feedback when they provide inadequate responses:

For example, a respondent was asked whether she had been sick or not feeling well at any time in the past two weeks. If illness was reported, this positive feedback was given—"That's the kind of information we need for this study." If the respondent gave a rapid "no" response, the feedback used was something like, "You answered quickly. Sometimes it's hard to remember these things. If you think about it again you may remember something" [1975: 20].

In essence, the interviewer makes it clear to the subject that conscientious responses are expected.

Problems of inaccuracy are also bound to arise if the interviewer asks questions about topics which are presently inaccessible to the respondent (e.g., not current or relevant to current life), and when the respondent does not understand the questions or concepts involved (Cannell and Kahn, 1968). For example, investigators have had difficulty asking respondents to indicate their perceptions of control over their environment (Langer and Rodin, 1976). Many persons are confused by the term *control* and different people define it differently. Such difficulties can be minimized by establishing a common frame of reference between interviewers and respondents.

MIMIMIZING ATTRITION

After obtaining the respondent's initial participation, the next problem faced by the researcher is maintaining participation for the duration of the project. We try to protect ourselves from this problem by stressing the importance of a longitudinal approach in our introduction to the project. We explain the problems created when subjects drop out and try to extract a commitment from the respondent to participate in the study for its duration. In an attempt to encourage continued participation, we stress the fact that the respondent is making a unique contribution which we value greatly. We also assign the same interviewer to each session with a respondent because it provides subjects with a greater sense of continuity. They are more likely to accept a follow-up visit from someone they have met before than from a stranger.

One step the researcher can take to minimize attrition is to try to understand precisely why dropout may occur with his or her population. In talking with Ann Wolbert Burgess, we learned that in studies on coping with rape, attrition is high not because rape victims lose motivation and drop out, but because they frequently move and are therefore difficult to recontact. In fact, Burgess and Holmstrom (1978) found that a very large percentage of rape victims move as a direct result of the attack. They were able to achieve an 85% follow-up rate, four to six years after attack, by "playing detective": asking respondents to provide more detailed information about their possible moving plans, soliciting information about how to reach them at work as well as at home, and doggedly persisting in their efforts to recontact the victims. Riecken et al. (1974) provide several practical suggestions as to how to find "lost subjects" including contacting the post office, utility companies, schools, and neighbors. Burgess noted that once the victims had been tracked down, they were usually receptive.

In the final analysis, the interview is a social process in which the respondents' perceptions of the interviewer largely determine their motivation to continue the interaction (Bernstein et al., 1974; Cannell and Kahn, 1968). If the social interaction between the parties is a successful one, respondents are not only likely to give complete, honest responses to questions but they are also likely to maintain their participation for the duration of the study.

CONCLUDING COMMENTS

The transition from the laboratory to the field may involve a parallel transition on the part of researchers from "expert" to "learner." As psychologists and researchers, we are accustomed to (and perhaps have grown too comfortable in) the role of expert/teacher. On the basis of our experiences, the best advice which we can offer to other researchers trying to make the transition from the laboratory to the field is that they should never underestimate how much they can learn from others. We feel that our work has been greatly enriched by our detailed discussions about coping and adjustment with agency and hospital personnel. Our interview schedules have been vastly improved by soliciting regular and detailed feedback from our interviewers. Moreover, we feel that we have learned a great deal about what is important from the respondents themselves. Our clinical work with these individuals was an important first step in educating ourselves about their concerns. Throughout the research process, we have tried to continue this educational process. For example, in piloting our protocol for the study on spinal cord injury; we included an open-ended question asking the respondent to identify his or her most important concerns. On the basis of their answers to this question, we learned that we were missing some important dimensions of their experience. Thus, the respondents are "experts" who can provide not only the answers but also the significant questions.

In addition to agency personnel, data collectors, and respondents themselves, investigators should recognize how much they can learn by interacting with other professionals who have had different training and experience than they have had. One of the most exciting aspects of our work at the Rehabilitation Institute of Chicago is that we have attended regular meetings that were designed to bring together a wide variety of people interested in spinal cord injury. This group included physicians, nurses, social workers, psychiatrists, clinical psychologists, and patients themselves. We have found such an interdisciplinary approach to be invaluable in shaping our research program. We have been fascinated by some of the insights about adjustment to disability that physicians and psychiatrists have shared with us. For example, one surgeon who has considerable experience with spinal-cord-injured patients told us that for a large percentage of these patients, the injury is less of a disaster than one might assume. He said that there are similarities among a large percentage of spinal-cord-injured patients: They are young, irresponsible men who would prefer significantly more attention from other than they receive. He suggested that for these patients, spinal cord injury is more of a solution than a problem. We have had some interesting discussions trying to determine whether such an unusual idea could possibly be true, or whether it merely reflects the surgeon's attempt to reduce his distress and make sense of the misery he encounters.

In this chapter we have tried to trace the development of our work on uncontrollable outcomes and have discussed some of the problems we have encountered in our transition from the laboratory to the field. We hope that this chapter has underscored the value of feedback from other professionals, data collectors, and respondents themselves in reaching solutions to these problems.

NOTES

1. This study is being conducted in collaboration with Stefan Harasymiw from the Rehabilitation Institute of Chicago and Ellen Wodika of Northwestern Memorial Hospital.

2. Riecken et al. (1974) argue that interviewers should be informed that 1 out of 10 of the respondents they interview will be reinterviewed by another member of the staff. Not only will this reduce the likelihood that interviewers will fabricate data, but it will also alert the researcher to problems with particular interviewers before they become severe. We know of a research project in which one-third of the data had to be discarded because of interviewer cheating. Use

of the above tactic may have helped the investigators avoid this problem.

REFERENCES

ABELSON, R.P., E. ARONSON, W.J. McGUIRE, T.M. NEWCOMB, M.J. ROSENBERG, and P.H. TANNENBAUM (eds.) (1968) Theories of Cognitive consistency: A Source Book. Skokie, IL: Rand McNally.

ABRAMSON, L.Y., M.E.P. SELIGMAN, and J.D. TEASDALE (1978) "Learned helplessness in humans: critique and reformulation." Journal of Abnormal Psychology 87: 49-74.

APSLER, R. and H. FRIEDMAN (1975) "Chance outcomes and the just world: a comparison of observers and recipients." Journal of Personality and Social Psychology 31: 887-894.

BAUM, A., J.R. AIELLO, and L.E. CALESNICK (1978) "Crowding and personal control: social density and the development of learned helplessness." Journal of Personality and Social Psychology 36:1000-1011.

BECK, B. (1970) "Cooking welfare stews" pp. 7-29 in R.W. Habenstein (ed.), Pathways to data Chicago: AVC.

BERNSTEIN, L., R.S. BERNSTEIN, and R.M. DANA (1974) Interviewing: A guide for health professionals. Englewood Cliffs, NJ: Prentice-Hall.

BREHM, J.W. (1966) A Theory of Psychological Reactance. New York: John Wiley.

————— and A.R. COHEN (1962) Explorations in Cognitive Dissonance. New York: John Wiley.

BREHM, J.W. and J. SENSENIG (1966) "Social influence as a function of attempted and implied usurpation of choice." Journal of Personality and Social Psychology 4: 703-707.

BULMAN, R.J. and C.B. WORTMAN (1977) "Attributions of blame and coping in the "real world": severe accident victims react to their lot." Journal of Personality and Social Psychology 35: 351-363.

BURGESS, A.W. and L.L. HOLMSTROM (1978) "Recovery from rape and prior life stress." Research in Nursing and Health 1: 165-174.

CANNELL, C.F. and F.J. FOWLER (1975) Interviewers and Interviewing Techniques. Advances in Health Survey Research Methods: Proceedings of a National Invitational Conference. DHEW Publication (HRA) 77-3154. Washington, DC: Government Printing Office.

————— and R.L. KAHN (1968) "Interviewing" pp. 526-595 in G. Lindzey and E. Aronson (eds.), The Handbook of Social Psychology. Reading, MA: Addison-Wesley.

COATES, D. and C.B. WORTMAN (1980) "Interpersonal control and depression maintenance" pp. 149-182 in A. Baum and J. Singer (eds.), Advances in Environmental Psychology (Vol. 2). Hillsdale, NJ: Lawrence Erlbaum Associates.

————— and A. ABBEY (1979) "Reactions to victimization" in I. Frieze and D. Bar-Tel (eds.), Applications of Attribution Theory. San Francisco: Jossey-Bass.

COMER, R. and J.D. LAIRD (1975) "Choosing to suffer as a consequence of expecting to suffer: why do people do it?" Journal of Personality and Social Psychology 32: 92-101.

CONVERSE, P.M. and H. SCHUMAN (1974) Conversations at Random: Survey Research as Interviewers See It. New York: John Wiley.

COOK, T.D. and D.T. CAMPBELL (1976) "The design and conduct of quasi-experiments and true experiments in field settings" pp. 223-326 in M.D. Dunnette (ed.), Handbook of Industrial and Organizational Psychology. Skokie, IL.: Rand McNally.

CORNWELL, J., B. NURCOMBE, and L. STEVENS (1977) "Family response to loss of a child by SIDS." Medical Journal of Australia 1(18): 656-658.

CRANO, W.D. and M.B. BREWER (1973) Principles of Research in Social Psychology. New York: McGraw-Hill.

DIENER, C.I. and C.S. DWECK (1978) "An analysis of learned helplessness: ongoing changes in performance, strategy, and achievement cognitions following failure." Journal of Personality and Social Psychology 36: 451-460.

DWECK, C.S. and C.B. WORTMAN (forthcoming) "Learned helplessness, achievement motivation, and anxiety: adaptive and maladaptive cognitions" in H.W. Krohne and L. Laux (eds.), Achievement, Stress, and Anxiety. Washington DC: Hemisphere.

ERLICH, J. and D. RIESMAN (1961) "Age and authority in the interview." Public Opinion Quarterly 25: 39-56.

FAIRWEATHER, G.W. and L.G. TORNATZKY (1977) Experimental Methods for Social Policy Research. New York: Pergamon Press.

FARBER, B. (1970) "Studying family and kinship" pp. 50-80 in R.W. Habenstien (ed.), Pathways to Data. Chicago: AVC.

FESTINGER, L. (1957) A Theory of Cognitive Dissonance. Palo Alto, CA: Stanford University Press.

FOXMAN, J. and R. RADTKE (1970) "Negative expectancy and the choice of an aversive task." Journal of Personality and Social Psychology 15: 253-257.

FRANKL, V.E. (1963) Man's Search for Meaning. New York: Washington Square.

GEER, B. (1970) "Studying a college" pp.81-98 in R.W. Habenstien (ed.), Pathways to data. Chicago: AVC.

GLASS, D.C. (1977) Behavior Patterns, Stress, and Coronary Disease. Hillsdale, NJ: Lawrence Erlbaum Associates.

_____ and J.E. SINGER (1972) Urban Stress: Experiments on Noise and Social Stressors. New York: Academic Press.

GLASS, D.C., M.L. SNYDER, and J. HOLLIS (1974) "Time urgency and the Type A coronary-prone behavior pattern." Journal of Applied Social Psychology 4: 125-140.

GULLO, W.V., D. CHERICO, and R. SHADICK (1974) "Suggested stages and response styles in life-threatening illness: a focus on the cancer patient" in B. Shoenberg et al. (eds.), Anticipatory grief. New York: Columbia University Press.

HAMMOCK, T. and J.W. BREHM (1966) "The attractiveness of choice alternatives when freedom to choose is eliminated by a social agent." Journal of Personality 34: 546-554.

HANUSA, B.H. and R. SCHULZ (1977) "Attributional mediators of learned helplessness." Journal of Personality and Social Psychology 35:602-611.

HYMAN, H. with W.J. COBB, J.J. FELDMAN, C.W. HART, and C.H. STEMBER (1975) Interviewing in Social Research. Chicago: University of Chicago Press.

JANIS, I.L. (1958) Psychological Stress. New York: John Wiley.

JANOFF-BULMAN, R. (1979) "Behavioral versus characterological self-blame: inquiries into depression and rape." Journal of Personality and Social Psychology 37: 1798-1810.

JONES, E.E., D.E. KANOUSE, H.H. KELLY, R.E. NISBETT, S. VALINS, and B. WEINER (1972) Attribution: Perceiving the Causes of Behavior. Morristown, NJ: General Learning Press.

KLECK, R. (1968) "Physical stigma and nonverbal cues emitted in face-to-face interaction." Human Relations 21: 19-28.

KLINGER, E. (1977) Meaning and void: Inner Experience and the Incentives in Peoples Lives.

Minneapolis: University of Minnesota Press.

LANGER, E.J. and J. RODIN (1976) "The effects of choice and enhanced personal responsibility for the aged: a field experiment in an institutional setting." Journal of Personality and Social Psychology 34: 191-199.

LAZARUS, R.S., J.B. COHEN, S. FOLKMAN, A. KANNER, and C. SCHAEFFER (forthcoming) "Psychological stress and adaptation: some unresolved issues" in H. Selye (ed.), Guide to Stress Research. New York: Van Nostrand-Reinhold.

LAZARUS, R.S. and R. LAUNIER (1978) "Stress-related transactions between person and environment" in L.A. Pervin and M. Lewis (eds.), Perspectives in Interactional Psychology. New York: Plenum.

LERNER, M.J. (forthcoming) A just world. New York: Plenum.

_____(1970) "The desire for justice and reactions to victims." in J. Macaulay and L. Berkowitz (eds.), Altruism and helping behavior. New York: Academic Press.

_____(1965) "Evaluation of performance as a function of performer's reward and attractiveness." Journal of Personality and Social Psychology 1: 355-360.

LIPOWSKI, Z.J. (1970) "Physical illness, the individual and the coping processes." Psychiatry in Medicine l: 91-102.

MASLACH, C. (1976) "Burned-Out." Human Behavior 5: 16-22.

MILLER, I.W. and W.H. NORMAN (1979) "Learned helplessness in humans: a review and attribution theory model." Psychological Bulletin 86: 93-118.

OVERMIER, J.B. and M.E.P. SELIGMAN (1967) "Effects of inescapable shock upon subsequent escape and avoidance learning." Journal of Comparative and Physiological Psychology 63: 23-33.

PENMAN, D.T. (1979) "Coping strategies in adaptation to mastectomy." Unpublished Ph.D dissertation. Yeshiva University, New York.

RICHARDSON, S.A. (1960) "A framework for reporting field-relations experiences" pp. 124-139 in R.N. Adams and J.J. Preiss (eds.), Human Organization Research: Field Relations and Techniques. Homewood IL: Dorsey Press.

_____B.S. DOHRENWEND, and D. KLEIN (1965) Interviewing: Its Forms and Functions. New York: Basic Books.

RIECKEN, H.W., R.F. BORUCH, D.T. CAMPBELL, N. CAPLAN, T.K. GLENNAN, J.W. PRATT, A. REES, and W. WILLIAMS (1974) Social Experimentation: A Method for Planning and Evaluating Social Intervention. New York: Academic Press.

ROTH, S. (forthcoming) "Learned helplessness in humans: a review and a revised model." Journal of Personality.

_____and R.R. BOOTZIN (1974) "Effects of experimentally induced expectancies of external control: an investigation of learned helplessness. Journal of Personality and Social Psychology 29: 253-264.

_____and L. KUBAL (1975) "Effects of noncontingent reinforcement on tasks of differing importance: facilitation and learned helplessness." Journal of Personality and Social Psychology 32: 680-691.

SCHATZMAN, L. and A.L. STRAUSS (1973) Field Research: Strategies for a Natural Sociology. Englewood Cliffs, NJ: Prentice-Hall.

SCHULZ, R. (1976) "Effects of control and predictability on the physical and psychological well-being of the institutionalized aged." Journal of Personality and Social Psychology 33: 563-573.

SELIGMAN, M.E.P. (1974) "Depression and learned helplessness" pp. 83-113 in R.J. Friedman and M.M. Katz (eds.), The Psychology of Depression: Contemporary Theory and Research. Washington DC: Winston.

_____ D.C. KLEIN, and W.R. MILLER (1976) "Depression" in H. Leitenberg (ed.), Handbook of Behavior Modification and Behavior Therapy. Englewood Cliffs, NJ: Prentice-Hall.

_____ S.F. MAIER, and J. GEER (1968) "The alleviation of learned helplessness in the dog." Journal of Abnormal Psychology 73: 256-262.

_____ S.F. MAIER, and R.L. SOLOMON (1971) "Unpredictable and uncontrollable aversive events" in F.R. Brush (ed.), Aversive Conditioning and Learning. New York: Academic Press.

SHAVER, K.G. (1970) "Defensive attribution: effects of severity and relevance on the responsibility assigned for an accident." Journal of Personality and Social Psychology 14: 101-113.

STITT, A. (1971) "Emergency after death." Emergency Medicine 3: 270-279.

SUDMAN, S. (1966) "Quantifying interviewer quality." Public Opinion Quarterly 30: 664-667.

TAYLOR, S.E. and S. LEVIN (1977) "The psychological impact of breast cancer: theory and practice" in A. Enelow (ed.), Psychological Aspects of Breast Cancer. London: Oxford University Press.

WALSTER, E. (1966) "Assignment of responsibility for an accident." Journal of Personality and Social Psychology 3: 73-79.

WEINER, B., H. HECKHAUSEN, W.V. MEYER, and R.E. COOK (1972) "Causal ascription and achievement behavior: a conceptual analysis of effort and reanalysis of locus and control." Journal of Personality and Social Psychology 21: 239-248.

WEISMAN, A.D. and J.W. WORDEN (1976) "The existential plight in cancer: significance of the first 100 days." International Journal of Psychiatry in Medicine 7: 1-15.

WEISS, C.H. (1972) Evaluation Research. Englewood Cliffs, NJ: Prentice-Hall.

WICKLUND, R. (1974) Freedom and Reactance. Potomac, MD: Lawrence Erlbaum Associates.

WORTMAN, C.B. (1976) "Causal attributions and personal control." in J.H. Harvey et al. (eds.), New Directions in Attributing Research. Hillsdale, NJ: Lawrence Erlbaum Associates.

_____ and J.W. BREHM (1975) "Responses to uncontrollable outcomes: an integration of reactance theory and the learned helplessness model" in L. Berkowitz (ed.), Advances in Experimental Social Psychology (vol. 8) New York: Academic Press.

_____ P.R. COSTANZO, and T.R. WITT (1973) "Effect of anticipated performance on the attributions of causality to self and others." Journal of Personality and Social Psychology 27: 372-381.

_____ and L. DINTZER (1978) "Is an attributional analysis of the learned helplessness phenomenon viable? A critique of the Abramson-Seligman-Teasdale reformulation." Journal of Abnormal Psychology 87: 75-90.

_____ and C. DUNKEL-SCHETTER (1979) "Interpersonal relationships and cancer: a theoretical analysis." Journal of Social Issues 35: 120-155.

_____ L. PANCIERA, L. SHUSTERMAN, and J. HIBSCHER (1976) "Attributions of causality and reactions to uncontrollable outcomes." Journal of Experimental Social Psychology 12: 301-316.

_____ and R.L. SILVER (forthcoming) "Coping with undesirable life events." in M.E.P. Seligman and J. Garber (eds.), Human Helplessness: Theory and Applications. New York: Academic Press.

WHYTE, W.F. (1960) "Interviewing in field research" pp. 352-374 in R.N. Adams and J.J. Preiss (eds.), Human Organization Research: Field Relations and Techniques. Homewood, IL: Dorsey Press.

YANCEY, W.L. and L. RAINWATER (1970) "Problems in the ethnography of the urban underclass" pp. 245-269 in R.W. Habenstein (ed.), Pathways to Data. Chicago: AVC.

MICHAEL S. PALLAK
DAVID A. COOK
JOHN J. SULLIVAN

9

COMMITMENT AND
ENERGY CONSERVATION

Consistent with the case study approach in this section of the volume, we would like to discuss the process by which we became involved in energy conservation research, move to a set of practical issues about energy conservation and field research, then discuss several sets of data regarding energy conservation by homeowners, and briefly touch on several broad issues concerning problem-oriented research.

FROM THE LAB TO THE FIELD: ATTITUDES AND BEHAVIOR

We became involved in energy conservation research as an outgrowth of a long-standing interest in attitude change processes and in issues concerning the relationship between attitudes and behavior. The core issue here is not so much "whether attitudes influence behavior" but rather one of "under what conditions" there is a relationship between one typical sort of measure of attitude (usually a verbal self-report measure exemplified by a checkmark on a scale) and other measures (usually nonverbal or overt behavior) related to attitude.

In our view, verbal self-report measures, such as a checkmark on an attitude scale, may be viewed simply as a summary of the individual's behavioral tendencies regarding the issue. For example, if an individual fills out a measure of attitudes toward a tuition increase and marks the position labeled "opposed," we would expect that the individual would choose subsequent action that also implies opposition to a tuition increase rather than an action that implied favorability to a tuition increase.

Of course, the research literature abounds with instances in which verbal measures do not seem to predict overt behavior with any degree of accuracy. On the other hand, a number of excellent reviews and analyses suggest that it is naive to assume that attitude is the only determinant of overt behavior. For example, overt behavior is often elicited in quite different situational settings than that in which initial self-report measures of attitude are obtained. As a result, the later overt behavior may be viewed as being under stimulus control of a new situation to some unknown extent. Situational cues eliciting such "attitude-related" behavior may imply that overt behavior is unrelated to attitudes, feelings, or personal values about an issue.

A study by Bickman (1972) nicely illustrates the difficulty in connecting verbal expressions of attitude with overt behavior. Bickman (1972) interviewed some 500 people about responsibility for picking up litter and 94% expressed an attitude favorable to removing litter. However, upon leaving the interview situation, only about 2% of the interviewees picked up litter that had been planted by the investigator.

In discussing the results in an attitude change seminar, we discovered that no one picked up litter in the halls or classrooms, largely because such situations were viewed as the responsibility of the custodial staff. Thus, the generally positive attitude about picking up litter did not influence behavior in the situation. Potential attitude-related behaviors were not (and probably very often are not) viewed as related to one's attitudes, in this case attitudes about litter. At the same time, failure to pick up litter does not seem to imply a negative attitude about picking up litter either, since the specific situation may be viewed by the individual as one in which attitudes are simply irrelevant to behavior.

People often explain or account for their behavior in terms of the situation rather than in terms of feelings or attitudes. More generally, of course, Jones and Nisbett (1971) pointed out that individuals, when asked, tend to explain their behavior in terms of situational cues rather than cues about internal states such as attitudes. In a series of recently completed studies we found that individuals who had performed an attitude-consistent act explained causality for the act in situational terms rather than in attitudinal terms about 50% of the time (as a reference point, however, all subjects who performed a counterattitudinal act explained their behavior in situational terms). Since people may see situations in nonattitudinal or in noninternal terms, it seems unlikely that individuals would ask themselves what their attitudes or values may imply for their behavior when deciding about a specific course of action. In short, situations often may not provide cues that suggest either that one's attitudes should guide behavior or that one's attitudes have some relevance for behavior.

Clearly, one's attitude position on an issue may be only one of several internal and external determinants of overt behavior related to the attitude issue. Thus, people may have well-articulated attitudes in the form of verbal expressions of affect, belief, and potential behavior, but such expressions may carry little weight when it comes to actual behavior. One implication for energy conservation behavior is that a decision about thermostat settings may be determined to a greater extent by one's feelings of comfort, by one's family, or by a variety of situational determinants unrelated to attitude rather than by one's attitude position that energy conservation is a "good thing." As with the broad issue of "under what conditions" attitudes may determine or shape behavior, the issue for energy conservation research may be one of establishing a link between the implications of an attitude position about energy usage and the subsequent behavior regarding thermostat settings. Phrased differently, one might ask about the sorts of variables or procedures that make cues about energy-related attitudes more salient relative to the potentially large array of nonattitudinal or situational cues that also determine energy-related behavior. One promising approach to the issue of making cues about attitudes (e.g., energy conservation) more salient in specific action situations concerned the effect of commitment to one's attitude (cf. Kiesler, 1971). Our eventual work on energy conservation was derived from the base provided by the commitment framework.

THE EFFECT OF COMMITMENT ON ATTITUDES

Briefly, one might summarize a substantial proportion of the literature in social psychology in the last 20 years as suggesting that the conditions under which an individual makes a decision to act may play a major role in determining how the individual responds to the outcomes or implications of the decision. Variables such as volition (e.g., incentive and justification) for an act or a decision, as well as the explicitness or public nature of the decision, influence later reactions to attack or support for the decision (cf. Kiesler, 1971; Pallak et al., 1972) as well as whether one assumes responsibility for postdecisional outcomes (cf. Pallak et al., 1974; Wicklund and Brehm, 1976). For example, theoretically when individuals "take a stand" on an issue by committing themselves publicly to an attitude position, the attitude position and the implications of the position may become more salient and less easily denied or forgotten in subsequent situations. Commitment is defined as a binding or pledging of the individual to an act or decision (cf. Kiesler, 1971). In laboratory studies (cf. Pallak et al., 1972; Sullivan and Pallak, 1976; Halverson and Pallak, 1978), commitment has been varied by whether the individual expected to be personally identified with a public speech advocating his or her attitude position (public commitment to the position) or not (private commitment). Individuals publicly committed to

their position were more susceptible to subsequent consonant communications advocating a more extreme position, were more resistant to an attack
on their position, and were more likely to comply with a subsequent request
for additional attitude-related behavior than individuals only privately committed to their position.

Taken together, these studies broadly suggested that the commitment
framework represented a useful approach to attitude-behavior issues and
offered one set of variables that might link expressions of attitude in one
situation to behavior in other situations. For example, when faced with a
behavioral choice, individuals may be more likely to ask themselves what
their past behavior or actions may imply for action in the present situation.
When the individual has previously taken a public stand (e.g., favoring
energy conservation), the previous decision and action may make cues about
the attitude position more salient relative to other cues in the immediate
situation. In this sense, one's initial public stand or commitment may form
an anchor that makes one's attitude a relatively salient guide for behavior in
subsequent situations (cf. Halverson and Pallak, 1978). Having acted previously by making a public commitment to their attitude position, individuals may be more likely to view later behavior in light of the implications of
their previous commitment to their position.

It seemed to us that a homeowner's energy-related behavior represented
an example of the "attitude-behavior problem" and that the perspective
represented by the commitment framework offered a plausible starting point
for field investigations. In short, it seemed likely that for homeowners who
publicly committed themselves to an attitude position favoring energy conservation, the attitude would be relatively salient when, for example, taking
actions such as setting thermostats.

Pragmatically, we had substantial experimental data from which to operate in terms of manipulations of commitment and in terms of an overall
paradigm. Residents of Iowa City, Iowa, were generally liberal and had
positive attitudes about issues such as energy conservation and it seemed
logical to expect that if a homeowner could be induced to support energy
conservation publicly, we should be able to observe reductions in energy
usage. In our planning, it seemed much simpler to use the utility-company
meter readings as a response measure of energy usage for several reasons
(given below) including the fact that meter readings did not depend on ad
hoc observers and were routinely collected by the utility system. Also for
these reasons we did not consider looking at heating oil consumption since
the latter was handled by a number of independent dealers not so readily
accessible as the local utility system for natural gas and for electricity.

ACCESS TO DATA IN THE FIELD

We began the series of studies (Pallak and Cummings, 1976), as it turned out, in autumn about two or three months prior to the oil embargo in 1973. At that time, energy-related issues were not in the forefront of the public's concern and did not represent a particularly reactive issue. Our major step was to engage in negotiations with officials in the local utility company including the area manager in order to ensure access to utility meter readings. We felt that cooperation would be easier and speedier to obtain by dealing with the senior official at the local level rather than by attempting to negotiate with officials in the main headquarters (located in an entirely different region). The officials were extremely helpful but expressed three sets of concerns.

The officials were very sophisticated about issues of privacy with regard to homeowners. We explained the procedure in detail (cf. Pallak and Cummings, 1976) in which the homeowners signed a release form permitting access to their utility records. The second concern was how much inconvenience the homeowner-subjects would have to experience as part of the study and whether the utility company would be seen as responsible for such problems. After some discussion, our procedure of telephoning for an appointment and following up with a 20-minute interview did not seem unreasonable. In addition, we left copies of a detailed script (as well as all other materials) for the interview. We also agreed that, if asked, we would explain that the utility company was "cooperating" with us rather than actually sponsoring the research. As it turned out, there were five or six homeowners who contacted the company to ask whether we were legitimate and so on.

The third issue raised in our discussions was one of how much disruption our data-gathering would cause the utility company. We worked out a procedure for one person to pull the records needed, make copies, and return the originals and made sure that we (the office manager, myself, and the data person) met each of the company employees with whom the data person would have to interact. The point here was that the local office was willing to cooperate so long as cooperation involved little strain for their system—an important issue when one takes their perspective. The discussions, the working out of details, and so forth reassured the company in this regard and led to a cooperative working relationship. In turn, having the cooperation at the local level meant that we did not have to read utility meters ourselves.

Although seemingly a minor point, the utility-meter readings were potentially a very difficult issue. Were we to read the meters it would have meant further intrusion into the homeowners' life-space with attendant potential "Hawthorne" effects. In addition, we would have had to substantially increase the number of people needed to complete the research—especially since we intended to take a more longitudinal perspective across the months following the induction (cf. Pallak et al., 1977).

In thinking about field research, one perspective that seemed crucial was that of "knowing the terrain." For example, as part of our discussions, we had to learn a fair amount about how the utility company gathers data for its use. The local area was divided into 21 geographic meter-reading districts and the period of time between any particular homeowner's readings varied between monthly readings and varied from month to month by district. Thus, any specific district could have a utility "month" that varied between 27 and 33 days in length. Since we had no a priori basis for guessing how large an effect the commitment procedure might produce, we kept a very detailed record of reading dates by district and homeowner (for example, a variation in meter period of three days would produce a variation of 10% usage in some months while not in others). Based on this set of information, however, we were able to interview each homeowner during the evening following the meter reading, thus reducing variance in the data base due to the data collection system.

Similarly, we planned to interview only one homeowner per residential block in each commitment condition (public, private) to minimize the amount of social interaction that might take place between homeowner subjects. Homeowners were randomly assigned to conditions including those (one per block also) in the control condition. The latter were interviewed in the evening preceding the end of the utility month for that district and permission for access to the utilty records was obtained at that time. These controls provided baselines for usage during the preceding month in which our subjects were presumably conserving energy. Thus a substantial amount of planning went into the sequencing of meter readings by the company and interviewing by our team across some seven or eight of the utility districts for each study.

Once we had a handle on the variation in utility periods, it then was relatively simple to convert the readings to a daily usage figure. For several reasons we used as the primary index a measure of change in usage level. It seemed desirable to use individual homeowners as their own control, especially since the timing of our studies was such that the "natural gas" study (Experiment I, Pallak and Cummings, 1976) went into gear at the beginning of the heating season in Iowa (September-October 1973) and in the "electricity" study (Experiment II, Pallak and Cummings, 1976) at the beginning of the air conditioning season (June-July 1974). Thus, the average daily use level for the month preceding the interview was the denominator for the index and the average daily use for the month after (or for succeeding months, see below) the interview was the numerator for the index and this ratio was converted to a percentage. An entry for a homeowner of 195% meant that the homeowner has used 195% as much natural gas or electricity in a month following the interview than in the month preceding the interview. Such an approach to meter readings seemed (really a simple-minded covariance) very useful in "smoothing out" or stablizing the distributions of readings.

THE COMMITMENT MANIPULATION

We might note that only 7 homeowners out of a total of 212 that participated in our studies indicated that they did not wish to participate when contacted by telephone to set up the initial interview. Those agreeing to the interviews were then randomly assigned to condition. In turn, only 3 homeowners out of the total refused to sign the release form (see below).

As part of the interview format, the interviewer (1 of some 12 or so undergraduate assistants) discussed a variety of energy conservation strategies and explained that we were a group that was concerned with whether or not individuals could save any energy—in short, whether personal efforts would in fact make much of a difference. The interviews also explained that we hoped to publicize our results and, in the public commitment condition, that we hoped to list the names of homeowners who had agreed to participate in the study.

In the private commitment conditions, however, the interviewers assured the homeowners of anonymity and explicitly stated that homeowners would not be personally identified. All homeowners signed a consent form that restated the above and that permitted access to the homeowner's utility records. Homeowners in the control condition were interviewed at the end of the utility period (as above). We might note that the utility readings pulled from company records were obtained only from an overall list of homeowners who had agreed to participate rather than from a list of homeowners separated by condition—again as a further precaution regarding experimenter bias (and interviewers did not have access to these records).

The results (Pallak and Cummings, 1976) were straightforward and are reproduced in Table 1. In both studies, homeowners who received the public commitment manipulation showed a lower rate of increase in natural gas and electricity consumption than homeowners in either the private commitment or control conditions. We might note that the mean usage level of natural gas in the base month was 177 ccf (hundred cubic feet) per month. In the electricity study for central air, the base month usage was 943 kwh (kilowatt hours) per month and for window air the base was 723 kwh per month.

TABLE 1   The Effect of Commitment on Rate of Increase
(over Base Month) of Natural Gas and Electricity
Consumption

Commitment:	Experiment I (natural gas)	Experiment II (electricity)	
		Central Air Conditioning	Window Unit Air Conditioning
Public	195.07%[b]	164.15%[d]	122.45%[f]
N	22	15	16
Private	215.88%[c]	204.36%[e]	155.83%[g]
N	19	17	16
Control	221.93%[c]	216.89%[e]	160.19%[g]
N	24	22	18

b. Entries with differing superscripts are statistically different. All entries are based on meter
  readings one month after interview.
  Adapted from Pallak and Cummings (1976)

LONG-TERM EFFECTS—NEW EVIDENCE

These results were based on observations for the month following the
interview. Consistent with our agreement with the homeowners, we sent a
brief communication stating that the project had been successful in saving
energy but that it would not be possible to identify homeowners publicly
(i.e., in the public commitment condition). We stated explicitly that the
study was concluded.

One issue here of interest was whether the effects obtained would persist.
On the one hand, it was encouraging to find an effect of a 20-minute interview procedure (about the same length of time as one spends with a subject
on the manipulation in a laboratory setting) reflected in meter readings
obtained a month or so later. In an actuarial sense that is a "long-term effect"
relative to the typical laboratory investigation. On the other hand, the differences obtained between conditions could have been the result of "energy-
conscious" behavior for a relatively few days following the interview that
then faded as the utility month progressed. Thus a relevant issue was that of
how fleeting the effect of commitment might be, or whether homeowners
were still behaving differently regarding energy use at the end of the utility
month.

As a result, Pallak et al. (1977) tracked the usage levels for participants in
the natural gas and electricity studies for a 12-month period. The results
from the 12-month analysis for natural gas usage are presented in Table 2.

Several points should be noted. Month 1 in Table 2 represents the results
reported in Table 1 for the utility month of November. The means and the
cell n s differ somewhat from the original in both studies due to homeowners

TABLE 2   The Effect of Commitment on Natural Gas
Usage Over 12 Months

Month:	Public Commitment (16)	Private Commitment (17)	Control (21)
November-1	187.85%[a]	213.12%	212.97%
December-2	295.34%	348.37%	342.98%
January-3	452.58%	515.94%	521.20%
February-4	370.76%	435.69%	431.67%
March-5	299.37%	336.79%	340.69%
April-6	277.29%	318.79%	317.85%
May-7	148.18%	159.29%	164.03%
June-8	87.93%	98.32%	95.10%
July-9	81.39%	96.16%	83.90%
August-10	72.22%	83.18%	83.91%
September-11	79.19%	81.37%	83.35%
October-12	140.95%	147.96%	140.21%

a. Each entry represents the usage level as a percentage of base month. Cell entries are in
   parentheses.
Adapted from Pallak et al. (1976).

who moved from the area during the 12-month period—11 homeowners in
the natural gas study and 13 homeowners in the electricity study—and these
losses did not differ by condition.

For the natural gas study, public commitment resulted in lower natural
gas consumption relative to the private commitment or control condition
throughout the 12-month period, 207.75% versus 235.88% + 234.82%, respectively, $F=7.11$, $p<.025$. Since all our homeowners used natural gas for
heating (some also used natural gas for hot water while some also used
electricity for hot water), it was not surprising that the repeated-measures
analysis also showed a Commitment × Month interaction indicating that
the commitment effect on natural gas usage depended on the month(s) of the
year, $F=2.75$, $p<.01$. We consulted monthly temperature norms for the Iowa
City area (Conway and Liston, 1974) and performed a median split on average monthly temperature. Based on the split the six months of November-
April can be described as "winter," i.e., the six months of highest usage of
natural gas, and the six months of May-October as "summer," i.e., the six
months of lower natural gas usage. Such a split seemed the easiest means of
breaking down the Commitment × Month interaction. Within the winter
(November-April) months, lower usage of natural gas was obtained in the
public commitment relative to private commitment and control, $F=10.34$,
$p<.01$. During the summer (May-October) months there was no difference
between conditions in usage of natural gas.

These results suggest that the effect of commitment on natural gas consumption persisted for some six months in the winter following our initial interview. As we all recall that winter involved shortage of fuel oil, gasoline, natural gas, higher prices for each of these commodities, and so forth. While it was gratifying to see that the effect was sufficiently robust to last for some six months (through April), it is unclear whether the diminution observed (Table 2) was due to a weakening of the effect of commitment or to a floor effect caused by the seasonal variation that resulted in reduced natural gas usage.

While we obviously thought the latter, the long-term data from the electricity study provide a base by which to assess those alternative interpretations. On the one hand, for homes heated with natural gas, electricity is also used to drive the fan in a forced-air system and so forth, as well as for central air conditioning in the summer months. Thus we expected that the multiple uses for electricity regardless of season would make potential floor effects (that would obscure an effect of commitment between conditions) less likely.

The results for the 12-month analysis of electricity usage for homeowners with central air conditioning are summarized in Table 3 and for homeowners with window air conditioners in Table 4. Recall that the electricity study (Experiment II, Pallak and Cummings, 1976) took place in the summer following the oil embargo—thus these results began about six months after the embargo. Again the means and cell n s for Month 1 (July) are from Table 1 for those homeowners who remained in the sample. The analysis confirmed that homeowners under public commitment showed less electricity usage than homeowners in the private commitment and control conditions, 89.82% versus 108.87%+114.47%, respectively, $F=6.61$ $p<.02$. Unlike the results from the natural gas study (above), there was no Commitment $\times$ Month interaction. As a result, the lessening of the commitment effect obtained over months in the natural gas study may be interpreted as the result of the drop in the natural gas usage caused by the onset of the summer, non-heating, months—in short, a floor effect.

The results for homeowners with only window air conditioning units are presented in Table 4. While Pallak and Cummings (1976) reported that window unit homeowners under public commitment used less electricity than in the private commitment or control conditions (for July-Month 1 in Table 4), the 12-month analysis showed only a Commitment $\times$ Month interaction, $F=2.14$, $p<.025$. As above, months were grouped as winter or summer and the effect of commitment was obtained for the summer months, $F=6.59$, $p<.01$, but not for the winter months when window air conditioning units were not in use.

TABLE 3 The Effect of Commitment on Electricity Usage over a 12-Month Period for Homeowners with Central Air Conditioning

Month:	Public Commitment (12)	Private Commitment (15)	Control (21)
July-1	166.72%[a]	202.63%	223.43%
August-2	96.78%	132.10%	141.75%
September-3	75.66%	90.54%	94.20%
October-4	70.12%	82.80%	87.26%
November-5	74.92%	90.24%	91.24%
December-6	80.03%	101.93%	102.09%
January-7	79.62%	99.73%	100.93%
February-8	82.30%	98.33%	102.12%
March-9	78.90%	92.15%	90.67%
April-10	68.82%	89.51%	90.99%
May-11	78.00%	90.93%	95.62%
June-12	126.02%	135.58%	152.33%

a. Each entry represents the usage level as a percentage of base month. Cell entries are in parentheses.
Adapted from Pallak et al. (1976).

TABLE 4 The Effect of Commitment on Electricity Usage over a 12-Month Period for Homeowners with Window Air Conditioning

Month:	Public Commitment (13)	Private Commitment (16)	Control (16)
July-1	124.97%[a]	156.35%	160.05%
August-2	102.56%	106.42%	117.25%
September-3	95.18%	83.15%	95.06%
October-4	83.75%	98.72%	86.70%
November-5	88.15%	97.43%	97.51%
December-6	103.01%	106.25%	102.11%
January-7	104.27%	101.94%	98.02%
February-8	93.88%	88.67%	94.51%
March-9	89.32%	86.69%	84.19%
April-10	89.67%	84.44%	81.28%
May-11	84.85%	85.44%	86.45%
June-12	107.88%	188.46%	135.96%

a. Each entry represents the usage level as a percentage of base month. Cell entries are in parentheses.
Adapted from Pallak et al. (1976).

Taken together, the long-term analysis of natural gas usage and electricity usage for central and window unit air conditioning seems very encouraging with regard to the effect of commitment. For homeowners in the natural gas study and in the window air conditioning sample of the electricity study, the effect of commitment was limited to the six-month season in which natural gas was being used for heating and electricity was being used for window unit air conditioners. The results for electricity with central air conditioning homeowners were not limited to a specific season.

This array of results suggests several interesting perspectives worth further empirical attention. For example, homeowners with central air as opposed to window air conditioning may differ in energy usage patterns as a function of differing air conditioning. In the case of central air conditioning, the thermostat controls are usually situated in a central, easily accessed, location. As a result, electricity usage may be more salient or more easily monitored. In contrast, owners of window units must rely on relatively primitive thermostat controls which usually do not permit a reading of actual room temperature. Thus, subjective estimates based on personal comfort may play a much larger role in determining usage—similarly usage of a window unit probably varies considerably more than usage of a central system.

When viewed in this light, our results suggested that energy conservation in terms of electricity usage (under public commitment) apparently became more habitual for homeowners with central air than for homeowners with window units. If we grant the not implausible assumption that window unit homeowners may have been more variable in their usage (turning a unit on or off more frequently), then one could speculate that energy conservation efforts may have been limited to, or cued to, usage of the window unit and hence less likely to generalize to energy usage in the non-air conditioning season relative to central air homeowners (an analogous argument can be made for natural gas usage also). For example, central air homeowners may have become more practiced or well-rehearsed in terms of observing thermostat settings—and if so may have generalized the behavior and/or concern for usage levels to the non-air conditioning season. While floor effects on electricity usage for window unit homeowners may be the most reasonable explanation for the Commitment × Month interaction, it seems plausible to assume that central air conditioned homeowners were behaving differently after the air conditioning season ended. If so, the question becomes a more general one of whether a more routine or systematic concern for thermostat settings or usage levels in the air conditioning season may be maintained across seasons.

We have no direct evidence that would let us assess the issue very precisely. For example, we have no direct evidence concerning the behaviors by which homeowners did or did not attempt to limit energy consumption, and we did not conduct any follow-up interviews. The latter was a deliberate decision as we had decided not to intrude further with the homeowners—again because we were concerned about issues of Hawthorne effects, surveillance, and such general issues concerning potential reactivity of such a procedure. In addition, we wanted to preserve the fact that as far as the homeowners were concerned, the study had been concluded. However, we did collect data related to the issue of whether more behavioral techniques that made energy usage salient to the homeowner would facilitate lower levels of electricity usage.

The Pallak and Cummings (1976) study included a "self-monitoring" condition. These homeowners received the private commitment procedure (as above) but were also asked to keep a simple "energy log" by noting appliance usage twice daily and utility-meter readings weekly. We reasoned that if the effect of commitment was related to persistence in behaviors resulting in reduced usage of window units, then a formal procedure that made these issues salient might also result in lower use levels. Since we were able to track electricity usage for homeowners in the self-monitoring condition also over 12 months, these results bear on the issue of whether concern for usage may generalize to other uses of electricity after the air conditioning season. These results are presented in Table 5 under the self-monitoring

TABLE 5   The Effect of Self-Monitoring of Usage on Electricity Consumption over a 12-Month Period for Homeowners with Window Air Conditioning

Month:	Self-monitoring (17)	Control (16)
July-1	136.25%	160.05%
August-2	96.30%	117.25%
September-3	79.99%	95.06%
October-4	74.97%	86.70%
November-5	78.47%	97.51%
December-6	86.85%	102.11%
January-7	85.50%	98.02%
February-8	83.16%	94.51%
March-9	77.22%	84.19%
April-10	78.00%	81.28%
May-11	85.12%	86.45%
June-12	130.31%	135.96%

a. Each entry represents the usage level as a percentage of base month. Cell entries are in parentheses. Adapted from Pallak et al. (1976).

(private commitment) for the window unit homeowners. Again July-Month 1 corresponds to the sample reported by Pallak and Cummings (1976) for window unit self-monitors and controls. The analysis (Self-monitoring versus Control × Month) indicated that self-monitoring resulted in lower usage levels relative to the controls, $F = 4.50$, $p < .05$, with no Self-Monitoring × Month interaction. Similarly the self-monitoring window unit homeowners (under private commitment) used less electricity than the window unit homeowners in private commitment (no self-monitoring) above, $F = 4.79$, $p < .05$, as one would expect.

These results suggest that the self-monitoring strategy may have engendered a set of actions concerned with a broader array of energy-related behaviors not so specifically cued or tied to simple usage of the window air conditioning unit. Thus, the self-monitoring procedure, which had been employed only for the month following the initial interview, may have become more routine or led to increased concern that in turn persisted once the air conditioning season had passed. Similarly, as above, central air homeowners may have been more likely to engage in thermostat monitoring regarding electricity usage as a result of initial public commitment and hence may have been more likely to persist in monitoring efforts after the air conditioning season in contrast to window unit homeowners.

Of course, one element of the self-monitoring procedure involved the homeowners in reading their own meter once a week thereby providing feedback, of a sort, linked to energy usage. Issues concerning feedback have received increased attention in the energy conservation literature and under some conditions are very effective in reducing energy usage (cf. Seligman and Darley, 1977; Kohlenberg et al., 1976). While the act of monitoring per se may bolster one's concern for energy conservation, the Seligman and Darley (1977) and Kohlenberg et al. (1976) studies suggest that having a baseline against which to compare and assess the effectiveness of one's efforts is crucial to the effect of self-monitoring. In our case, however, it is not clear what exactly may have provided a baseline for comparison of the meter readings by which homeowners could have assessed the effectiveness of their efforts in the self-monitoring condition.

THE EFFECT OF COMMITMENT: SUMMING UP

We began investigations of energy usage initially as a test of the power of the commitment variable. Thus, it seemed that taking a stand or the expectation that one's stand would become public led to behaviors resulting in reduced levels of natural gas and electricity usage. The effect of the commitment manipulation persisted even though the homeowners had been informed that the study was concluded and that their stand would not become public. These results were consistent with the framework suggesting that commitment may lead to later behavior consistent with the attitude implied by one's initial stand. Although encouraging as an approach to issues of attitude-behavior relationships, we should note that more direct evidence would have involved deriving a scale (or scales) concerning energy attitudes and then relating attitude position as a pretest measure with later usage levels under public or private commitment. That is, we made the assumption that homeowners were initially favorable to some degree toward energy conservation—a plausible assumption in many respects since few homeowners refused the interview when contacted and few refused to sign the agreement form. However, we do lack the sort of precise data concerning attitudes that would let us more directly assess the effectiveness of the commitment approach to attitude-behavior consistency.

We became increasingly committed to issues of energy conservation per se and to the question of techniques or strategies that could be brought to bear. During the period that the studies above were conducted (about three years), we became increasingly involved in energy conservation issues through participation in a team-taught course entitled "Energy and Contemporary Society." As one might predict, we became much more interested in the question of techniques or strategies suggested by a behavioral science or social psychological perspective that could be brought to bear on a major social and technological issue such as energy and energy conservation. In thinking about our research, for example, the procedure of interviewing homeowners seemed cumbersome, time consuming, and inherently limited in terms of potential direct applications by a utility company. Our studies, however, did suggest that energy-related behavior was malleable and amenable to the sorts of approaches with which psychologists are familiar from their laboratory and applied experience.

ENERGY CONSERVATION AND FEEDBACK: NEW EVIDENCE

The self-monitoring procedure originally was designed to assess whether inducing homeowners to perform monitoringlike behaviors would also induce energy conservation. On the one hand, we attempted to demonstrate a possible set of actions that might plausibly explain why commitment led to reductions in energy usage. On the other, we were interested in developing a procedure, stemming in a sense loosely from the commitment approach, that would be effective while not being so tied to the expectation that one's agreement to participate would be public. In turn, the self-monitoring results suggested that the procedure may have led to a set of concerns and behaviors that homeowners maintained after the air conditioning season had elapsed.

In the course of our interviews, we found that homeowners expressed the fact that they had little basis on which to assess the effectiveness of their efforts. In one sense, as the heating or air conditioning seasons develop, homeowners only receive feedback in the form of a utility bill and comparisons across months for a homeowner rarely permit this kind of assessment. As we thought about the feedback issue, it seemed that the component of the self-monitoring procedure involving reading one's own meter was useful (cf. Seligman and Darley, 1977). If one thinks about homeowners as trying new behaviors in order to reduce energy usage, then feedback about effectiveness of one's efforts may play a critical role in maintaining those behaviors. In our case, having a social comparison theory orientation, we thought that feedback in terms of group averages might indicate effectiveness of one's own efforts. In line with our concern for procedures that a utility company might adopt usefully, we thought that utility district averages could be included eventually in one's monthly utility statement—thus allowing a homeowner to compare usage and effectiveness relative to comparable others.

The procedure that we (Pallak et al., 1976) developed was closely modeled on the private commitment procedure above. Homeowners with central air conditioning were interviewed and signed an agreement permitting access to their utility records. However, we told homeowners that we wanted to read their meters ourselves every two weeks for a six-week period. In turn, we explained that we would send them a postcard noting their meter readings. In the usage feedback condition, homeowners simply received a card stating their actual electricity usage for the preceding two-week period— exactly as they received usage feedback from the utility company in their monthly statement. For homeowners in the comparative feedback condition, however, we also included the average electricity usage for other homeowners in the study, as well as the individual homeowner's usage level. As before, each homeowner received a statement from us at the end of the six-week period stating that the study had concluded and so forth.

The results summarized in Table 6 are based on the utility-company readings. Month 1 (June) represented the meter readings at the end of the second two-week period (i.e., one month after the interview and homeowners had received a third card from us between Month 1 and Month 2). Month 3 readings were obtained after homeowners had learned that the study had concluded—allowing us to assess the longer term effect of comparative feedback after the procedure had been terminated.

Again the cell entries are in terms of percentage usage relative to the base month preceding the interview (May 1976). As may be seen, the comparative feedback resulted in lower rates of increase during the air conditioning season than the simple usage feedback, $F = 7.53$, $p < .01$, and the effect held for six weeks after comparative feedback had been withdrawn.

TABLE 6   The Effect of Comparative or Usage Feedback on Electricity Usage for Homeowners with Central Air Conditioning Over a Three-Month Period

Month:	Comparative Feedback (20)	Usage Feedback (18)
June-1	134.06%[a]	166.22%
July-2	142.10%	173.05%
August-3	121.95%	144.43%

a. Each entry represents the usage level as a percentage of base month. Cell entries are in parentheses. All *ns* are in parentheses.
Adapted from Pallak et al. (1976).

These results nicely complement Kohlenberg et al. (1976) and Seligman and Darley (1977). The latter employed feedback concerning individual performance relative to the individual's previous performance, while in the present case our comparative feedback allowed the homeowner to compare performance with that of others. In addition, we were able to assess the effect after feedback had stopped. Taken together, these sets of results suggest that the feedback procedures lead to changes in energy-related behavior that persist over time. The intriguing implication, of course, is that utility companies could incorporate various sorts of feedback with some reprogramming of the utility billing system. Alternatively, the feedback strategy represents a potentially useful strategy as one means of reducing consumption during the peak air conditioning season when generating capacity may be inadequate leading to brown-outs.

Unfortunately, we were not able to pursue this possibility further as each of us moved from the geographic area. Our next step would have been to discuss the possibilities of reprogramming billing statements within a subset of the utility meter districts as one means of a broader scale test of the comparison feedback procedure. Similarly, we had planned a study involving the comparison feedback procedure on an acute basis—that is introduction of comparison feedback just prior to the peak air conditioning and peak heating season. It seemed that the local utility company would have been willing to implement such a strategy based on our history of rather constructive cooperation.

Our particular brand of energy conservation research developed from a series of laboratory investigations conducted in the context of attitude change issues. Our paradigm represented really a transfer of the sorts of single-subject-at-a-time procedures from the lab to single-homeowner-at-a-time in the field. Because we were accustomed to that level of analysis, we never pursued other interesting aspects of the array of energy research issues. For example, we worked with homeowners who paid their own utility bills. What about people who do not and hence have no direct access to information about personal behavior and energy consumption? Similarly, because of the specific case-study approach of the specific chapters in this annual, we have not tried to provide a particularly broad view of the variety of approaches, expertise, paradigms, and critical analyses that psychologists are able to bring to bear. However, an excellent analysis of many of these issues had been provided by McClelland and Canter (forthcoming) and is well worth reading.

While remaining basic laboratory researchers, the energy research experience led to several changes in our perspective on social psychology. On the one hand, social psychology has had a robust history in the field, in applications, and in laboratory settings. Thus, it always seemed reasonable to move from the lab, to the field, and back to the lab. On the other hand, we began to view our particular research as an instance of problem-oriented research rather than as "action-research" or as "applications-research," i.e., research that is based on the question "how can we conserve energy" and that borrows freely from the relatively sophisticated knowledge and data base in psychology. Thus, our research is not so much a test of the commitment notion in the field setting (although it is that) as one point of entry or one perspective by which we moved into a series of issues in a relatively thoughtful manner. The concern at a problem level is how do we induce energy conservation over the long haul in those areas where simple compliance procedures (i.e., the 55-mph speed limit) or surveillance mechanisms are not useful.

At a broader level one can think of the science system in psychology as providing a great deal of information about theoretical process and conceptual variables and as representing an excellent basis by which to begin a systematic analysis of problems such as energy conservation. In one sense our collective data base allows psychologists to begin thinking about the sorts of intervention strategies (and to assess their effectiveness) in ways that would be useful and easily adaptable at a policy level. While we did not develop our particular line of research further, the main thrust, I think, is that a problem-oriented perspective leads one to think about both what we know and what we could recommend as starting points for policy development in a fashion that is consistent with our values and approaches as a science.

REFERENCES

BICKMAN, L. (1972) "Environmental attitudes and actions." Journal of Social Psychology 87: 323-324.

CONWAY, H.M. and L.L. LISTON [eds.] (1974) The Weather Handbook. Atlanta: Conway Research.

HALVERSON, R.R. and M.S. PALLAK (1978) "Commitment, ego-involvement, and resistance to attack." Journal of Experimental Social Psychology 14: 1-12.

JONES, E.E. and R.E. NISBETT (1971) The Actor and the Observer: Divergent Perceptions of the Causes of Behavior. Morristown, NJ: General Learning Press.

KIESLER, C.A. (1971) The Psychology of Commitment: Experiments Linking Behavior to Belief. New York: Academic Press.

KOHLENBERG, R.J., T. PHILLIPS, and W. PROCTOR (1976) "A behavioral analysis of peaking in residential electricity energy consumers." Journal of Applied Behavior Analysis 9: 13-18.

McCLELLAND, L. and R.J. CANTER (forthcoming) "Psychological research on energy conservation," in A. Baum and J.E. Singer (eds.), Advances in Environmental Psychology (vol. 3): Energy Conservation—Psychological Perspectives. Hillsdale, NJ: Lawrence Erlbaum Associates.

PALLAK, M.S., D.A. COOK, and J.J. SULLIVAN (1976) "The effects of comparison feedback on electricity usage." University of Iowa. (unpublished)

————— and N. CUMMINGS (1976) "Commitment and voluntary energy conservation." Personality and Social Psychology Bulletin 2: 27-31.

—————M. MUELLER, K. DOLLAR, and J. PALLAK (1972) "The effect of commitment on responsiveness to an extreme consonant communication." Journal of Personality and Social Psychology 23: 429-436.

————— S. SOGIN, and A. VanZANTE (1974) "Bad decision: the effect of volunteering, locus of causality, and negative consequences on attitude change." Journal of Personality and Social Psychology 30: 217-227.

—————J.J. SULLIVAN and D.A. COOK (1977) "The long-term effects of commitment on voluntary energy conservation." Presented at the meeting of the Midwestern Psychological Association, Chicago.

SELIGMAN, C. and J.M. DARLEY (1977) "Feedback as a means of decreasing residential energy consumption." Journal of Applied Psychology 62: 363-368.

SULLIVAN, J.J. and M.S. PALLAK (1976) "The effect of commitment and reactance on action-taking." Personality and Social Psychology Bulletin 2: 179-182.

SHERIF, C.W., M. SHERIF, and R.E. NEBERGALL (1965) Attitude and Attitude Change. Philadelphia: W.B. Saunders.

WICKLUND, R.A. and J.A. BREHM (1976) Perspectives on Cognitive Dissonance. Hillsdale, NJ: Lawrence Erlbaum Associates.

BERTRAM H. RAVEN
ROBERT W. HALEY

10

SOCIAL INFLUENCE
IN A MEDICAL CONTEXT

HOSPITAL-ACQUIRED INFECTIONS AS A PROBLEM
IN MEDICAL SOCIAL PSYCHOLOGY

In 1847, Dr. Ignaz Philipp Semmelweis was appointed to the maternity department of the Allegemeines Krankenhaus (General Hospital) in Vienna. At the time of his appointment, as many as 10% of the women admitted to one division of the hospital's obstetric service died of puerperal fever. To elucidate this problem, Semmelweis began his now classic study into the causes of maternal mortality. Through meticulous research and an insight gained through the death of a close friend and colleague, he finally felt that he had discovered the answer: The culprit, it seemed, was "the examining finger" of the physician who would first examine the cadavers of women who had just died of puerperal fever and then immediately proceed to the examination of healthy patients in adjacent rooms. Though he did not yet have the benefit of the germ theory of disease still being developed by Pasteur and Koch, Semmelweis proposed a simple solution to the problem: He recommended that before proceeding from autopsy to delivery room, and just before examining each patient, each physician first wash his hands in an antiseptic solution. Though his recommendations were considered controversial, they were followed, and the maternal death rate at Allegemeines Krankenhaus dropped dramatically.

One would have hoped that with such clear evidence, the policy advo-

AUTHORS' NOTE: We gratefully acknowledge the essential scientific contributions of the following: Howard E. Freeman, Sharon Reeder, T. Grace Emori, David Redfearn, Susan Rakow, Eve Fielder, and Vi Dorfman; and the editorial assistance of Deborah L. Jones.

This research was supported by contracts 200-75-0510 and 200-76-0600 from the Center for Disease Control.

Portions of this article were originally presented at the International Congress of Applied Psychology in Munich, Federal Republic of Germany, August 3, 1978, in a paper entitled, "Social Influence Processes and Infection Risk in Hospitals."

cated by Semmelweis in Germany (and a few years earlier by Dr. Oliver Wendell Holmes, 1843, see Holmes, 1977, in this country) would have been accepted for all time. Unfortunately, such was not to be the case, and Semmelweis, rejected by his peers as something of an aberration, eventually died tragically in a mental hospital—ironically, himself a victim of a hospital-acquired infection.

This parable, as pointed out by Schaffner (1977), has great relevance for the research on hospital infection control today: Patients—then as now—were developing infections which they had contracted after hospitalization; there was misunderstanding as to the mode of transmission; epidemiologic research suggested a solution; the solution (in this case, handwashing), though conceptually simple, proved difficult to enforce, physicians being particularly reluctant to accept the practice; implementation of the solution was not supported by the hospital's administration. One of the critical factors in that situation, as well as in those that we face today, was the need to change the behavior of hospital personnel through social influence.

The potential role of social psychology and other social sciences in medicine and medical practice is being increasingly recognized (Taylor, 1978). Medical professionals are becoming ever more aware that innovative techniques and procedures cannot improve the welfare of patients unless they can be implemented. Newly developed medications for an illness such as high blood pressure, for instance, cannot be effective unless the medical practitioner can be persuaded to prescribe them and the patient can be persuaded to take them (Caplan et al., 1976). Likewise, a new technique for aseptically handling patients' urinary catheters which might reduce the risk of infection will have no effect unless the nurses or other relevant hospital personnel are persuaded to use it. Theories and research on social influence methods and on the bases of social power, then, have critical implications for medical practice.

Such research in medical settings can be grouped into three major categories: studies of (1) the influence of medical practitioners on patients, (2) the influence of medical practitioners and hospital personnel on one another, and (3) the influence of hospital authorities and administrators on patient-care personnel. In this article we focus upon the latter two categories. Our particular concern will be on social influence factors which might contribute to the problem explored by Semmelweis—the prevention and control of *nosocomial infections.*

THE DEFINITION OF THE PROBLEM

Derived from "nosokomeion," the Greek word for hospital, nosocomial infection is defined as one that develops during hospitalization and that was not present or incubating at the time the patient was admitted. This problem received new attention and emerged as a major public health issue following the serious hospital-based epidemics of staphylococcal disease that swept the country in the 1950s (Communicable Disease Center [now Center for Disease Control], 1958).

Today, the problem is still considerable. It is estimated, probably conservatively, that 5% (Bennett et al., 1971) of the 32 million patients admitted to U.S. hospitals each year acquire such an infection during their stay; 15,000 of these patients die. In addition to these human costs in excess morbidity and mortality, the financial costs of hospital care have been significantly increased by the problem: In the United States alone, patients who contract these infections will spend an average of seven extra days in the hospital, for an additional cost of over $1.1 billion per year. Other nations face similar burdens.

Despite the magnitude of the problem, one might be tempted to write off nosocomial infections as an inevitable risk of hospitalization. To be sure, no one suggests that all such infections could be eliminated. However, authorities in the field have argued convincingly that the rate could be reduced by as much as half, with tremendous savings in lives, health, and hospital costs (Sencer and Axnick, 1975; Bennett, 1978).

THE DEVELOPMENT OF INFECTION SURVEILLANCE AND CONTROL PROGRAMS

With the guidance and encouragement of the Center for Disease Control (CDC), the American Hospital Association (AHA), and other organizations, many hospitals during the past decade sought to combat nosocomial infections by voluntarily implementing infection surveillance and control programs (ISCPs). Then, in 1976, in recognition of the enormity of the problem, the Joint Commission on the Accreditation of Hospitals (JCAH; 1976), a private accrediting organization, issued an extensive set of guidelines recommending that each hospital have an ongoing ISCP as one of the conditions of accreditation. A model program is designed to monitor the frequency and kinds of nosocomial infections and thereby foster the development of policies and procedures to control them. There is, of course, additional expense involved in ISCPs. However, it is estimated that if such programs reduce nosocomial infection rates by even 6%, they will have paid for themselves financially and certainly in terms of the health and lives of hospitalized patients (Sencer and Axnick, 1975).

Although the most effective organization for an ISCP is still being debated, most experts agree that the personnel should include the following:

(1) an Infection Control Practitioner (ICPrac), usually a registered nurse with clinical experience and knowledge of epidemiology (study of the prevalence and spread of disease) and infectious disease, to be responsible for detecting and recording nosocomial infections, analyzing the data, advising hospital personnel about policy, and taking other measures to reduce nosocomial infections; (2) a Medical Epidemiologist (ME), usually a physician with knowledge and interest in epidemiology, infectious disease, and fundamental biostatistics, to work closely with the ICPrac, giving direction, guidance, and support to develop infection surveillance and control measures and presumably to serve as the chairman of the Infection Control Committee; (3) an Infection Control Committee, including, in addition to the ICPrac and the ME, representatives of the major clinical departments, the pathologist, the director of nursing, an administrative representative, and various other ex officio members (Pharmacy, Housekeeping, Inhalation Therapy, Housestaff, and so on). The Infection Control Committee should meet regularly (at least monthly, but more often if data on infections so warrant), review surveillance and other significant information, and play a major role in determining the hospital's infection control policies. It should provide for meaningful implementation of these policies, offering guidance and support for the ME and ICPrac.

In short, the job of these hospital personnel, organized as an ISCP, is to maintain awareness of infection risks existing in the hospital, formulate strategies for reducing the risks (e.g., isolation of infectious patients and proper aseptic patient-care practices), and implement the policies that will prevent infection (Center for Disease Control, 1972). A further important objective of these ISCP personnel is to influence the physicians, nurses, and other hospital employees who care for patients to incorporate the preventive patient-care concepts, advocated by the ISCP, into their daily patient-care practices.

AN EVALUATION OF INFECTION SURVEILLANCE
AND CONTROL PROGRAMS

OVERALL PROJECT STUDY DESIGN

Although, as mentioned, all hospitals have been urged—and to maintain accreditation are now required—to have an ISCP, the efficacy of such programs had not, until the inception of our project, been evaluated in a scientifically sound, nationwide study. Thus, it was to test the assumptions about the preventability of nosocomial infections and the effectiveness of control efforts that CDC in 1974 launched the Study on the Efficacy of Nosocomial Infection Control, or SENIC Project.

While the SENIC study design has been described in detail elsewhere (Haley et al., forthcoming a), we will summarize its major features here, before focusing on the segment of the project dealing specifically with social influence. The project has three primary objectives:

(1) to determine whether (and, if so, to what degree) the implementation of ISCPs has lowered nosocomial infection rates in major categories of U.S. hospitals

(2) to describe the current status of ISCPs and infection rates in these hospitals

(3) to study in detail the relationships among (a) the characteristics of hospitals and patients, (b) the components of ISCPs, and (c) changes in the components of infections (for example, their distribution at specific anatomical sites and on specific hospital services).

Given these primary objectives, planners at CDC outlines a three-phase nationwide evaluatcon project. Phase I, the Preliminary Screening Questionnaire, was designed to survey the universe of U.S. hospitals—some 7,000 in all—to determine the extent of infection control activity in the country and to pinpoint the beginning of formal ISCPs. Using this information the designers planned to stratify the respondents and select a random sample for more intensive study in Phases II and III. Phase II, the Hospital Interview Survey, and the phase on which we will concentrate here, was designed to measure in detail the activities gauged only grossly in Phase I. This information was to be gathered by extensive on-site interviews in the sample hospitals. Phase III, the Medical Records Survey—another on-site evaluation, this time by specially trained medical chart reviewers—was designed to measure each hospital's nosocomial infection rate over time (1970 and 1976). By comparing the rates in these two years and by assessing the impact of various programs implemented during the same period, the study's designers sought to determine which combination of program components is most effective in reducing nosocomial infections for the least cost to hospitals.

CONCEPTUAL MODEL OF HOSPITAL INFECTION CONTROL PROGRAMS

An important prerequisite to studying ISCPs was defining the characteristics, likely causal pathways, and measurement parameters of such programs. This proved no simple matter, even to the CDC hospital epidemiologists who had been involved in nosocomial infection research for a number of years. The main difficulties arose from the imprecise terminology used to refer to ISCP activities and concepts and to the wide variety of approaches to infection control being practiced in the nation's hospitals. Early in the project's design phase, therefore, the CDC staff designed a series of conceptual models expressing the complex interrelationships in terms given precise definitions. Although the models are discussed in more detail elsewhere (Haley et al., forthcoming a), we will present a simplified conceptual model

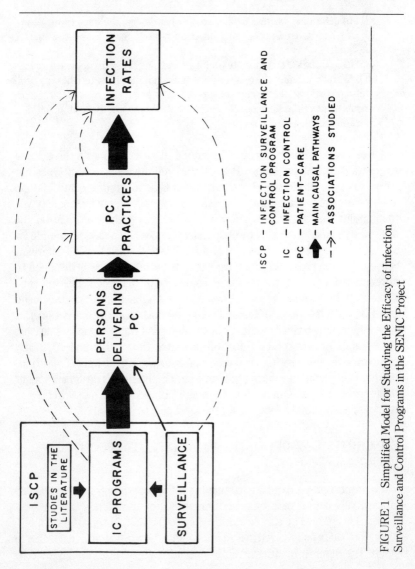

FIGURE 1   Simplified Model for Studying the Efficacy of Infection Surveillance and Control Programs in the SENIC Project

here to illustrate the relationships among factors which contribute to noso-comial infection.

According to the model (Figure 1), an Infection Surveillance and Control Program (ISCP) is an organized unit which draws upon (1) preexisting knowledge found largely in studies in the literature and (2) ongoing surveil-lance of nosocomial infections as a basis for developing its active infection control programs. Although the infection control program's interventions are aimed ultimately at reducing nosocomial infection rates, they must operate largely through the influencing of *patient-care personnel* (e.g., nurses, physicians, and paramedical personnel) to adopt and use consistently certain *patient-care practices* that reduce infection risks directly. Exam-ples of patient-care practices that have the most effect are (1) collecting a urine specimen by aspirating the wall of a patient's indwelling urinary cathe-ter (rather than disconnecting the catheter), (2) changing the site of an intravenous catheter needle at least every three days, and (3) washing hands between patient contacts.

Consequently, the change in the nosocomial infection rate over time, measured in the Medical Records Survey phase of the project, will be the ultimate dependent variable of the analysis, and patient-care practices (pri-marily of the nursing staff) will be analyzed as important intervening varia-bles. A more detailed model specifies all the ISCP characteristics and func-tions aimed at influencing the practices of the patient-care personnel. Poten-tially one of the most important of these is the variety of social influence techniques used by the ISCP staff members (e.g., the ME and ICPrac) to alter the behavior of the patient-care personnel.

THE DEVELOPMENT OF THE HOSPITAL INTERVIEW SURVEY

Having outlined the fundamental scientific problems to be examined, we now describe briefly the research process itself. The CDC project planners developed these conceptual models and several alternative study designs early in 1974 and convened a multidisciplinary task force of consultants to discuss and various alternatives under consideration. The consensus of the task force was that the quasi-experimental study design could be adopted if two important methodological innovations could be made: namely, the de-velopment of a new method for accurately measuring nosocomial infection rates retrospectively in the study hospitals and the development of a way to measure and control for the impact of the personal effectiveness—or as it came to be known, the "charisma factor"—of the ICPrac of ME that might confound the analysis of ISCP efficacy. The measurement of nosocomial infection rates was a problem the CDC epidemiologists were familiar with and had already been working on. Measuring the charisma factor of ISCP personnel, however, was another matter. Paraphrasing a prominent member of the task force: "Some ISCP personnel are just effective people, and effective people may control infections mainly by their own personal magnetism rather than primarily through the surveillance activities they practice. This phenomenon would confound the ability to evaluate the efficacy of the actual program elements."

The conclusion of the task force meetings led to a two-year period of intensive methodological development. The CDC epidemiologists designed a method for measuring nosocomial infection rates by retrospective review of patients' medical records. In this effort, they enlisted the collaboration of a group in the Department of Biostatistics at the University of North Carolina (UNC) at Chapel Hill to assist in the validation of the method and its implementation in the national Medical Records Survey (Haley et al., forthcoming b). To measure the charisma factor the CDC staff decided upon the Hospital Interview Survey to measure the characteristics and activities of the ISCP personnel and, more important, to query the members of the hospitals' nursing staffs on the personal effectiveness of the ISCP personnel. After all, should not charisma be measured by querying the people whose behavior in patient care was the target of the ISCP's influence?

Realizing that sociopsychological measurements of this type were not within the realm of expertise of medical epidemiologists, the project staff at CDC decided to enlist a group of social scientists to contribute the technology for making these measurements. To begin this multidisciplinary research effort, CDC initiated open bidding for a research contract by placing an advertisement in the *Commerce Business Daily,* a U.S. government publication that lists all government procurement invitations, contract awards, and so forth. At that time, a member of Institute for Social Science Research (ISSR) at the University of California at Los Angeles (UCLA) was routinely scanning the *Commerce Business Daily* for research opportunities and came upon the announcement of the SENIC contract for developing "a data collection form that could be used . . . to document quantitatively staff members' competence and influence (charisma, etc.) which are likely to affect the success of Infection Surveillance and Control Programs (ISCPs) in influencing nosocomial infection rates." Given the experience of the ISSR staff in studying social power and influence, evaluation research, and the conduct of surveys, they responded to an official "Request for Proposal" (RFP) with a formal research protocol in which they redefined the "charisma factor" as "effectiveness in using social influence techniques." In the ensuing competitive bidding process, ISSR's proposal was selected and an initial research contract was negotiated. Therein began an intensive collaboration to measure and study, among other things, social influence in hospitals.

ALTERNATIVE RESEARCH STRATEGIES

By the time the social science team of ISSR became involved in the SENIC Project, the CDC staff had already made the basic decision to utilize a field-survey approach with a large sample of hospitals for their study of hospital infections. As we noted earlier, the objectives were not only to study what factors of ISCPs were related to greater effectiveness in infection control but also to obtain indications of the extent of actual reduction in infection rates, to determine the status and form of the ISCPs, and to examine the distribution of various forms and sites of hospital infections. These objectives argued against the use of some alternative research strategies. (An evaluation of these alternatives and the rationale for choosing the final design are discussed elsewhere, (see Haley et al., forthcoming a).

The reliance on self-report data in our interview schedules and questionnaires was of considerable concern to us, despite assurance that all responses would remain confidential. We were aware of studies such as that of Hofling et al. (1966), which indicated discrepancy between what hospital personnel reported that they and others would do and their actual observable behavior. We did try to deal with this problem by phrasing some questions so as to minimize social desirability bias (e.g., asking how *other* nurses would be likely to behave, rather than depending on their estimation of their own behavior). We also included some parallel items on different forms (e.g., reports regarding physicians' behavior were included both in the nurses' questionnaire and in the medical epidemiologists' schedule to help guard against biased perceptions and reporting). However, these solutions were not completely satisfactory, and we must remain circumspect in our evaluation of some of our self-report data, looking toward other research data to supplement our findings.

Instead of an interview survey approach, we might also have considered an intensive field observational approach, with carefully trained observers attached to a variety of hospitals and instructed to observe carefully the behavior of ISCP personnel in implementing their policies. The observational method might have had some advantages in avoiding dependence on self-report data. However, it would have been extremely difficult or impossible to have observations carried out unobtrusively, and we might have expected that the presence of observers would have had a marked effect on the behavior of hospital personnel. Furthermore, in order to examine the vast range of differing ISCPs and their implementation in various types of hospitals, a sizable number of observers would have been necessary, at tremendous cost. These, then, were some of the factors which led to the adoption of the field interview survey approach, which we describe here.

DETERMINATION OF CONTENT

In the early stages of development of the Hospital Interview Survey, ideas and information were exchanged through a series of meetings of the UCLA social scientists, the CDC medical epidemiologists, and the collaborating statisticians from UNC. From these meetings, a number of working documents emerged. The UCLA staff also attended several training conferences on nosocomial infection at CDC and elsewhere and reviewed the extensive literature on the subject.

In February 1975, the UCLA and CDC staff visited 20 hospitals to observe firsthand a variety of approaches to infection control. At these visits the two groups held informal interviews with key hospital personnel and later compared field notes with preconceived hypotheses from CDC's infection control experience and ISSR's social science concepts. The interviews were supplemented by discussions with consultants with broad experience in infection control. Based on these experiences, the collaborating investigators developed a comprehensive list of several thousand ISCP components and characteristics that appeared to be important and seemed to vary between hospitals. The items to be included were keyed to the conceptual models, and four criteria were used to reduce the mammoth list to a still large but manageable one. Specifically, an item was included if it measured an activity that was (1) likely to be effective, (2) commonly used in hospitals, (3) expensive, or (4) recommended by CDC, AHA, or JCAH. The final list included some 500 discrete topics which, accounting for multipart questions and multiple responses, resulted in more than 2,500 individual response items per hospital.

SELECTING AND DEFINING THE RESPONDENTS

The next serious problem was to select and define the respondents to be interviewed in the hospitals. We initially focused on developing a structured personal interview form, or instrument, by which a trained interviewer could obtain correctly form the ICPrac the characteristics of the ISCP and the social influence techniques used by the ISCP personnel. After initial experiences with the ICPrac instrument, however, we extended the scope of the survey, developing an interview instrument for the ME and a paper-and-pencil self-administered instrument for the hospital's staff nurses involved in direct patient care. The nursing staff instrument was also designed to measure the effects of the social influence techniques from the viewpoint of the "target" personnel and their actual patient-care practices. Much later, we added shorter interview instruments for the hospital administrator, to assess his/her interaction with the ISCP staff, and for other hospital personnel who frequently take part in infection control activities (Table 1).

At this point, it occurred to us that, although all hospitals have (at least on paper) an infection control committee, not every hospital has an ICPrac or an ME; and furthermore, even when these positions exist, there is substantial variation in the types of activities, division of responsibilities, and dependence on other hospital departments or outside consultants. There was even such variation in the titles given to the different infection control positions (e.g., infection control practitioner, infection control nurse, nurse epidemiologist, surveillance officer) that defining our respondents in a consistent way appeared at first to be a serious obstacle. To overcome it, we defined a number of "prototypic roles" in operational terms that could be recited verbatim in each hospital to define the respondents in a standardized fashion to obtain comparable responses in all of the hospitals.

By the end of an intensive planning period, we had crystallized the theoretical model of infection control, and we had designed and pretested interview instruments for 12 respondents. The final instruments contained

TABLE 1   Hospital Personnel Interviewed in Phase II of
the SENIC Project and Length of Interviews

Hospital Personnel	Approximate Interview Time
1. Chairman of the Infection Control Committee and/or Medical Epidemiologist	60 minutes
2. Infection Control Nurse (Practitioner) (if none, the nursing representative on the Infection Control Committee or other most knowledgeable infection control person	3½ hours
3. Hospital Administrator (or Assistant Administrator more directly in charge of infection control)	20 minutes
4. Director of the Microbiology Laboratory	30 minutes
5. Technician in the Microbiology Laboratory	20 minutes
6. Director of the Nursing Service	20 minutes
7. Operating Room Supervisor	20 minutes
8. Head of Pharmacy	5 minutes
9. Head of Inhalation Therapy	15 minutes
10. Head of Intravenous Team (if IV team present)	10 minutes
11. Head of Housekeeping	15 minutes
12. Person in charge of cleaning anesthesia equipment	10 minutes

more than 2,500 questions on such topics as the characteristics and activities of ICPracs, MEs, and infection control committees; the techniques of infection surveillance and outbreak investigation; environmental monitoring; isolation practices; the relationships between the ISCP and the hospital administration and other departments; nurses' patient-care practices; methods used to train staff members in correct care; techniques of influencing the behavior of patient-care personnel; housekeeping and disinfection techniques; and the role of the microbiology laboratory. In the actual survey, 55 interviewers obtained responses from some 13,000 hospital personnel in 433 hospitals, including about 7,200 staff nurses. Details of the logistical management of the field work, statistical sampling techniques used to select the staff nurses, quality control procedures, and other important management concepts will be described in subsequent reports.

DATA PROCESSING

Because of the size and complexity of the interview data base, extensive development went into data processing and the editing and cleaning of the computerized data files. Initially, the forms were sent from the field to CDC where they were logged in and microfilmed. They were then sent to ISSR where coders converted the interviewers' recordings to numerical codes in preprinted spaces in the right-hand margins of the instruments. At this stage, the small number of open-ended questions and the "other, specify" responses were coded numerically according to a code book that was developed from examining a random sample of the completed instruments.

RESULTS

Drawing from different sections of the complex model and concentrating on the responses of the ICPrac, the ME/Infection Control Committee Chairman (hereafter referred to as the ME/ICC-Chm), and the nursing staff, we present some representative results from the data analyzed thus far.

APPROVAL AND SUPPORT OF HOSPITAL AUTHORITIES

An item included on the instruments for both the ME and the ICPrac asked how helpful various hospital staff members, particularly those in authority, were in implementing the ISCP. There was, of course, a variety of responses, but in general both respondents agreed that the hospital administration could have been more helpful: Only 40% of the ICPracs and 54% of the

MEs rated the hospital administration as "very helpful."

AUTHORITY OF ISCP STAFF TO IMPLEMENT INFECTION CONTROL POLICY

A question, also included on both forms, asked whether the ISCP personnel could implement certain policies on their own—such as closing a ward harboring infected patients, setting up staff education programs, and warning staff about negligence—or whether they need prior approval. Approval and support of hospital authorities was significantly correlated with the ISCP staff's perceived authority in implementing policy. These, in turn, were significantly related to the item described below: readiness to take action with respect to a violator.

READINESS TO SPEAK UP TO VIOLATOR OF POLICY

We asked the ICPrac, "Would you say something if you saw (someone) enter a strict isolation room without masking? . . . discard an unprotected hypodermic needle in a regular wastebasket? . . . after handling a contaminated dressing . . . proceed to "clean" procedures such as drawing blood or handling clean linen without first washing hands?" Violators of differing status were substituted for the "someone" in the question: head nurse, staff nurse, attending physician, and laboratory technician. Readiness to say something differs with the situation ($F=19$, $p<.001$ by analysis of variance). But even more important is the effect of the target: ICPracs were significantly less likely to speak up to physicians than to others ($F=171$, $p<.001$).

Further analysis shows that readiness to deal directly with the violator of infection control policy, rather than to ask someone else to take action, is determined by the status of the influencing agent as well as the status of the target. Considering in Table 2 the responses of both the ICPrac and the ME/ICC-Chm on dealing with a staff nurse, an attending physician, or the head of the inhalation therapy department, we see that the ICPrac would be most likely to deal directly with a nurse violator, while the ME/ICC-Chm would be more likely to deal directly with a physician violator (interaction effect, analysis of variance, $F=123$, $p<.001$). Such action, however, often cannot be delayed until the matter is referred to some other authority. Suppose, for instance, that a staff nurse sees a physician do something that she thinks places a patient at risk. Should she be ready to take action herself immediately? We asked the staff nurses whether they would say something if they saw various personnel: (1) disconnecting a urinary catheter in order to take a urine specimen (clearly an inappropriate procedure according to CDC guidelines); (2) performing their duties with a boil on their arms (thus exposing patients to possible infection); (3) handling an infected wound or dressing and then proceeding to another patient without washing their hands. The mean responses indicated that most nurses believe that they probably *would* say something. However, here again, we note that nurses are much more reluctant to speak up to physicians than to nurses or other personnel (housekeepers, orderlies, and so on; $F = 7122$, $p < .001$).

TABLE 2   Proportion of Infection Control Practitioners
and Medical Epidemiologists/Infection Control Committee
Chairmen Who Would Take Direct Action Against
Violators of Differing Status

	Respondent		
Violator	*ICPRAC* *(N=429)*	*ME/ICC-Chm* *(N=412)*	*Marginals*
Staff Nurse	.83	.40	.62
Attending Physician	.65	.86	.76
Inhalation Therapy Head	.73	.76	.75
Marginals	.74	.68	.71

Note. Effects of respondent significant at $p < .01$, effects of violator of variance and interaction effects significant at $p < .001$, by repeated-measures analysis of variance (BMDP2V).

As an alternative to speaking up directly, we asked the staff nurses whether they would report the violator to someone else? The same pattern was reported: Staff nurses said that they are not only *less* likely to say something to a physician who violates policy than to other personnel they are also *less* likely to report him/her to others for corrective action ($F = 839$, $p < .001$). Still, they were more likely to report a physician than to speak to him/her directly.

BASES OF POWER UTILIZED BY THE ICPRAC AND ME

We were especially interested in the methods used by ISCP personnel to get hospital staff members to comply with prescribed policy and the relative effectiveness of these methods. In our preliminary informal interviews, we learned of a number of highly complex and involved influence strategies used by various personnel in differing situations. While the richness of these approaches could not be examined fully in a massive survey, we were able to make use of a scheme which had proven useful in other studies of social influence processes. The background for this approach is described in greater detail elsewhere (French and Raven, 1959; Raven, 1974; Raven and

Rubin, 1976). *Social power* is defined in terms of potential methods of influence which might be utilized by an influencing agent. *Social influence* is defined as a change in a person's *(target's)* cognitions, attitudes, or behavior, which has its origins in another person or group (the influencing agent). Essentially six differing *bases of power* were examined: coercive, reward, legitimate, referent, expert, and informational. In our study we presented the ME/ICC-Chm, ICPrac, and the staff nurses with hypothetical situations in which an agent might want to correct the behavior of a violator of infection control policy. Listed below are the six bases of power, followed, as an example, by the possible responses offered to the ICPrac who might want to correct the behavior of a staff nurse who "breaks technique":

(1) *Coercive power* stems from the ability of the influencing agent to mediate punishment for the target: "Warn the nurse of possible disciplinary action or possible dismissal."

(2) *Reward power* stems from the ability to mediate rewards: "Point out to the nurse that your evaluations carry some weight; that you might be able to help the nurse in the future."

(3) *Legitimate power* grows out of the target's acceptance of a role relationship with the agent that obligates the target to comply with the request of the agent: "Emphasize your position as Infection Control Nurse and the nurse's obligation to comply with your recommendation in this matter."

(4) *Referent power* occurs when the target uses the other as a "frame of reference," as a standard for evaluating his/her behavior: "Emphasize that other nurses in the hospital follow proper procedures."

(5) *Expert power* stems from the target's attributing superior knowledge or ability to the agent—in other words, the agent knows best, knows what is correct: "Emphasize your expertise regarding infection control procedures."

(6) *Informational power* is a result of the persuasiveness of the information communicated by the agent to the target: "Indicate the basis for techniques, citing available evidence, hospital data or journal references, and so forth."

To evaluate the approach used with additional targets, a corresponding set of six alternatives was presented for influencing an errant physician and a head of inhalation therapy. Both the ICPrac and the ME/ICC-Chm were asked to rate their use of these six bases of power as "very likely," "somewhat likely," or "unlikely." From the bases rated "very likely," they then selected the "most likely" bases of power. The same procedure was repeated to find out which of the various vases of power were seen as most effective in changing behavior.

What bases of power did the ICPrac and the ME/ICC-Chm report that they would be likely to use? From Table 3, we see that a clear first choice for both respondents is *informational* power, with expert power the second

TABLE 3   Mean* Reports of Use of Differing Power
Bases by Infection Control Practitioners and Medical
Epidemiologists/Infection Control Committee Chairmen in
Influencing Staff Nurses, Attending Physicians, and
Inhalation Therapists

Likelihood of Use

a.   As Reported by the ICPrac (N=427)

| | Target Person | | | |
Power Base	Staff Nurse	Attending Physician	Inhalation Therapy Head	Marginals
Coercive	.71	.17	.42	.43
Reward	.57	.06	.10	.24
Legitimate	.86	.65	.83	.78
Expert	.70	1.54	1.54	1.26
Referent	.86	.88	.81	.85
Informational	1.88	1.79	1.88	1.85
Marginals	.93	.85	.93	.90

b.   As Reported by the ME/ICC-Chm (N=410)

| | Target Person | | | |
Power Base	Staff Nurse	Attending Physician	Inhalation Therapy Head	Marginals
Coercive	.96	.56	.90	.81
Reward	.50	.17	.22	.30
Legitimate	1.16	1.02	1.14	1.11
Expert	.72	1.62	1.49	1.28
Referent	1.24	1.29	1.10	1.21
Informational	1.70	1.81	1.80	1.77
Marginals	1.05	1.08	1.11	1.08

*Scores ranged from 0: "unlikely" to 2: "very likely".

Note. Main effects and interaction effects significant by repeated-measures analysis of variance (p<.001; BMDP2V).

most likely choice. Only reward power seems to be almost completely
rejected. However, the ICPrac seems more selective in the use of differing
bases of power, as can be seen in the right marginals: Bases other than expert
and informational power were used sparingly. In contrast, the overall mean
for each base of power (except informational power) is higher for the
ME/ICC-Chm: In general, these respondents, then, tend to use a greater
variety of power bases. The target by bases of power interactions are highly

significant for both of the influencing agents—some bases of power (coercive, reward, and legitimate) are more likely to be used for nurses than for physicians. Note that ICPracs are more likely to use expert power with physicians than with nurses and that the ME/ICC-Chm shows a much greater tendency to use coercive power with physicians than does the IC-Prac.

PERCEIVED SUCCESS IN IMPLEMENTING CHANGES IN POLICY

How successful do the ICPracs and the ME/ICC-Chm feel that they would be in influencing staff members to change procedures if they needed to do so to minimize infection risk? To examine this question, both sets of respondents were presented with a number of situations in which they might want to influence nurses, physicians, and other ancillary staff members to change their mode of operation: getting nurses to wear a different hair style, persuading assistants to change their method of disinfecting X-ray tables, changing the procedure for review of antibiotic usage by physicians, changing the requirement for inservice training for physicians, asking nurses to report illness in their households. The respondents were then asked to rate the situations in terms of how successful they would be in implementing change. As we can see in Table 4, both sets of respondents tended to feel that they would be at least somewhat successful overall. Their expectancy of success was somewhat greater with nurses, least with physicians. However, this comparison must be made with caution, since the sort of activity to be influenced was different for different positions. For example, we were com-

TABLE 4   Mean* Perceived Success of Infection Control
Practitioners and Medical Epidemiologists/Infection
Control Committee Chairmen in Getting Staff to Comply
with ISCP Policies

| | *Means*(N=834)* | | |
| | Respondent | | |
Target	ICPrac	ME/ICC-Chm	Marginals
Housekeeper	.94	.95	.94
Staff Nurse	1.21	1.19	1.20
Attending Physician	.78	.81	.80
Marginals	.98	.98	.98

*Scores ranged from 0: "Not at all successful" to 2: "Very successful."

Note: Effects of target significant by repeated-measures analysis of variance ($p<.001$), effects of respondent and interaction effect not significant (BMDP2V).

paring getting physicians to change their review of use of antibiotics with getting nurses to report illnesses in their households.

GENERAL COMPLIANCE WITH THE HOSPITAL'S ISOLATION POLICY

Earlier we pointed out that the status of the violator determines whether the violator would be spoken to by an observer and/or reported and what bases of power would be used in attempting to change his/her behavior. Might we also expect that general compliance with the hospital's isolation policy differs with status? We asked two sets of respondents—the staff nurses and the ME/ICC-Chm—how likely it would be that various staff members would comply with the following isolation policies: (1) wearing mask, gloves, and gown when entering the room of a patient with a skin infection and (2) wearing a mask in a room with a tubercular patient. The results indicated that the staff nurses report a general belief that most of the target personnel would probably comply. However, there is a significant difference according to the status of the personnel, with attending physicians seen as less likely to comply than the others ($F = 1924$, $p < .001$). Could this perception represent a bias on the part of the staff nurses? Apparently not, since similar results were found when the ME/ICC-Chm made the same estimate.

NURSES' COMPLIANCE WITH THE REQUESTS OF PHYSICIANS

Finally, does it sometimes happen that a staff member of higher status will make a request that tends to increase infection risk and that a person of lower status will comply? To measure this occurrence, we presented the staff nurses the following hypothetical situations in which physicians: (1) asked them to move a child out of isolation for psychological reasons, even though the child had a contagious staph infection; (2) ordered the nurse to continue catheterization of a patient even though the catheter had clearly been accidentially contaminated; (3) ordered the nurse to allow a child to keep a pet turtle in his/her room for psychological reasons, despite the hospital's regulation opposing such because of the risk of salmonella.

As Table 5 shows, the majority of the staff nurses report they would tend to refuse to follow the improper requests (both with and without stating the reason). However, we cannot disregard the sizable minority who say that they would comply. Furthermore, we might expect nurses to *underestimate* the extent to which they would comply. Indeed, when we asked whether the other nurses, in general, would comply with such requests, 73.2% reported

TABLE 5 Percentage of Staff Nurses Reporting Whether
They Would Comply with Improper Orders from
Physicians, by Situation

	Situation		
Category Response	Transfer patient out of isolation while still infectious	Continue with contaminated catheterization	Allow child to keep pet turtle in room
Follow order	2.6	4.2	4.3
Follow order, express reservations	36.7	18.3	20.1
Refuse, state reasons	57.1	41.6	62.0
Just refuse	3.6	35.9	13.6
Total	100.0	100.0	100.0
	(N=7066)	(N=7131)	(N=7089)

that they would, at least sometimes, while 27.6% reported that they would
comply frequently. Still, the staff nurses did not believe that doctors made
such requests often: 60.2% said that such requests were made "rarely" or
"almost never," 33.3% said that such requests were made "sometimes," and
5.5% said that such requests were made "frequently." Thus, these requests,
though not frequent, are not unheard of, and when they are made, a substantial minority of staff nurses say that they comply with them. Why would staff
nurses comply with a physician's inappropriate request? The greatest number (46.4%) said that the most likely reason was the attribution of expert
power to the physician. The use of informational power was rated second
(39.7%).

CONCLUDING REMARKS

The prevention and control of infections within hospitals is an area within
health research to which the concepts of social power and influence are
extremely applicable. As noted experts in hospital epidemiology have
pointed out, "there is already a sufficient body of knowledge available that, if
conscientiously applied, would effect a significant reduction in hospital-
associated infections" (Hewitt and Sanford, 1972; Eickhoff, 1975). Thus,
despite the ever-present need for additional knowledge and techniques to
combat nosocomial infections, there is also a great need for more effective
methods of motivating health-care professionals to implement the preventive measures that are already available.

The study of social influence in a hospital setting is certainly no simple undertaking. It requires firm grounding in social theory and methodology as well as an intimate knowledge of the hospital milieu, including current concepts of hospital epidemiology and infection control. One of the objectives of the SENIC Project was to bring togehter a multidisciplinary research team to develop and carry out such an effort. The resulting collaboration has turned out to be almost as interesting an example of social interaction and influence as the subject under study. This is well exemplified by the types of problems faced in designing and implementing the project and the solutions jointly worked out. Among the problems illustrated in this article were (1) defining the complex social influence system called an ISCP; (2) developing explicit and testable hypotheses; (3) defining measurable characteristics for study; (4) defining a list of respondents to ensure comparable measures in all hospitals; (5) developing and pretesting an efficient set of interview instruments for application in a nationwide survey; (6) selecting, recruiting, and training the right types of interviewers; and (7) processing and editing an immense sociological data set. We found that neither the social psychologists nor the medical epidemiologists alone could have worked out entirely satisfactory solutions; instead, each group had to become partially proficient in the discipline of the other. Through this intellectual "cross-fertilization," we developed together, over three years, a common body of terminology and experience with which to tackle these problems.

As with the conceptual and logistical development of the project, we are finding that the analysis of the data is likewise an evolving process benefiting greatly from multidisciplinary contributions. This collaborative analysis began with the preliminary review of data collected during the various pretests of the interview instruments. These early efforts allowed us not only to improve the discriminating ability of the interview instruments but also to refine somewhat the proposed hypotheses before beginning analysis on the final data set.

The results of these collaborative efforts are apparent in the initial main analyses reported here. We are finding that relationships postulated to be occurring in hospitals are, in fact, being documented. For instance, we found that, as expected, the perceived helpfulness and support from authorities such as the hospital administration play a significant role in determining the perceived autonomy of the ISCP staff and its readiness to take action. Kanter (1977) has pointed out the importance of the "reflected power" of sponsors in organizations' higher other authorities who can provide support for the supervisors. She also argues that this sponsorship is particularly necessary for female supervisors and, given that the ICPracs are usually female, there is obvious relevance to the infection control situation.

We also found that the status of both the influencer and the target affects the uses and perceived results of social influence in infection control; more specifically, ISCP personnel and staff nurses were somewhat more reluctant to speak up to a physician than to a nurse or to another staff member whom they see violating infection control policy, and the ME/ICC-Chm was more likely to take direct action with a physician violator than was the ICPrac. We confirmed a general impression that, although policies regarding isolation of patients with infectious diseases are generally followed by all health professionals, when they are broken, physicians are more likely than others to be in violation. We showed that, as expected, physicians exert a substantial degree of influence over the behavior of staff nurses. When confronted with an extreme example—a hypothetical physician's order to act contrary to an established infection control policy—a sizable proportion of staff nurses reported that they would comply with the physician's command. This finding stresses the importance of the ISCP staff's implementing infection control policies through the cooperation and the influence of the hospital's medical staff.

Early analyses on the bases of social power used in implementing infection control policy were similarly confirmatory. We found that both the ICPrac and the ME/ICC-Chm were most likely to use informational power and, second, expert power—the two bases that they also perceived as the most effective. However, though informational power seemed to be consistently favored, the preference for other bases of power varied according to the influencing agent and target. In dealing with attending physicians and inhalation therapy heads, the ICPrac's preference for expert power seemed to approach quite closely the likelihood of use of informational power; however, in dealing with nurses, bases other than informational power were seen as considerably less likely, with legitimacy, reference, and coercion all surpassing expert power. The ME/ICC-Chm reported a greater likelihood of using a variety of bases of power, with expertise being particularly likely in influencing attending physicians and inhalation therapy heads. However, in dealing with nurses, their second most likely choice was the referent power of other nurses ("emphasize that other nurses in the hospital follow proper procedures").

An important implication can be drawn from the ICPrac's reports that she is most likely to use informational power with nurses, while nurses believe that they are more likely to be influenced by the ICPrac's expert power. Such discrepancy in usage and effectiveness of power should be explored in more depth so that the most effective basis of influence can be determined. The finding that reward power is ranked very low in both usage and effectiveness also warrants further consideration. Bennis et al. (1958), this their study of an outpatient clinic, found that compliance by nurses with prescribed policies and procedures (as well as the morale of nurses) was highly related to the extent to which desired rewards were correlated with expected rewards and with the extent to which supervisors correctly estimated the desirability of various rewards which they might mediate for nurses. Perhaps it is such discrepancies which account for the low effectiveness of reward indicated in the current study.

On the basis of preliminary analyses such as these, we are currently studying in more detail the types of relationships presented and the effects of various ISCP components and alternative approaches on the change of nosocomial infection rates in the study hospitals. The main object of these efforts is to derive a set of recommendations, based on the best available empirical evidence, that hospitals can use to guide their infection control efforts more effectively and efficiently.

REFERENCES

BENNETT, J.V. (1978) "Human infections: economic implications and prevention." Annals of Internal Medicine 89 (Supplement): 761-763.

————W.E. SCHECKLER, D.G. MAKI, and P.S. BRACHMAN (1971) "Current national patterns, United States" pp. 42-49 in Proceedings of the International Conference on Nosocomial Infections, Atlanta, Center for Disease Control, August 3-6, 1970.

BENNIS, W..G., N. BERKOWITZ, M. AFFINITO, and M. MALONE (1958) "Authority, power, and ability to influence." Human Relations 11: 143-155.

CAPLAN, R.D., E.A.R. ROBINSON, J.R.P. FRENCH, Jr., J.R. CALDWELL, and M. SHINN (1976) Adhering to Medical Regimens: Pilot Experiments in Patient Education and Social Support. Ann Arbor, MI: Institute for Social Research.

Center for Disease Control (1972) Outline for Surveillance and Control of Nosocomial Infections. Atlanta: Author.

Communicable Disease Center (now Center for Disease Control) (1958) "Hospital-acquired staphylococcal disease." In Proceedings of the National Conference, September. Atlanta: Author.

CUNDY, K.R. and W. BALL [eds.] (1977 Infection Control in Health Care Facilities. Baltimore: University Park Press.

EICKHOFF, T.C. (1975) "Reviews and commentary: nosocomial infections." American Journal of Epidemiology 101: 93-97.

FRENCH, J.R.P., Jr. and B.H. RAVEN (1959) "The bases of social power" pp. 150-167 in D. Cartwright (ed.), Studies in social power. Ann Arbor: University of Michigan.

HALE, R.W., and D. QUADE, H.E. FREEMAN, J.V. BENNETT, and the CDC SENIC Planning Committee (forthcoming a) "Study on the efficacy of nosocomial infection control (SENIC Project): summary of study design." American Journal of Epidemiology.

HALEY, R.W., D.R. SCHABERG, D. McCLISH, D. QUADE, K. CROSSLEY, J.E. Mc-GOWAN, R.H. SHACHTMAN and J.V. BENNETT (forthcoming b) "The accuracy of retrospective chart review in measuring nosocomial infection rates: results of validation studies in four hospitals." American Journal of Epidemiology.

HEWITT, W.L. and J.P. SANFORD (1974) "Statement from the National Institutes of Health

Workshop on Hospital-Associated Infections." Journal of Infectious Diseases 130: 680-686.

HINTON, N.A. (1971) "Why infection control programs fail." Canadian Hospital 77: 48-49.

HOFLING, C.K., E. BROTZMAN, S. DALRYMPLE, N. GRAVES, C.M. PIERCE (1966) "An experimental study in nurse-physician relationship." Journal of Nervous and Mental Disease 143: 171-180.

HOLMES, O.W. (1977) "The contagiousness of puerperal fever." Medical Essays: 1842-1882. Darby, PA' Arden Library.

Joint Commission on the Accreditation of Hospitals (1976) "Infection control" pp. 49-56 in Accreditation Manual for Hospitals. Chicago: Author.

KANTER, R.M. (1977) Men and Women of the Corporation. New York: Basic Books.

KNIGHT, V. (1967) "Instrments and infection." Hospital Practice 2.

MISUMI, J. (1978) "The effects of organizational climate variables particularly leadership variable and group decision on accident prevention." Presented at the 19th International Congress of Applied Psychology, Munich, Federal Republic of Germany.

_____(1974) "Action research on the development of leadership, decision making processes and organizational performance in a Japanese shipyard." Presented at the 18th International Congress of Applied Psychology, Montreal, Canada.

PERRY, E. (1971) "Setting up an infection control program." Canadian Hospital 77: 45-46.

RAVEN, B.H. (1974) "The comparative analysis of power and power preference" in J.T. Tedeschi (ed.), Perspectives on Social Power. Chicago: AVC.

_____ and J.F. RUBIN (1976) "Interpersonal influence and social power" pp. 200-242 in Social Psychology: People in Groups. New York: John Wiley.

SCHAFFNER, W. (1977) "Humans: the animate reservoir of nosocomial pathogens" pp. 57-70 in K.R. Cundy and W. Ball (eds.), Infection Control in Health Care Facilities. Baltimore: University Park Press.

SENCER, D.J. and N.W. AXNICK (1975) "Utilization of cost/benefit analysis in planning prevention programs." Acta Medica Scandanavia 556 (Supplement): 123-128.

TAYLOR, S.E. (1978) "A developing role for social psychology in medicine and medical practice." Personality and Social Psychology Bulletin 4: 519-523.

THORFINNSON, A.R. (1971) "Infection control: the physician's viewpoint." Canadian Hospital 77: 39-42.

WALTER, G.W. (1964) "Surfaces, their importance and control" pp. 24-34 in Proceedings of 1963 National Conference on Institutionally-Acquired Infections (Public Health Service Publication 1188). Washington, DC: Goverment Printing Office.

WILLIAMS, R.E.O. (1971) "Changing perspectives in hospital infection." Proceedings of the International Conference on Nosocomial Infections. Chicago: American Hospital Association.

RICHARD I. EVANS   **11**

BEHAVIORAL MEDICINE:
A New Applied Challenge
to Social Psychologists

EARLY PROBLEMS FACING APPLIED SOCIAL PSYCHOLOGISTS

Since Beers' (1953) classic, *A Mind That Found Itself: An Autobiography,* was first published at the turn of the century, there has been a concerted effort on the part of some concerned individuals to promote a national interest in the so-called mental health movement. The tragic picture of bleak, primitive institutions housing dependent, alienated mental patients with no hope of even a limited interest in them from society, soon began to raise the consciousness of many more responsible individuals in our culture. Federal government funding eventually became available for research and rehabilitation relating to mental illness. Even previously indifferent state legislatures began to recognize the horrors that existed within mental institutions in their states and slowly began to support improvement of staff and facilities. Soon community psychiatry, psychology, and preventive mental health began to play an increasingly important part in our society (Bierer and Evans, 1969). Prevention and treatment of mental illness thus became a challenge to many behavioral scientists and among them were many social psychologists.

But even before behavioral scientists had developed sufficient knowledge to cope fully with mental health problems, they were also encouraged to become involved in solving broader types of social problems, such as juvenile delinquency, crime, and poverty. Stimulated by considerable funding in the administrations of Presidents Kennedy and Johnson, such efforts as Project Head Start, designed to enrich the preschool environment of underprivileged children, involved the theories and insights of many individuals in social psychology. However, the war on poverty and attacks on other social problems hardly have been unconditional successes. Although many in the behavioral sciences became involved, the solutions to the problems inherent in delinquency, crime, and poverty could obviously not have been solved in such a relatively short period of time, even with massive funding. In fact, in the areas of general mental health and broad social problems, it is unlikely that any of the behavioral sciences, including social psychology, has yet developed the necessary theoretical and basic research foundations to create completely adequate control and prevention strategies.

THE EMERGENCE OF BEHAVIORAL MEDICINE

A new field, "behavioral medicine," has developed which presents still another difficult challenge to social psychologists: the prevention and treatment of physical disease. Of course, psychosomatic medicine, which encompasses the notions that the mind and body are intricately interrelated, has been a focus of interest for the behavioral sciences since their inception (e.g., Dunbar, 1947). However, one critical aspect of behavioral medicine is the challenge to intervene in health problems in the normal population to actually reduce the incidence of disease and death. But behavioral medicine emerged from a very complex social system and the boundaries of the field are not clearly outlined. Some attempts have been made to define the area. For example, the newly formed Academy of Behavioral Medicine Research has defined behavioral medicine as:

The interdisciplinary field concerned with the development and integration of behavioral and biomedical science, knowledge and techniques relevant to the understanding of health and illness and the application of this knowledge and these techniques to prevention, diagnosis, treatment and rehabilitation [Baldwin, 1978: 16].

Here behavioral medicine is specifically defined as an interdisciplinary field rather than a discipline or science, and there are no preconceived limits of knowledge or methods. Therefore, the area can involve a number of social scientists and health professionals including psychologists from various subspecialties, sociologists, anthropologists, physicians, nurses, epidemiologists, biostatisticians, physiologists, health educators, researchers, public health professionals, pharmacologists, dentists, and others. They are unified not by their training, but by their goals and activities related to reaching these goals. These activities can occur in a wide variety of settings, including hospitals, clinics, universities, medical schools, schools of public health, rehabilitation centers, public schools, the community at large, and private and public agencies.

Of obvious relevance to social psychology is that aspect of behavioral medicine which is related to lifestyle interventions. For example, the Framingham study (e.g., Haynes et al., 1978), a well-controlled longitudinal investigation of the determinants of cardiovascular disease, indicated that various aspects of the lifestyle (e.g., cigarette smoking, diet, exercise) of the individual places him or her at greater risk for the development of heart disease. Research has strongly suggested the notion that if certain aspects of the individual's lifestyle can be altered, he or she is less likely to become seriously incapacitated or die at an early age. In the mental health movement, the social psychologist had to deal with developing behaviors that may be less clearly linked to psychopathology or social problems than these lifestyle patterns are related to physical disease or death. For example, there is probably no behavior as closely linked to the development of mental health or social problems as cigarette smoking is to physical disease (National Cancer Institute, 1977).

To provide some perspective on the phrase *behavioral medicine,* it should be mentioned that at the meeting at the National Academy of Sciences on April 10, 1978, where the Academy of Behavioral Medicine Research was founded, a discussion concerning the appropriate name for the organization took place. Not surprisingly, among the interdisciplinary charter membership group present, social psychologists were concerned about the term *medicine* in the title. Clearly, this implied to some social psychologists that the field would be perceived as focusing on the centrality of the clinical physician. This would be troublesome to social psychologists involved in nonclinical health research areas.

In an effort to clarify this issue, Matarazzo (1979), in his presidential address to the newly formed Division 38 (Health Research) at the 1979 American Psychological Association meetings, introduced the notion of "behavioral health." He defined behavioral health as an interdisciplinary field dedicated to promoting a philosophy toward one's own health which stresses *individual responsibility* in the application of behavioral and biomedical science, knowledge, and techniques to the *maintenance* of health and the *prevention* of illness and dysfunction by a variety of self-initiated individual or shared activities. Yet he still uses the phrase *behavioral medicine* in his presentation as a generic delineation of the field. I suspect that the phrase *behavioral medicine* will finally become the generic one in the field of health research, because the term has been already widely used to refer to this emerging field by various National Institutes of Health agencies, at least one new journal *(Journal of Behavioral Medicine),* various books (including those involving contributions of social psychologists), and various academic departments and programs. It should be mentioned that even in titling this chapter, this issue had to be considered.

In the remainder of this chapter, I will describe the activites of our social psychology research group as it entered the field of health research, by extending the earlier social psychological investigations of fear arousal in persuasive communications research into the area of preventing oral disease. This will be followed by a discussion of our entry into research in prevention of cardiovascular disease as our group was funded by the National Heart, Lung, and Blood Institute as part of the newly formed National Heart and Blood Vessel Research and Demonstration Center at Baylor College of Medicine. Our research in this area began with the development and evaluation of social psychological strategies to deter the onset of cigarette smoking in adolescents. Our pre- and postdoctoral research training program for social psychologists who wish to enter the health research area will then be discussed. Because of the novelty of this program, it will be presented in some detail. This description of our own research and training activities in behavioral medicine is followed by a description of another health research area in which social psychologists have become involved, Type A or coronary-prone behavior. Finally, some basic concerns which the social psychologist might have as he or she enters the health research field are discussed.

DESCRIPTION OF PERSONAL INVOLVEMENT WITH BEHAVIORAL MEDICINE

My personal perspective and experience as our social psychology research group became involved in some aspects of physical disease prevention may illustrate some of the issues the social psychologist faces as he or she becomes involved with health research.

The first thing a social psychologist entering the health field may discover is what many health professionals and biomedical scientists have long known: Prevention of disease involves some form of lifestyle intervention. If psychologists have problems developing successful strategies for modifying lifestyles of the mentally ill, delinquent youngsters, criminals, or those who are in the throes of poverty, certainly no fewer difficulties are encountered in developing strategies to effect the kinds of lifestyle modifications that are involved in preventing physical disease. In fact, the biomedical sciences have identified "risk factors" which when present in individuals increase the probability that they will contract various diseases. We are all aware of many of these risks such as excessive use of alcohol and other drugs, smoking cigarettes, and eating improperly. But being made aware of the dangers of these behaviors through intensive educational programs has rarely discouraged us from starting them and, once starting them, from continuing. Such educational programs appear to be of only limited value in effecting a discontinuation of self-destructive behaviors by individuals. For example, in research which we have been carrying out with thousands of school children, we found that by the time they are 12 years old, virtually all children believe that smoking cigarettes may be dangerous to their health (Evans et al., 1978). Yet even before they reach their teens, many of these same children begin smoking. Most drug addicts were aware of the dangers of drugs before they began using them. Even after recovery from a heart attack, when fear of death may be at a peak, many heart patients continue to take the risks which contribute to heart disease, such as smoking or consuming improper foods or even failing to take important medications (Marston, 1970).

FEAR AROUSAL AND PREVENTION OF ORAL DISEASE

So when we first became interested in health research, an examination of the effects of fear arousal became a focus of our social psychology research group. We decided to conduct a series of experiments to learn more about why fear arousal as a means of motivating us to alter our lifestyle to protect our health is so ineffective. First, we searched for a health area in which the general public was still relatively uninformed of the relationship between certain specific behaviors and health maintenance. Preventive dentistry appeared to be such an area. It seems that it was well known to dental scientists but not to society at large that by merely brushing and flossing our teeth properly, it is possible to eliminate virtually all tooth decay and gum disease (Arnim, 1963). Here was significant information concerning disease prevention behaviors, unlike widely held knowledge such as the relationship between smoking and cancer, of which most people were not aware.

This would, therefore, be an ideal situation for setting up experimental situations which would allow us to learn at a grassroots level more about why simply being made aware of the dangers of a disease does not motivate us to do what is necessary to prevent that disease. As Higbee (1969) has pointed out in his extensive review of the fear arousal literature, and more recently supported in an assessment of this field by Janis (see Evans, forthcoming), no blanket statement can be made concerning the value of fear as a motivator. An earlier examination of this problem was made by Janis and Feshbach (1953) who reported in a now classic study that a minimal fear appeal with general toothbrushing instructions was more effective in increasing the incidence of toothbrushing than a *strong* fear appeal. However, this study had to rely on subjects' *reports* of toothbrushing. No more adequate estimate of actual toothbrushing behavior was involved. Furthermore, in this study only the emotion of fear was investigated as a "motivator." Also of importance, and not considered by Janis and Feshbach, is the question of whether a positive appeal, one that emphasizes a favorable result to the individual, may not be more powerful as a motivator than fear. Subsequently, Leventhal et al. (1965) not only challenged the importance of fear as a "motivator" to change behavior but also found in their research (involving persuasion to encourage tetanus inoculations) that highly *specific* instructions, even without fear, might be the most effective way of motivating individuals to engage in health practices. My social psychology research group further pursued this problem of the relative effectiveness of fear arousal in two basic studies in preventive dentistry (Evans et al., 1968, 1970).

Very briefly, these studies involve as subjects junior high school students. They include a pretest of these students which includes: (1) photographing their pink-stained teeth to determine the cleanliness of their teeth before oral hygiene instructions are given; (2) obtaining reports of their brushing behavior; and (3) administering certain behavioral tests.

One week after the pretesting, students in one experimental group were subjected to general oral hygiene instructions plus a very *high* fear message, such as was used by Janis and Feshbach. Another group in addition to the general oral hygiene instructions received a positive appeal, providing information which stressed many of the favorable effects of brushing. A third group received more specific instructions with no accompanying fear or positive appeals. A last group served as the control. The students were retested after five days, two weeks, and six weeks.

The results clearly indicated that reported oral hygiene behavior differed significantly from actual behavior as determined from the photographs of the students' teeth, suggesting that studies which rely on *reported* behavior as a criterion of change may be misleading. Perhaps of greatest interest was the fact that merely exposing the students on only *one* occasion to elaborated, specific instructions without using emotional appeals (fear or positive) resulted in sufficiently heightened oral hygiene behavior to result in significantly cleaner teeth than was evident in the pretest. Furthermore, the general oral hygiene instructions coupled with a positive appeal were nearly as effective. Effective, but significantly less so, were the fear appeals when coupled with general oral hygiene instructions. When this type of investigation was extended to longer periods of time (Evans et al., 1975), it was discovered that behavior changes were maintained and that even simply testing the subjects (possibly perceived as monitoring) at irregular intervals was almost as effective in increasing brushing behavior as various persuasive messages including those using fear arousal.

Skinner (see Evans, 1968) and Rogers (see Evans, 1975) have independently concluded that failures in our educational system may be partly due to depending too much on motivating students through fear of punishment for failure rather than stressing individual satisfaction in learning. Difficulties in child rearing in general may result from too much emphasis on fear of punishment as a motivation device. So perhaps we should not be too surprised by the limited impact of primarily stressing fear arousal in health education as well.

Of course, even as Janis and Feshbach (1953) originally suggested, fear probably does have some impact on us, at least to effect short-term changes in our health behavior. For example, right after a heart attack, individuals may change their lifestyles to prevent a recurrence. But as suggested earlier, many patients will return to their previous risk-taking lifestyles (Marston, 1970). So, even under conditions of intense fear of the consequences of behavior such as experienced by postcoronary patients, *permanent* changes in health habits may not occur. In fact, after a habit such as smoking cigarettes which is probably destructive to our health has become especially well integrated into our lifestyles, health professionals are rarely able to permanently alter that behavior using fear arousal or, for that matter, any other approach (Evans, et al., 1979b).

DETERRENCE OF CIGARETTE SMOKING IN ADOLESCENTS

The difficulties in altering behaviors such as cigarette smoking which involve drug addiction or dependence, and which have been integrated into our lifestyles in a complex manner, suggested to us that we might focus more of our efforts toward developing strategies that would influence children to resist the pressures to begin a high-risk behavior, that is, focus on prevention rather than cessation. McGuire (1974) investigated verbal inoculations against the influence of persuasive communications which were directed at altering cognitions. Why could not inoculation strategies be developed against the pressures to begin a behavior such as smoking? So we developed a five-year longitudinal investigation which began with this conceptual base. This would involve training adolescents to resist the social pressures to begin smoking or advance toward frequent, addictive smoking. In-depth interviews, conducted prior to both a pilot study (Evans, 1976) and the longitudinal study (Evans et al., 1978), with a large population of seventh graders, suggest that peer pressure, models of smoking parents, and the mass media (e.g., cigarette advertising) may, individually or collectively, outweigh the belief of children that smoking is dangerous. Recent explorations of this problem at Stanford and Minnesota corroborate our findings (Hurd et al., 1978; McAllister et al., 1978).

Furthermore, we now have some evidence (Evans et al., 1979a) that in addition to depending too heavily on fear as a deterrent to smoking, anti-smoking messages in schools fall into a "time perspective" trap. That is, they focus too much on the future consequences of smoking. To be more mean-ingful to teen-agers who tend to be present oriented, smoking messages should emphasize more immediate effects of smoking on the teen-ager.

We are using this strategy of inoculation against pressures to smoke predicated on the following theoretical notion concerning the development of addicted smokers: If students can be "nursed" through the period during which they are particularly vulnerable to social influences to smoke (the junior high years), they will be sufficiently fortified so that the heavy addic-tive smoking which is generally first found as students progress into high school will be less likely to occur. By then, students may be more indepen-dent and may be less likely to respond to social pressures to begin smoking.

To summarize our methods and results, first the 10-week pilot investiga-tion was completed with 750 male and female students entering the seventh grade in the Houston Independent School District. The message portion of the pilot study consisted of short videotapes approximately 10 minutes in length. Rather than relying upon adult authority figures as communicators as health education programs generally do, the videotapes feature adoles-cents of approximately the same age as the target population, who present the smoking information and role play certain social situations in which the pressure to smoke is encountered (see *Figure 1*). Furthermore, the roles of the students in the tapes are presented honestly, since the student spokesper-sons state that they have been asked to present the messages and to play certain roles. This approach has appeared to be better received by student viewers who may have been adversely affected by the authority figures and the artificiality of many health communication efforts, such as drug control films.

Figure 2 summarizes the research design of this investigation. Four different videotapes were presented to subjects on each of four consecutive days. The videotapes presented on the first day included information about the dangers of smoking to health and, most prominently, a section describing and illustrating peer pressure and its effect on smoking behavior.

The videotape presented on the second day recapped the first tape and presented information about parental influence on smoking behavior, in-cluding a depiction of parental pressure to smoke and not to smoke and

FIGURE 1   Scene from *Resisting Pressures to Smoke* Film

children's modeling of parents' smoking behavior.

The third videotape recapped the first two tapes and presented information dealing with pressures to smoke emanating from the mass media. This tape included a pictorial analysis of such advertising techniques as artistically hiding the Surgeon General's warning on cigarette packages and appeals based on implied sexual attractiveness and popularity.

The fourth and final videotape was a general recap of the first three tapes. The message portion of the pilot study was either present in its entirety (all four videotapes presented) or absent (no videotapes presented) in various experimental and control groups.

Following the videotapes, students were involved in written and oral responses to questions. The experimenter distributed brief questionnaires for subjects' written responses. Four sets of questions were prepared, one presented in conjunction with each videotape. The questions which incorporated a quasi-role-playing device of allowing the respondent to make decisions concerning whether or not to respond to social pressures to smoke were formulated in such a way as to (1) attribute motivation to resist pressures to smoke to persons who have seen the videotape and (2) attribute ability to decide whether or not to smoke to persons subjected to smoking pressures.

Present in some experimental classes and absent in others was feedback

GROUP		PRETEST	EXPERIMENTAL CONDITION	2 DAY POSTTEST	8 WEEK POSTTEST	10 WEEK POSTTEST
1	EXPERIMENTAL	O_1	MESSAGE FOCUSED DISCUSSION FEEDBACK *	O_2 F_1	O_3 F_2	O_4 F_3
2	EXPERIMENTAL	O_1	NICOTINE VIDEOTAPE PLUS TESTING	O_2	O_3	O_4
3	EXPERIMENTAL	O_1	FEEDBACK ON MEASUREMENT	O_2 F_1	O_3 F_2	O_4 F_3
4	CONTROL	O_1	NICOTINE VIDEOTAPE PLUS PRETEST & POSTTEST ONLY			O_4
5	CONTROL		NICOTINE VIDEOTAPE PLUS POSTTEST ONLY			O_4

O: Observation
F: Feedback Delivery
*   Discussion of Coping Alternatives

FIGURE 2   Social Psychological Deterrents of Smoking in School's 1975 Pilot Study Research (Evaluation) Design

to subjects concerning group smoking behavior in their respective classes. The experimenter presented this feedback with a chart that reflected the degree of smoking or smoking-related behavior. This feedback was delivered during each posttest, with feedback given at the time of the second posttest based on the data gathered in the first posttest, and so on. Feedback on each occasion was delivered after the administration of that day's posttest to avoid contamination by the feedback.

Following each videotape presentation and accompanying a discussion designed to reinforce the messages in the videotape, a carefully designed poster representing a scene from the videotape was displayed in the classroom. Figure 3 is the poster dealing with peer pressure. It portrays a student visibly turning down an offer of a cigarette from members of a group of students who are all smoking. The wording on the poster is: "You don't have to smoke just because your friends do. YOU can resist peer pressure."

FIGURE 3

Figure 4 is the poster dealing with parent pressure. It depicts a daughter obviously annoyed at smoke from her mother's cigarette. The message reads: "Even if your parents smoke, you don't have to imitate them. YOU can decide for yourself."

Even if your parents smoke, you don`t have to imitate them.
YOU can decide for yourself.

FIGURE 4

Finally, following the media pressure videotape, a poster (Figure 5) is displayed. It depicts a large "Marlboro man" reaching out from a billboard and offering a cigarette to a passing student, who visibly indicates that he does not want the cigarette. This poster states: "Cigarette ads are a rip-off! YOU can resist media pressure to smoke."

Cigarette ads are a rip-off! YOU can resist media pressure to smoke.

FIGURE 5

The posters served as a continuous reminder of the videotape messages. A preliminary test of student reaction to them indicated that they were attention getting and were preferred to other poster formats which we had designed.

As the studies mentioned earlier indicate (Evans et al., 1970, 1975), repeated testing may be perceived by subjects as a monitoring of their behavior. Therefore, testing is treated as an independent variable, and a testing-only group is included to assess the effect of testing by itself on the dependent variables.

The five dependent variables measured include smoking information, smoking attitudes, intention to smoke, reported smoking behavior, as well as Horning et al.'s (1973) nicotine-in-saliva analysis, which was used as an objective measure of the presence or absence of smoking. The amount of nicotine present in the saliva samples is determined by a mass spectrometric analysis, and inferences can be made about the degree of smoking behavior practiced by the subjects. Cost of operation of the mass spectrometer precludes analysis for each subject on each testing occasion, but saliva samples were collected from each subject on each occasion, and a sampling of specimens from each group was analyzed. A study by Evans et al. (1977) found that when subjects learned from a short film that their saliva could be analyzed, their self-reports on smoking became more accurate. This technique was used to increase the validity of self-reports of smoking.

As indicated in Figure 6 and as reported in Evans et al. (1978), rates of onset of smoking in the full treatment, the feedback, and the testing-only groups were significantly lower than the onset rates in the pretest single posttest control groups. Over 18% in the control groups had begun smoking, while less than 10% in the experimental groups had begun smoking. (The

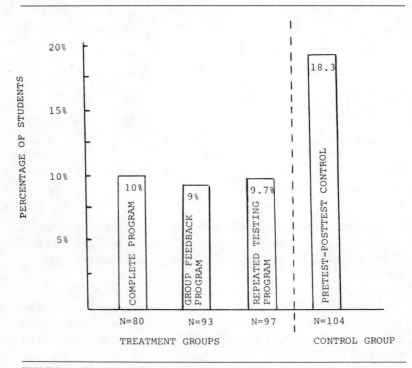

FIGURE 6   Results of 1975 10-Week Pilot Study:
Percentage of Students Who Began Smoking (One or More
Cigarettes a Month) During the First Quarter of the Seventh
Grade, as Reported at the End of the Term (Treatment
Versus Experimental Groups $\chi_2 = 4.51$, p < .05)

small number of already smoking subjects in the various experimental groups precluded a statistical comparison of onset rates among the experimental groups and the control group.) These results suggest that such interventions may prove more useful in deterring smoking among junior high students than merely instructing them in the long-term dangers of smoking. Perhaps most important, these findings suggest that various kinds of interventions may be effective, particularly if they have a reasonable conceptual base supported by data from the target audience concerning their perceptions of the determinants of smoking.

The five-year longitudinal study initially involving approximately 4,500 students is presently underway—using modifications of the pilot study methodology—tracking students through the 7th, 8th, 9th, 10th, and 11th grades. Through the second year of the study, preliminary data analysis suggests promising impact of the interventions. As indicated in Figure 7, 80% of the students in a random sample of all students in the experimental

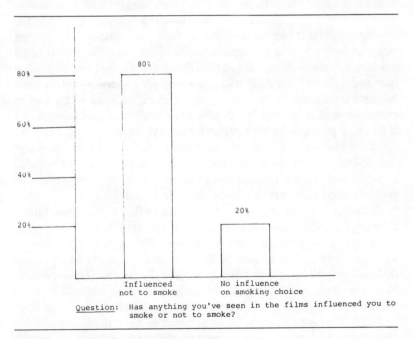

Question: Has anything you've seen in the films influenced you to smoke or not to smoke?

FIGURE 7   Three-year Longitudinal Study of
Social Psychological Deterrents of Smoking in Schools
Project (Open-Ended Interviews with a Sample of 61
Students in the Full-Treatment Condition Following the
Second-Year Intervention, 1977-978)

groups claim that the films had influenced their decision not to smoke. More systematic analysis of both qualitative and quantitative data will be reported as the analyses of the data are completed.

SPIN-OFF SMOKING STUDIES

Several individual research studies were carried out by social psychology graduate students in conjunction with this project. They are summarized as follows. The first study is entitled: "Feedback about immediate consequences: strategy to control children's smoking" (Hansen and Evans, 1978). Within the context of our larger field study of smoking in adolescents, the smoking behavior of an additional sample of 365 sixth-grade children was examined. Subjects in treatment conditions were presented information about the immediate consequences of smoking and, as is suggested by social learning theory, subjects were also presented several forms of direct and vicarious feedback about the levels of carbon monoxide found in the breath. After viewing a film about how carbon monoxide immediately enters the smoker's body and can be measured in the breath, subjects were given vicarious feedback via a live demonstration of the detection process using smoking and nonsmoking adult models. Subjects in the first feedback group then had their breath tested for carbon monoxide and received immediate feedback on the results. A second group received feedback on the carbon monoxide content of their breath after a one-week delay and subjects in a third group produced breath samples but were never given feedback on the results. A fourth feedback group was not monitored for carbon monoxide but did view the vicarious feedback demonstration. Control conditions included a pretest and posttest-only control group as well as an information-only control group which only viewed the carbon monoxide film.

Although low rates of smoking prohibited a sufficiently rigorous statistical analysis of the results, rates of smoking indicated that the numbers of subjects who reported smoking in the immediate feedback and the information-only conditions were reduced, while the subjects who received delayed feedback had the smallest increase in the number of new smokers. Further analysis revealed that subjects in the delayed and withheld feedback conditions made significant decreases in their estimates of how soon large amounts of carbon monoxide could be found in their bodies. Overall, this study suggests a social psychological technique for presenting meaningful information to children which may be used to reduce or deter their experimenting with the use of cigarettes. However, the sixth grade may be too early for the maximum effectiveness of feedback programs, because of the still-limited smoking experience of the group.

Another spin-off study completed is entitled: "Role of information and belief in adolescents' smoking behavior" (Bane and Evans, 1978). This study dealt with the possibility that the apparent failure of traditional attempts to deter smoking among school children may be in the children's failure to attend to or to believe the information presented. To explore this possibility, a social psychological investigation of the relationships between 498 sixth, seventh, and eighth graders' smoking behavior and their awareness of the belief in the negative consequences of smoking was undertaken also within the context of our larger longitudinal study. Junior high school (eighth-grade) subjects in a separate sample responded to questionnaire items measuring their recall of smoking-and-health information and their belief in that information. Smoking behavior was determined by the use of the nicotine-in-saliva technique used in the principal investigation.

Correlations between subjects' reported frequency of cigarette smoking and their beliefs about several negative consequences of smoking suggest that antismoking campaigns may have had some impact on the incidence of smoking. However, the variance unaccounted for by the belief items included in this investigation was so great (about 66% for the eighth grade) as to suggest that traditional antismoking programs were unable to overcome immediate pressures to smoke for a substantial percentage of the children studied. The fact that 85% of the self-identified eighth-grade smokers indicated beliefs in the unhealthiness of smoking demonstrates the inadequacy of using merely informational messages as a smoking deterrent and appears to support the value of the approach utilized by our major study. Students are being trained to cope with immediate social pressures and other social influences to smoke rather than depending primarily on communicating information concerning the dangers of smoking.

Still another investigation is entitled: "Communicating imminent health consequences: smoking control strategy for children" (Mittelmark and Evans, 1978). A low-fear appeal smoking control intervention stressing immediate effects of smoking (i.e., *carbon monoxide*) was compared to a high-fear appeal Cancer Society-developed, long-term consequences message in a 10-week field study. Also within the context of our larger study, a separate sample of 240 sixth-grade students participated. Subjects in the *carbon monoxide* message group viewed two films, saw in-class demonstrations, and participated in short question-and-answer sessions. The *cancer* message group was exposed to a typical school health antismoking program. The pretest-multiple posttest study design also included repeated testing and pretest-final posttest control groups.

It was hypothesized that, as compared to the *cancer* message and control groups, the *carbon monoxide* message group would (1) evidence a lower smoking onset rate, (2) less frequently report intentions to begin smoking, (3) show evidence of having gained new knowledge, (4) be more likely to perceive smoking as an immediately detrimental behavior, and (5) judge immediate effects to be the most important health consideration for children exposed to pressures to begin smoking.

To increase the validity of responses obtained on the dependent measure instrument, a three-stop procedure employed in the major investigations was used during testing occasions. Subjects were first shown how specimens of their saliva could be analyzed for nicotine content by a mass spectrometer. They were then requested to produce saliva specimens. Finally, subjects responded to a 19-item questionnaire which included items which elicited responses concerning self-reports of smoking.

Due to the very low smoking onset rates which were also observed in this study sample as a whole, the hypothesized reduced smoking onset rate was not observed in the *carbon monoxide* message group. However, results did confirm the remaining hypotheses. It was concluded that low-fear appeal messages which stress short-term consequences of smoking may be more successful deterrents against early experimentation with cigarettes than are high-fear appeal messages which stress long-term serious health consequences. Again some support was gained for the use of another component of the major study, emphasizing *immediate* physiological effects.

Based at least on our research so far (Evans, 1978c, 1978d), it would appear useful to deal with the problem of influencing preaddictive smokers to curtail the incidence of smoking before they become addicted or nicotine dependent or to focus on preventing individuals from beginning to smoke in the first place. This would, of course, necessitate the increased targeting of smoking prevention programs to nonsmokers or preaddicted smokers beginning with preteen-aged children and progressing to teen-agers. Strategies for intervention with this group must move away from depending solely on fear arousal and the mere dissemination of facts about the long-term health consequences of smoking. Preteens and teens must be taught to cope "on the spot" with the pressures to smoke they encounter. We should encourage efforts to build into school curricula sophisticated programs which inoculate against the social pressures to smoke, in lieu of the frequently used high-fear arousal, information-centered programs, which may well even be counterproductive.

TRAINING SOCIAL PSYCHOLOGISTS IN BEHAVIORAL MEDICINE RESEARCH

A vital issue to be raised is how social psychologists can be trained to enter the field of behavioral medicine research. An earlier social psychology doctoral research training program (Evans, 1966) in the context of which the dental fear arousal studies were carried out addressed itself to one field of behavioral medicine, oral disease. Our curent pre- and postdoctoral social psychology research training program addresses itself to a far broader aspect of behavioral medicine, the prevention of cardiovascular disease (Evans, 1978a). This program might serve as at least one model for future graduate research training in the field. It was funded by the National Heart, Lung, and Blood Institute in 1978 for five years. The rationale for the program suggests that if we accept the assumption that a significant impact on morbidity and mortality would result if individuals could be trained in modifying behaviors involved in *preventing* as well as in rehabilitating heart attack and stroke patients, then the role of the social psychologist in such programs would obviously be an important one.

Examples of research areas in which the trainees could be involved include evaluation of strategies for enhancing communication between post-coronary patient and cardiologist, the evolution of sociopsychological stress in the developing child as related to hypertension, the problem of increasing adherence to various therapeutic regimens described by cardiologists, the evaluation of the effects of training cardiologists in dealing with the post-coronary patient and his or her family, the evaluation of strategies for dealing with lifestyle changes of patients with heart disease, and the whole range of developing and evaluating strategies for modifying various types of coronary-prone behavior (e.g., smoking, diet, Type A, exercise).

In addition to carrying out research dealing with such problems, the trainees in this program are required to attend a series of monthly presentations coordinated by cardiovascular investigators which deal with such topics as environmental factors in hypertension, advances in lipid and atherosclerosis research, practice of medicine with consideration of risk factors, problems of individual compliance with physicians' instructions, basic correlates of hypertension, and conscious and conditioned control of cardiovascular function. Attendance is required at the regularly scheduled weekly meetings of the Baylor College of Medicine National Heart and Blood Vessel Research and Demonstration Center. Also required is participation in the regularly scheduled orientation to cardiovascular disease sessions for cardiovascular fellows.

To engage in such new program development, the social psychologist should have a reasonable knowledge of the physiological components of the risk factor as it relates to cardiovascular disease. The social psychologist developing intervention programs should learn how to select and collaborate with appropriate researchers and clinicians dealing with cardiovascular disease. In this program, such individuals are available to work with the trainees throughout the course of the training program.

In order to obtain the skills necessary to develop intervention and research programs of their own, both the pre- and postdoctoral trainees are active in ongoing research projects in the Baylor National Heart Center. These include our long-range adolescent smoking prevention project, a diet modification program, a neighborhood clinics hypertension control program, and various public education and school education programs. Theoretical training to conceptualize such interventions and research is obtained in social psychology seminars which deal in part with social psychological concepts as they pertain to program development in health behavior.

Perhaps one of the most vital skills a social psychologist should have if he or she is to work effectively in a preventive medicine or health care setting is how to evaluate programs once they are developed. In my opinion, such evaluation skills must be predicated on both extensive knowledge of classical experimental design and quasi-experimental research methodology (Campbell and Stanley, 1963), general program evaluation skills, and proficiency with appropriate statistical techniques and computer resources. All trainees in the program are required to enroll in seminars in program evaluation and research methodology.

In the last several years, social psychology has been investigating the use of several *specific* techniques that might be useful in dealing with problems such as patient compliance in taking drugs (e.g., hypertension control), self-management following input from health professionals, and improving already existing health maintenance programs. Examples of specific techniques that are proving to be useful are behavior modification, modeling and other derivatives from the social learning paradigm, skills for enhancing group interaction (group dynamics), attribution theory, survey research, focused interviewing and testing, and use of persuasive communication models. The trainees in this program are required to enroll in various seminars that acquaint them with such techniques as well.

The training related to prevention and control of cardiovascular disease is a full-time three-year program including summer sessions. As we have gained experience with previous National Institute of Health research training programs, it has become clear that the best structure for the formal academic training is a balance between a standard set of requirements in the first stage to insure a reasonable level of basic competence and enough flexibility in the second stage to allow for individual interests and abilities. Depending on the extent of previous training in psychology of the predoctoral trainees and particularly the postdoctoral trainees, aside from the fairly structured training of the Ph.D. Program in Social Psychology, the training is shaped to particularly focus on the prevention and control of cardiovascular disease as described earlier.

The trainees are required to engage in independent study and research and are supported in any independent research that they begin to develop. Examples of such possible research areas were mentioned earlier, but to illustrate how this works some current research activities of the trainees might be mentioned. In response to the interest of several of the trainees, Dr. Ray Roseman, codeveloper of the Type A research area, was invited to spend several days in Houston with our group, sharing all aspects of the state of the art in this field. Theodore Dembroski, a Ph.D. from our earlier program and now a leader in the Type A research area, also visited our program and is helping us develop a research program. (A brief description of the Type A behavior in general as an example of a possible research area for social psychologists will be presented in the next section of this chapter.)

Examining the various cardiovascular interdisciplinary multirisk factor intervention programs supported by the National Heart, Lung, and Blood Institute within the Baylor College of Medicine National Research and Demonstration Center as a model, it is evident that there is a developing employment base for graduates of such a training program in medical schools (e.g., Department of Community and Preventive Medicine, Internal Medicine, Continuing Education Programs, or Epidemiology). For some time now schools of public health, as they look at cardiovascular disease prevention and control, have indicated an interest in individuals with such training. Also, as our own experience has indicated, faculty members of psychology departments can profitably work in this area. Graduates of this program employed by university psychology departments are continuing research in this field by developing an appropriate interface with medical schools or schools of public health. As more programs in behavioral medicine begin to develop during the next several years as encouraged by the Yale Conference on Behavioral Medicine, support by the National Institutes of Health, and the creation of the Academy of Behavioral Medicine Research, openings for graduates of a Social Psychology program in various aspects of behavioral medicine should become increasingly available. The bottom line for such interest in social psychologists trained in behavioral medicine research may be cost effectiveness. Preventing disease is far less costly than treating it.

TYPE A BEHAVIOR AND SOCIAL PSYCHOLOGY

Perhaps one of the problems the social psychologist has as he or she enters this new area is to maintain the balance between starting from a solid base of social psychological conceptualization and the demands for application of knowledge to solve an immediate problem. The temptation might be great to latch on to an existing definition of a problem in behavioral medicine without bringing to bear on it any unique definitions of the problems which might emerge from a social psychological perspective.

One current area of investigation, Type A behavior, illustrates this problem. In a well-controlled eight and one-half year longitudinal study, Friedman and Rosenman (1974; Rosenman et al., 1975) found that the presence of certain behaviors which they labeled Type A proved to be highly related to coronary-heart disease. The Type A individual is described as highly impatient, competitive, overly preoccupied with work and hostile (Dembroski et al., 1978a, 1977). This is in contrast to the Type B who is at a lower point on the spectrum of these behaviors. Some creative social psychologists (e.g., Glass, 1977; Dembroski et al., 1978b) are among the researchers who are tying in these Type A behaviors with physiological measures which demonstrate sympathetic nervous system arousal or biochemical changes in response to various stress-arousing social situations.

These investigations extend to real-life settings the social pressures which are designed to elicit Type A behaviors in the assessment interview. Social pressures are presented in a microcosm in the brief assessment interviews used to categorize subjects as A's or B's by Friedman and Rosenman's Western Collaborative Group Studies (Friedman and Rosenman, 1974; Rosenman, 1978). However, it would be interesting to extend the work of Glass and Dembroski to examine further social influences which trigger these Type A behaviors. Perhaps some variations of attribution or social exchange theory or concepts from social learning theory could be introduced in various investigations in this area. Social psychological concepts might be one basis for building a more global model of the provocation of Type A behaviors than is present in the assessment interviews. Since nonpsychologically trained clinical cardiologists Friedman and Rosenman first observed, developed, and reported that important lifestyle variables, such an input by social psychologists could become crucial in establishing their ultimate validity.

So far Type A behavior has not been sufficiently linked to cardiovascular disease across cultures or adequately studied in females, in children, in older individuals, and in the context of changing social influences in total lifespan development. If one ultimately embarks on developing and evaluating intervention programs to modify Type A behaviors, something which is currently being done in a few essentially clinical behavior modification-oriented investigations, it would seem that contributions from social psychologically oriented investigators could be profitably built into the intervention programs, since the concept of Type A appears to be largely a response to perceived pressures in one's social environment.

SOME BASIC CONCERNS

If social psychologists have learned from their past experiences of working with social problems, they will not enter the field of behavioral medicine with overly optimistic promises for the solutions to problems. It is now well known that many of the optimistic promises of success made by some social scientists as they entered the war on poverty backfired. Individuals in the political system consequently became suspicious of the claims of social scientists. They may be reflected to this day in the lowered funding priorities for behaviorial research. If individuals in the health care system are led to expect too much from the contributions of the social psychologist, the results for behavioral medicine would be unfortunate. A cautious, judicious approach which makes only modest claims of the possible contribution of the social psychologist would appear to be the best tack.

Furthermore, on becoming involved in this new field, social psychologists face many critical entry problems. The field of medicine has been heavily exposed to the techniques of behavior modification, so much so that virtually all psychologists are now referred to as "behaviorists" by many physicians. Explaining the particular capabilities, interests, and values of the social psychologist may often prove to be difficult. For example, the importance of the need for prefield investigations involving fairly basic social psychological research may not be easily communicated to many members of the biomedical community. The very rigor of evaluation procedures demanded by social psychologists can be threatening to some of the health professionals who employ interventions at an essentially clinical level. In addition, as we move into an applied area, social psychologists need to learn to recognize new types of methodological problems which arise when real-world settings become the context of research.

Although those of us in social psychology who are involved in field interventions characteristically conceive them with a critical eye toward rigorous evaluation, such projects are subject to occasional whims of fate or the unavoidable impact of real-world events on controlled research. One example of this occurred recently when Joseph Califano, Secretary of Health, Education and Welfare, dropped in on our rigorously controlled social psychological deterrence of smoking in schools project. The impact of his news media entourage, as well as Califano's personal presence, is difficult to assess. Although this certainly may be the only instance of the "Califano effect" on an applied social psychological investigation, similar but less dramatic confounding effects may be expected in a field situation at any time.

Government policy implications of social psychological projects in behavioral medicine are evidenced in other ways. For instance, our research group was invited to write a chapter in the U.S. Surgeon General's Report on Smoking and Health (Evans et al., 1979a). In addition, I was requested to testify before Senator Kennedy's U.S. Senate Subcommittee on Health after the senator visited Houston and viewed some of the intervention materials we had produced (Evans, 1978b). More recently I have been working with the Federal Trade Commission concerning policies relating to effects of cigarette advertising on youth. Certainly public policy issues were important in many programs in the past in which applied social psychology was involved (e.g., Project Head Start). Once we leave the laboratory, it is difficult to escape public scrutiny if society has an immediate stake in what we are doing.

SUMMARY

In this chapter an attempt has been made to define the area of behavioral medicine and to represent it as a challenge to social psychologists. I traced my own involvement in this area in both research and training to illustrate the movements of social psychologists into this field. A line of research designed to explore means of effecting behavior to reduce oral disease began to point to the limitations of fear arousal in persuasive communications. It also focused on the need to challenge the validity of simple self-reports of health behaviors as dependent measures. It indicated how even testing health behavior in itself may effect such behavior significantly. I used description of the line of research of my social psychology research group in the prevention of smoking in adolescents to further illustrate the involvement of social psychologists in behavioral medicine. I also presented detailed description of my program designed to train social psychologists in health research. I also discussed a typical current area in behavioral medicine of possible interest to social psychologists, the Type A behavior pattern. Finally, I offered some words of caution for the social psychologist as he or she enters the environment of the health professional.

REFERENCES

ARNIM, S.S. (1963) "The use of disclosing agents for measuring tooth cleanliness." Journal of Periodontology 34: 227-245.

BALDWIN, D. (1978) "Health behavior researchers create new professional organization." APA Monitor, August: 16.

BANE, A.L. and R.I. EVANS (1978) "Role of information and belief in adolescents' smoking behavior." Presented at the meeting of the American Psychological Association, Toronto, Canada, August 28-September 1.

BEERS, C.W. (1953) A Mind That Found Itself: An Autobiography. Garden City, NY: Doubleday.

BIERER, J., and R.I. EVANS (1969) Innovations in Social Psychiatry. London: Avenue Publishing.

CAMPBELL, D.T. and J.C. STANLEY (1963) Experimental and Quasi-Experimental Designs for Research. Skokie, IL: Rand McNally.

DEMBROSKI, T.M., J.M. MACDOUGALL, and J.L. SHIELDS (1977) "Physiological reactions to social challenge in persons evidencing the Type A coronary-prone behavior pattern." Journal of Human Stress 3: 2-10.

—————J. PETITTO, and R. LUSHENE (1978a) "Components of the coronary-prone behavior pattern and cardiovascular responses to psychomotor performance challenge." Journal of Behavioral Medicine 1: 159-176.

—————T.M., S.M. WEISS, J.L. SHIELDS, S.G. HAYNES, and M. FEINLEIB (1978b) Coronary-Prone Behavior. New York: Spring-Verlag.

DUNBAR, H.F. (1947) Mind and Body: Psychosomatic Medicine. New York: Random House.

EVANS, R.I. (forthcoming) The Making of Social Psychology: Discussions with Creative Contributors. New York: Gardner Press.

—————(1978a) Social psychology in preventing cardiovascular disease. (Grant proposal to the National Heart, Lung, and Blood Institute, 1 T32 HL 7258-01A.)

—————(1978b) "Summary of testimony presented to the United States Senate Subcommittee on Health." (unpublished)

—————(1978c) "Social psychological deterrents of smoking in schools: further results." Presented at the meeting of the American Psychological Association, Toronto, Canada, August 28-September 1.

—————(1978d) "Deterring smoking in adolescents: a social psychological perspective." Presented at the Symposium on Primary Prevention in Childhood of Atherosclerotic and Hypertensive Diseases, Chicago, Illinois, October 18-20.

—————(1976) "Smoking in children: developing a social psychological strategy of deterrence." Preventive Medicine 5: 122-127.

—————(1975) Carl Rogers: The Man and His Ideas. New York: E.P. Dutton.

—————(1968) B.F. Skinner: The Man and His Ideas. New York: E.P. Dutton.

—————(1966) "A new interdisciplinary dimension in graduate psychological research training: dentistry." American Psychologist 21: 167-172.

—————W.B. HANSEN, and M.B. MITTELMARK (1977) "Increasing the validity of self-reports of behavior in a smoking in children investigation." Journal of Applied Psychology 62: 521-523.

—————A.H. HENDERSON, P.C. HILL, and B.E. RAINES (1979a) "Smoking in children and adolescents—psychosocial determinants and prevention strategies" Chapter 17 in U.S. Public Health Service, Smoking and Health: A Report of the Surgeon General. Washington, DC: Government Printing Office.

—————(1979b) "Current psychological, social, and educational programs in control and prevention of smoking: a critical methodological review" pp. 203-243 in A.M. Gotto and R. Paolelli (eds.), Atherosclerosis reviews (vol. 6). New York: Raven Press.

—————R.M. ROZELLE, T.M. LASATER, T.M. DEMBROSKI, and B.P. ALLEN (1970)

"Fear arousal, persuasion and actual versus implied behavior change: new perspective utilizing a real-life dental hygiene program." Journal of Personality and Social Psychology 16: 220-227.

—————(1968) "New measure of effects of persuasive communications: a chemical indicator of toothbrushing behavior." Psychological Reports 23: 731-736.

—————R.M. ROZELLE, M.D. MITTELMARK, W.B. HANSEN, A.L. BANE, and J. HAVIS (1978) "Deterring the onset of smoking in children: knowledge of immediate physiological effects and coping with peer pressure, media pressure, and parent modeling." Journal of Applied Social Psychology 8: 126-135.

—————R.M. ROZELLE, R. NOBLITT, and D.L. WILLIAMS (1975) "Explicit and implicit persuasive communications over time to initiate and maintain behavior change: a new perspective utilizing a real-life dental hygiene program." Journal of Applied Social Psychology 5: 150-156.

FRIEDMAN, M. and R. ROSENMAN (1974) Type-A Behavior and Your Heart. New York: Alfred Knopf.

GLASS, D.C. (1977) Behavior Patterns, Stress, and Coronary Disease. Hillsdale, NJ: Lawrence Erlbaum Associates.

HANSEN, W.B. and R.I. EVANS (1978) "Feedback about immediate consequences: strategy to control children's smoking." Presented at the meeting of the American Psychological Association, Toronto, Canada, August 28-September 1.

HAYNES, S.G. and S. LEVINE, N.A. SCOTCH, M. FEINLEIB, and W.B. KANNEL (1978) "The relationship of psychological factors to coronary heart disease in the Framingham study. I: Methods and risk factors." American Journal of Epidemiology 107: 362-383.

HIGBEE, K.L. (1969) "Fifteen years of fear arousal: research on threat appeals: 1953-1968." Psychological Bulletin 72: 426-444.

HORNING, E.C., M.G. HORNING, D.I. CARROLL, R.N. STILLWELL, and I. DZIDIC (1973) "Nicotine in smokers, non-smokers, and room air." Life Science 13: 1331-1346.

HURD, P.D., C.A. JOHNSON, and T. PECHACEK (1978) "Peer, physiological monitoring, and commitment effects in antismoking interventions." Presented at the meeting of the American Psychological Association, Toronto, Canada, August 28-September 1.

JANIS, I.L. and S. FESHBACH (1953) "Effects of fear-arousing communications." Journal of Abnormal and Social Psychology 48: 78-92.

LEVENTHAL, H., R. SINGER, and S. JONES (1965) "Effects of fear and specificity of recommendations upon attitudes and behavior." Journal of Personality and Social Psychology 2: 20-29.

MARSTON, M.V. (1970) "Compliance with medical regimes: a review of the literature." Nursing Research 19: 312-323.

MATARAZZO, J. (1979) "Behavioral health and medicine: new frontiers for psychology." Presented at the meeting of the American Psychological Association, New York City, September 1-5.

McALLISTER, A.L., C. PERRY, and N. MACCOBY (1978) "Systematic peer leadership to discourage onset of tobacco dependency." Presented at the meeting of the American Psychological Association, Toronto, Canada, August 28-September 1.

McGUIRE, W.J. (1974) "Communication-persuasion models for drug education: experimental findings" pp. 1-26 in M. Goodstadt (ed.), Research on Methods and Programs of Drug Education. Toronto, Canada: Addiction Research Foundation.

MITTELMARK, M.B. and R.I. EVANS (1978) "Communicating imminent health consequences: smoking control strategy for children." Presented at the meeting of the American Psychological Association, Toronto, Canada, August 28-September 1.

National Cancer Institute (1977) The smoking digest. Progress report on a nation kicking the habit. Washington, DC: Government Printing Office.

ROSENMAN, R.H. (1978) "The interview method of assessment of the coronary-prone behavior pattern" pp. 55-69 in T.M. Dembroski et al. (eds.), Coronary-Prone Behavior. New York: Spring-Verlag.

ROSENMAN, R.H., R.J. BRAND, R.I. SHOLTZ, M. FRIEDMAN, R. STRAUS and M. WURM (1975) "Coronary heart disease int he Western Collaborative Group Study: final follow-up experience of eight and one-half years." Journal of the American Medical Association 233: 872-977.

ABOUT THE AUTHORS

ANTONIA ABBEY is a Ph.D. candidate in social psychology at Northwestern University. Her dissertation, which is currently in progress, is designed to assess the effects which rape victims' attributions of responsibility have on their long-term adjustment. She has also done research focusing on the reactions of others to rape victims. Her other research interests include commitment, sex roles, and social judgment.

ELLIOT ARONSON is Professor of Psychology at the University of California, Santa Cruz. He is the coeditor of *The Handbook of Social Psychology* (five volumes, 1968) and *Theories of Cognitive Consistency* (1968), coauthor of *Methods of Research in Social Psychology* (1975) and *The Jigsaw Classroom* (1978) and author of The Social Animal (1980).

LEONARD BICKMAN is a Professor in the Department of Psychology at Loyola University of Chicago and director of the Westinghouse Evaluation Institute in Evanston, Illinois. He has published over 70 research papers and he is also the editor of the *Applied Social Psychology Annual*. Bickman is the current president of the American Psychology—Law Society and president-elect of the Society for the Psychological Study of Social Issues.

JOHN S. CARROLL is Associate Professor of Psychology at Loyola University of Chicago, where he is a member of the Applied Social Psychology Program. He coedited with John Payne a book that brought together their interests in social psychology and cognitive psychology, *Cognition and Social Behavior* (1976). A second book has recently been published called *New Approaches to Social Problems: Applications of Attribution Theory,* coedited with Irene H. Frieze and Daniel Bar-Tal (1979). His research focuses on the parole decision process and upon his multi-disciplinary interests in social psychology, cognitive psychology, and criminal justice. These include the use of base-rate information in prediction, the effect of imagining an event upon expectation, and how people choose whether to commit crime.

ROBERT B. CIALDINI is currently Professor of Psychology at Arizona State University where he has been since 1971. He has also served as a visiting faculty member at Ohio State University in 1973-1974 and was a Visiting Scholar at the University of California, San Diego, in 1978.

DAN COATES is an Assistant Professor at the University of Wisconsin—Madison. He has coauthored a number of journal articles and book chapters, most of which have dealt with the social problems encountered by victims of crime and other aversive events. His current research interests include parole decision making and further work on social reactions to victims.

DAVID A. COOK received his Ph.D. in 1976 from the University of Iowa in Social Psychology. He has published in the areas of attribution, attitude change and behavior change, and attraction. His research interests also include time perception and applied social psychology issues. Currently, he is Assistant Professor of Psychology at Ball State University in Muncie, Indiana.

ABOUT THE AUTHORS

ANTONIA ABBEY is a Ph.D. candidate in social psychology at Northwestern University. Her dissertation, which is currently in progress, is designed to assess the effects which rape victims' attributions of responsibility have on their long-term adjustment. She has also done research focusing on the reactions of others to rape victims. Her other research interests include commitment, sex roles, and social judgment.

ELLIOT ARONSON is Professor of Psychology at the University of California, Santa Cruz. He is the coeditor of *The Handbook of Social Psychology* (five volumes, 1968) and *Theories of Cognitive Consistency* (1968), coauthor of *Methods of Research in Social Psychology* (1975) and *The Jigsaw Classroom* (1978) and author of The Social Animal (1980).

LEONARD BICKMAN is a Professor in the Department of Psychology at Loyola University of Chicago and director of the Westinghouse Evaluation Institute in Evanston, Illinois. He has published over 70 research papers and he is also the editor of the *Applied Social Psychology Annual*. Bickman is the current president of the American Psychology—Law Society and president-elect of the Society for the Psychological Study of Social Issues.

JOHN S. CARROLL is Associate Professor of Psychology at Loyola University of Chicago, where he is a member of the Applied Social Psychology Program. He coedited with John Payne a book that brought together their interests in social psychology and cognitive psychology, *Cognition and Social Behavior* (1976). A second book has recently been published called *New Approaches to Social Problems: Applications of Attribution Theory*, coedited with Irene H. Frieze and Daniel Bar-Tal (1979). His research focuses on the parole decision process and upon his multi-disciplinary interests in social psychology, cognitive psychology, and criminal justice. These include the use of base-rate information in prediction, the effect of imagining an event upon expectation, and how people choose whether to commit crime.

ROBERT B. CIALDINI is currently Professor of Psychology at Arizona State University where he has been since 1971. He has also served as a visiting faculty member at Ohio State University in 1973-1974 and was a Visiting Scholar at the University of California, San Diego, in 1978.

DAN COATES is an Assistant Professor at the University of Wisconsin—Madison. He has coauthored a number of journal articles and book chapters, most of which have dealt with the social problems encountered by victims of crime and other aversive events. His current research interests include parole decision making and further work on social reactions to victims.

DAVID A. COOK received his Ph.D. in 1976 from the University of Iowa in Social Psychology. He has published in the areas of attribution, attitude change and behavior change, and attraction. His research interests also include time perception and applied social psychology issues. Currently, he is Assistant Professor of Psychology at Ball State University in Muncie, Indiana.

habit. Washington, DC: Government Printing Office.

ROSENMAN, R.H. (1978) "The interview method of assessment of the coronary-prone behavior pattern" pp. 55-69 in T.M. Dembroski et al. (eds.), Coronary-Prone Behavior. New York: Spring-Verlag.

ROSENMAN, R.H., R.J. BRAND, R.I. SHOLTZ, M. FRIEDMAN, R. STRAUS and M. WURM (1975) "Coronary heart disease int he Western Collaborative Group Study: final follow-up experience of eight and one-half years." Journal of the American Medical Association 233: 872-977.

THOMAS D. COOK is Professor in Psychology Department at Northwestern University. He is the coauthor of *Sesame Street Revisited: A Case Study in Evaluation Research, Quasi-Experimentation: Design and Analysis in Issues for Field Settings, The Evaluation Review Annual* (Vol. 3), and *Qualitative and Quantitative Methods in Evaluation.* He is currently on the editorial board of seven journals.

LEONARD DINTZER is currently in the Societal Analysis Department of the General Motors Research Laboratories. He received his Ph.D. in Social Psychology from Northwestern University. His research areas include social integration, applied social psychology, and time series methodology.

RICHARD I. EVANS received his Ph.D. from Michigan State University and is currently Professor of Psychology at the University of Houston. He is the Director of a National Heart, Lung and Blood Institute-supported pre- and postdoctoral social psychology training program and he is a Principal Investigator in the Baylor College of Medicine National Heart and Blood Vessel Research and Demonstration Center. His most recent books include *The Making of Psychology, The Making of Social Psychology,* and *Social Psychology in Life* (with Richard Rozelle). His Social Psychology/Behavioral Medicine Research Group received APA Division 13 Research Excellence Awards in 1973 and 1977. He is the recipient of the 1977-1980 Phi Kappa Phi Distinguished Scholar Award.

MICHELLE FINE is a social psychologist and Research Associate at the Industrial Social Welfare Center at Columbia University. Her major theoretical interests are in the areas of the perception of injustice and the role of options in awakening a sense of injustice. She is particularly interested in issues related to women in work and family settings. She is the coauthor of the forthcoming text, *Toward the Experimenting Society: Methods for the Design and Evaluation of Social Experiments.* She is also involved in research on multiplicity sampling techniques for hard-to-find populations.

ROBERT W. HALEY is currently a physician epidemiologist serving as Assistant to the Director, Bacterial Diseases Division, Bureau of Epidemiology, at the Center for Disease Control in Atlanta, Georgia. Since joining the epidemiology staff at the Center for Disease Control, he has studied epidemics, nosocomial infections, and related risk factors and control measures; has served as a consultant to hospitals in various regional and national policy-making bodies on these matters; and has been the project chief of the study on ethics advocacy of Nosocomial Infection Control (SENIC Project).

ELIZABETH HOLLAND is a doctoral candidate in social psychology at Northwestern University and is currently on leave at the University of Michigan. Her research interests include issues in helping relationships and coping with victimization. Her master's thesis involved the study of burn-out among hot-line volunteers. For her dissertation, she is conducting a longitudinal study on the effects of others' reactions to rape victims on their adjustments to the attack.

RONNIE JANOFF-BULMAN is currently an Assistant Professor of Psychology at the University of Massachusetts — Amherst. While working on her Ph.D. at Northwestern University, she and Camille B. Wortman studied the relationship between spinal-cord-injured patients' attribution of blame for their accident and their ability to cope with permanent paralysis. Her current research interests include attribution of self blame among victimized populations and the effects of such attributions on subsequent coping.

CHARLES A. KIESLER is currently Walter Van Dyke Bingham Professor of Psychology at Carnegie-Mellon University and Editor of the *American Psychologist.* He was Executive Officer of the American Psychology Association and has continued to be involved in such national issues as mental health policy and science policy. His books include *Attitude Change: A Critical Analysis of Theoretical Approaches* (with B.E. Collins and N. Miller), *Conformity* (with S. Kiesler), and *The Psychology of Commitment.* He recently edited the collection *Psychology and National Health Insurance: A Sourcebook* (with N. Cummings and G. Vanderbos).

MELVIN M. MARK is Assistant Professor of Psychology at The Pennsylvania State University. He received his Ph.D. in social psychology from Northwestern University in 1979. A coeditor of *Evaluation Studies Review Annual,* Vol. 3, he is interested in the application and extension of social science methodology, particularly in the areas of program evaluation and time series methodology. His research interests also include distributive justice.

NEAL OSHEROW received his B.A. from Wesleyan University in 1976 and is currently an advanced graduate student at the University of California, Santa Cruz, conducting research on cooperative methods of education, self-disclosure and interpersonal attraction, and psychology and law.

MICHAEL S. PALLAK received his Ph.D. in 1968 from Yale University in Social Psychology and was on the faculty at the University of Iowa from 1968 to 1976. He has published extensively in the areas of attitude change and action taking while developing strong interests in energy conservation and the role of psychology in national issues concerning science and mental health policy. He is currently the Executive Officer of the American Psychological Association.

BERTRAM H. RAVEN is Professor in the Department of Psychology at University of California, Los Angeles, where he also is Director of a National Institute of Mental Health-sponsored pre- and postdoctoral program in social and personality factors in health. A Past-President of the Society for the Psychological Study of Social Issues, he has also served as general editor of the *Journal of Social Issues.* He is coauthor of *Social Psychology: People in Groups* (Wiley) and *Discovering Psychology* (Science Research Associates). His research and writing has focused on small group behavior and especially on interpersonal influence and social power. Most recently he has been applying social influence and power theory to medical and health issues.

LEONARD SAXE is currently Assistant Professor of Psychology and Senior Research Associate of the Center for Applied Social Science at Boston University. During 1979, he served as a Fellow at the U.S. Congress' Office of Technology Assessment. His interests include both methodological issues of conducting applied research and substantive issues of person perception and interpersonal relations. He is the coeditor of *The Social Psychology of Education: Theory and Research* and is the coauthor of the forthcoming text, *Toward the Experimenting Society: Methods for the Design and Evaluation of Social Experiments.* He is also an Associate editor of the *Personality and Social Psychology Bulletin.*

ROXANE L. SILVER is a Ph.D. candidate in social psychology at Northwestern University, where she was a National Science Foundation graduate fellow for three years. Her doctoral research is a longitudinal investigation of the predictors of successful adjustments to spinal cord injury. She is also conducting similar research on the coping process of parents who have lost an infant to Sudden Infant Death Syndrome.

JOHN J. SULLIVAN received his doctorate in social psychology at the University of Iowa. Since then he has served on the faculty at the University of Wisconsin—Milwaukee and at Illinois State University. During this time, he research both applied and theoretical aspects of attitude-behavior relationships. Since leaving academia, Sullivan has been employed as a market researcher by the Quaker Oats Company in Chicago.

CAMILLE B. WORTMAN received her Ph.D. from Duke University in 1973 and spent the next seven years on the faculty at Northwestern University. Her research interests include reactions to uncontrollable life events and predictors of good psychological adjustment among those victimized by illness, physical disability, or rape. This work is summarized in a chapter with Roxane Silver, which will appear in Seligman and Gerber's forthcoming book on human helplessness. In 1979, she accepted a position on the psychology faculty at the University of Michigan. She is currently studying problems in the social support system that often accompanies life stress.